Frontiers in Economic History

Economic historians have contributed to the development of economics in a variety of ways, combining theory with quantitative methods, constructing new databases, promoting interdisciplinary approaches to historical topics, and using history as a lens to examine the long-term development of the economy. Frontiers in Economic History publishes manuscripts that push the frontiers of research in economic history in order to better explain past economic experiences and to understand how, why and when economic change occurs. Books in this series will highlight the value of economic history in shedding light on the ways in which economic factors influence growth as well as social and political developments. This series aims to establish a new standard of quality in the field while offering a global discussion forum toward a unified approach in the social sciences.

Claude Diebolt • Michael Haupert
Editors

The State of Economic History

A Global Perspective

Springer

Editors
Claude Diebolt
BETA/CNRS
University of Strasbourg
Strasbourg, France

Michael Haupert
University of Wisconsin-La Crosse
La Crosse, WI, USA

ISSN 2662-9771 ISSN 2662-978X (electronic)
Frontiers in Economic History
ISBN 978-3-032-01623-2 ISBN 978-3-032-01624-9 (eBook)
https://doi.org/10.1007/978-3-032-01624-9

This Springer imprint is published by the registered company Springer Nature Switzerland AG
The registered company address is: Gewerbestrasse 11, 6330 Cham, Switzerland

Introduction

This project began with a session at the American Economic Association meetings in January of 2019. We put together a session titled *What Role (if any) Should Economic History Play in the Training of an Economist?* That session featured four papers focusing on the titled topic for the American PhD program. The ensuing discussion led us to consider the same question for other countries around the world. What was the role of economic history in the training of future economists, What role did the discipline play in the larger realm of economics research and considerations? So, we proposed a session on this wider topic, and it was accepted for the World Economic History Congress meetings to be held in Paris … in the summer of 2020. Of course, we all know that did not happen. In fact, those meetings were delayed 2 years. But when they finally did occur, we were able to assemble seven of the nine authors of chapters in this volume (some virtually, given the circumstances and the fact that those meetings were hybrid). The session was a huge success. We had a standing room only crowd that spilled out into the hallway, with dozens more attending remotely. The response was so enthusiastic that we decided it could not stop there. We wanted to include those authors who had originally agreed to participate in our session, but were prevented from joining us in Paris due to the pandemic's lingering effects on travel and budgets. At long last, our journey is complete, and we are proud and excited to present to you this volume of essays that collectively look at the place of economic history across the globe. We thank Springer for publishing this volume as part of its *Frontiers in Economic History* series.

In 1954, Joseph Schumpeter argued that economics rested on three pillars, with economic history being the most important. A decade later, at the American Economic Association (AEA) meetings, a session was dedicated to the significance of economic history in the training of future economists. In 1981, the AEA hosted a session addressing the broader question of what content should be included in an economics major. Then, in 1994, Christina Romer published an article in the *Journal of Economic Education* titled "The End of Economic History?" She concluded that economic history had not disappeared but had instead been integrated into the broader discipline, raising questions about whether it still constituted a distinct field. At the 2012 World Congress in Stellenbosch, a session was organized that focused on globalizing economic history beyond the Western canon. Over the past decade, the AEA has regularly featured sessions examining the role of economic history in the United States. Thus, economic history continually reflects on its role within economics.

With our session at the July 2022 World Economic History Congress in Paris, we aimed to broaden the discussion beyond the typical Western-focused curriculum and explore how economic history fits within the discipline globally. We brought together leading economic historians from around the world to assess the state of economic history on every continent where economics is taught. The question we asked them to consider was broad, and thus approached in different ways by each author. Each contributor addressed topics such as the role of economic history in graduate training, the major questions economic historians are uniquely equipped to answer, and how economic history integrates into the economic landscape across different regions. The common thread among the essays is the examination of the impact of economic history on the education of economists, how it has evolved, how it has manifested itself, and in some cases, what that portends for the future.

To open the volume, we harken back to the origins of the project at the 2019 AEA meetings. In "*American Made: The Role of Economic History in the Training of PhD Candidates*," *Michael Haupert* examines the evolution of the role that economic history has played in the training of economics PhD students in the United States. Economic history was once a cornerstone, along with theory and econometrics, in graduate economics education, but has seen its place in the doctoral curriculum steadily decline, despite its significant contributions to the discipline. He looks at the impact economic history, particularly in its cliometric form, has had on the empirical testing of economic theory, the construction of historical datasets, and our understanding of the dynamics of long-term growth. He looks at the current state of the field by examining the top ranked PhD programs in economics in the United States, and finds that only a minority still offer economic history courses, with very few including it as either a core or optional field. This erosion is troubling: economic history offers contextualized understanding of data, promotes empirical rigor, and develops analytical tools that are highly relevant to current debates on institutions, growth, and inequality, and as such, he argues for its inclusion as an essential part of the training of an economist.

In his chapter "*Economic History in Western Europe: Bridging Verstehen and Erklären*," *Claude Diebolt* moves the discussion to the cradle of economic history: the European continent. He explores the enduring methodological tension between understanding (Verstehen) and explaining (Erklären) in economic history. The field emerged in the late nineteenth century amidst the *Methodenstreit*, separating itself from both theoretical economics and traditional political history. In Western Europe, economic history evolved unevenly, gaining institutional independence in some countries (e.g., the UK), while remaining marginal in others. The discipline flourished during the 1960s–70s, embracing quantification, long-term trends, and integration with the social sciences. However, by the 1980s, it faced decline. Historians moved toward cultural and micro-histories, while economists favored increasingly abstract, mathematical models, deepening the divide between the two disciplines.

This divergence has led to a crisis of identity for economic history: historians often lack economic training, while economists show limited historical awareness. Each community speaks a different methodological language—historians emphasize context and interpretation, whereas economists emphasize generalization and modeling. As a result, economic history has become a marginal, hybrid field caught between disciplines that no longer intersect, raising critical questions about its future relevance and institutional survival.

The chapter "*Cliometric Approaches to Central, East, and Southeast Europe, 2019–2022*" by *Matthias Morys* explores the relatively recent rise of quantitative economic history in the CESEE region. This field only took root after the fall of the Berlin Wall (1989) and the dissolution of the Soviet Union (1991), as political and economic transformations created the conditions for its development. Focusing on research published between 2019 and 2022, Morys builds on some of his previous work to identify three main research areas. The first theme focuses on long-term barriers to economic growth in the region, often citing serfdom alongside factors such as demographics, weak institutions, and limited market integration. Second, research investigates how economically "backward" the region was at the onset of communism, not merely through GDP but by evaluating structural and developmental factors—raising counterfactuals about the region's potential under liberal regimes. The third major theme assesses the economic outcomes of the state socialist period. This involves questioning whether central planning was essential for industrialization and how successful it was, especially when compared to pre-communist trajectories.

The next chapter moves our attention to the United Kingdom, which, along with continental Europe, is the progenitor of economic history as a discipline. "*The State of Economic History: Credible or Incredible?*" is *Jane Humphries* argument that economic history has long found itself marginalized between its disciplinary parents, economics and history. She outlines its struggle to maintain institutional visibility, intellectual autonomy, and student interest. The rise of cliometrics in the 1960s and the 1970s marked a turning point, embedding economic history within quantitative methods and economic theory. While this shift helped align the field with an increasingly mathematical economics, it also distanced it from historians drawn to cultural and postmodern approaches. Traditional narrative methods endured, particularly outside the USA, and professional associations continued to promote methodological pluralism. Nevertheless, institutional barriers and declining undergraduate interest gradually weakened the discipline's foundations. Graduate programs, with their emphasis on technical economics, left little space for the historical depth that economic history demands. Recent research suggests a growing integration of economic history into economics. However, this convergence is not without trade-offs. While integration brings greater visibility and analytical rigor, it also risks eroding the field's breadth, interpretive nuance, and historical sensitivity.

With the contribution of *Bishnupriya Gupta*, "*New Perspectives of Economic History of South and Southeast Asia and the Middle East*," our focus shifts to the Southeast. Gupta examines how colonialism has shaped the economic trajectories of regions like South and Southeast Asia and parts of the Middle East. Early scholarship emphasized descriptive, macro-level narratives about trade, resource extraction, and deindustrialization within a Marxist framework, highlighting unequal imperial relationships. Some imperialist interpretations, in contrast, emphasized modernization through colonial infrastructure investment. However, these accounts often lacked systematic, large-scale data. Economic historians have helped transform the field by leveraging digitized archival materials, including company records, colonial censuses, and maps, allowing for detailed, sub-regional analyses. Commodity-level trade data, geospatial tools, and emerging text analysis techniques offer new insights into old issues. This new wave of work employs rigorous empirical methods to investigate living standards, labor markets, gender roles, investment patterns, and the legacy of colonial rule. Gupta's contribution showcases how this granular data has shifted the focus from broad development narratives to nuanced, evidence-based investigations of economic change and divergence.

Yutaka Arimoto, Tomoko Hashino, Masaki Nakabayashi, Tetsuji Okazaki, Osamu Saito, Kaoru Sugihara, and Yoshihiro Sakane explore the evolution and current directions of economic history research in Japan in "*The State of Economic History in Japan.*" Japan's Socio-Economic History Society, founded in 1930, reflects a long-standing scholarly tradition, predating many similar institutions globally. In recent decades, the field has undergone significant transformation, marked by increasing internationalization and the growing influence of economics and econometrics. Japanese economic historians are publishing more frequently in leading international journals and adopting quantitative methods alongside traditional narrative approaches. These methodological shifts have enabled research on new topics, ranging from institutional development and market integration to demographic and environmental history. The chapter emphasizes how Japanese scholars are blending domestic historical depth with global academic standards, broadening the scope and relevance of their work. This convergence signals a dynamic and outward-looking future for economic history in Japan.

The chapter "*The Rise and Fall and Rise (?) of Economic History in Australia*" by *Andrew Seltzer, Martin Shanahan, and Claire Wright* documents the significant fluctuations that economic history has endured in Australia since its establishment, shaped by colonial record-keeping and post-WWII academic expansion. The field grew steadily, supported by prominent scholars like Noel Butlin and the development of cliometrics, but faced decline from the late 1980s due to university funding cuts and corporatization, resulting in department closures and a "missing generation" of scholars. This decline diminished Australia's engagement with advancements driven elsewhere by the rise of cliometrics. However, since the early 2000s, there has been a cautious revival with renewed hiring, courses, and research output, though the field remains smaller and more precarious than in its mid-twentieth-century heyday. Since its origin, economic history in Australia has been caught between the economics and history disciplines, which shaped its evolving identity. Scholars have debated its future extensively, especially during periods of institutional change and funding pressures. Today, while facing challenges such as data accessibility, internationalization, and university structures, there is cautious optimism about the field's renewal, buoyed by new research and emerging scholars. The authors conclude by reflecting on these challenges and offering perspectives on the discipline's future in Australia.

Johan Fourie explores the revival of African economic history since 2010 in "*Opportunities and Challenges in African Economic History.*" This resurgence has been driven largely by economists and influenced by the rise of New Historical Economics and the creation of the African Economic History Network. Once marginalized, Africa has become increasingly central to the field, with studies on diverse topics such as health, violence, and intergenerational mobility appearing in top economics and science journals. Four key factors have spurred this renaissance: methodological advances, new data availability, specialized academic platforms, and global interest in Africa's economic potential. However, the resurgence has also brought two major challenges: a growing divide between the "history matters" and "historical reconstruction" schools, and the persistent underrepresentation of African-based scholars. This fragmentation risks limiting the field's relevance and inclusivity. Fourie analyzes publication patterns and urges strategies to promote interdisciplinarity and African participation in order to ensure that African economic history remains both methodologically rigorous and contextually grounded.

Continuing our journey around the world, *Adolfo Meisel* explores the evolution of economic history in South America in his contribution, "*From Dependencia Back to the Original Sin: Economic History in South America in the Twenty-First Century.*" His focus is on the key intellectual shifts from the mid-twentieth century to the present and their influence on the field of economic history in South America. The field gained prominence in the 1960s and 70s, a period referred to as its "Golden Age," when scholars deeply influenced public policy through structuralist and dependencia theories. However, the decline of these paradigms in the 1980s led to a loss of academic and political influence. In their place, the cliometric movement, emphasizing quantitative methods and economic theory, began to take root, particularly through the influence of U.S.-based scholarship. Concurrently, the New Institutional History, championed by figures like North, Acemoglu, and Robinson, reshaped debates around institutions, growth, and inequality. More recently, there is a growing interest in monetary and banking history, drawing on Friedman and Schwartz's legacy. Together, these trends illustrate a transition toward empirically grounded, internationally connected, and methodologically diverse economic historiography in South America.

Coming full circle, we return to North America. "*Recent Trends in Economic History in Mexico,*" by *Gustavo A. Del Angel*, examines recent developments in economic history research in Mexico through a review of academic publications over the past quarter century. While economic history in Mexico has deep roots dating back to the early twentieth century, the last 25 years have seen notable growth and diversification. The field has expanded beyond national topics, with increasing attention to the twentieth century, fiscal history, and particularly business history. Despite this evolution, most research still originates from historians rather than economists. Mexico serves as a regional hub for economic history, fostering interdisciplinary dialogue. Del Angel highlights international debates on the integration of economic history into economics, especially through cliometrics. Though this integration is more advanced in North America, Latin America and Mexico have engaged with these trends while maintaining distinct features. Overall, the field remains positioned between history and economics, contributing crucial insights to both disciplines while navigating methodological and disciplinary tensions.

The world is a bigger place than we have covered in these ten chapters. Unfortunately, we were not able to cover every region of the world. The omission of China and Canada, for example, is noteworthy. But the constraints of time and other obligations prevented the inclusion of more participants. We are not claiming to have examined all facets of economic history in every corner of the globe. Rather, what we have accomplished in this volume is to collective the viewpoint of leading scholars on the role of economic history in their part of the world. Economic history has a rich and varied background, has a legacy of outstanding and influential research, and has evolved into a vibrant and important contributor to the fields of economics and history. As the authors in this volume have shown us, the discipline has proud past, a vibrant present, and a promising future.

Claude Diebolt
Michael Haupert

Contents

Contributors

Gustavo A. Del Angel Department of Economics at CIDE, Centro de Investigación y Docencia Económicas (CIDE), Mexico, Mexico

Yutaka Arimoto Metrics Work Consultants Inc. and Hitotsubashi University, Tokyo, Japan

Claude Diebolt BETA/CNRS, University of Strasbourg, Strasbourg, France

Johan Fourie Stellenbosch University, Matieland, South Africa

Bishnupriya Gupta University of Warwick, Coventry, UK

Tomoko Hashino Kobe University, Kobe, Japan

Michael Haupert University of Wisconsin-La Crosse, La Crosse, WI, USA

Jane Humphries University of Oxford, Oxford, UK

London School of Economics, London, UK

Adolfo Meisel Universidad del Norte, Barranquilla, Colombia

Matthias Morys University of York (UK) and Leibniz Institute for East and South-East European Studies, Regensburg, Germany

Masaki Nakabayashi The University of Tokyo, Tokyo, Japan

Tetsuji Okazaki Meiji Gakuin University, Tokyo, Japan

Osamu Saito Hitotsubashi University, Tokyo, Japan

Yoshihiro Sakane Hiroshima Shudo University, Hiroshima, Japan

Andrew Seltzer Royal Holloway, University of London, London, UK

London School of Economics, London, UK

Martin Shanahan University of South Australia, Adelaide, SA, Australia

University of Gothenburg, Göteborg, Sweden

Kaoru Sugihara Research Institute for Humanity and Nature, Kyoto, Japan

Claire Wright University of Technology Sydney, Ultimo, NSW, Australia

List of Figures

List of Charts

Recent Trends in Economic History in Mexico

List of Tables

Opportunities and Challenges in African Economic History

Recent Trends in Economic History in Mexico

American Made: The Role of Economic History in the Training of PhD Candidates

Michael Haupert

Abstract I examine the role of economic history in the training of economics PhD students in the United States. Economic history—once a cornerstone of graduate economics education alongside theory and econometrics—has seen its place in the doctoral curriculum steadily decline, despite its significant contributions to the discipline. Economic history, particularly in its cliometric form, has been instrumental in testing economic theories, building historical datasets, and shedding light on long-term growth dynamics. Finally, I provide empirical evidence on the current state of the field by examining 50 PhD programs in economics, and find that only a minority still offer economic history courses, with very few including it as either a core or optional field. This erosion is troubling: economic history offers contextualized understanding of data, promotes empirical rigor, and develops analytical tools that are highly relevant to current debates on institutions, growth, and inequality, and as such it should be an essential part of the training of an economist.

> I do not approve of Economic History courses quite unaccompanied by any Economic Theory.—Sir William Ashley (1927)

Introduction

At the 1964 meetings of the American Economic Association (AEA) in a session on the current state of economic history, several papers were delivered on the role of economic history in the education of an economist. In 1981, an AEA session was devoted to the broader question of what content should be included in the economics major. Another generation of economists has been trained since then, and it is time once again to consider the role of economic history within the economics discipline. Specifically, what role does it play in the training of graduate students?

M. Haupert (✉)
University of Wisconsin-La Crosse, La Crosse, WI, USA
e-mail: mhaupert@uwlax.edu

C. Diebolt, M. Haupert (eds.), *The State of Economic History*, Frontiers in Economic History, https://doi.org/10.1007/978-3-032-01624-9_1

Economic historians have contributed to the development of economics in many ways, combining theory with quantitative methods, constructing and revising databases, and discovering and creating entirely new ones. This has made it possible to question and reassess earlier findings, thus increasing our knowledge, refining earlier conclusions, and correcting mistakes. In addition, this field has added greatly to our understanding of economic growth and development, affording the economic historian the valuable element of time as a variable. The use of history to examine economic theory has deepened our knowledge and understanding within fundamental areas of research as to how, why, and when economic change occurs. It is perhaps in this area where the greatest contributions of economic historians have appeared.

What should an economist know? In an effort to determine what it is that academic economists believe they should master, I look at 50 of the top ranked economics Ph.D. programs in the United States to see how they train their students. Admittedly, the students at the top 50 programs only make up a small percentage of the total number of academic economists, but they make up a much larger percentage of the economists who train future generations of economists. So it is worth looking at what they believe are the vital tools for all future economists to master.

Why Economic History?

Economic history is a subset of history. Both economists and historians are trying to tell plausible stories about the past, and they succeed or fail by narrative standards to connect one event to another. The cliometric revolution in the late 1950s transformed the study of economic history from a narrative to a mathematical format by combining theory with quantitative methods and exploiting rich databases to test economic theories, thus expanding the frontier of our knowledge of the past and its ability to portend the future. The use of history as a crucible to examine economic theory has deepened our knowledge of how, why, and when economic growth occurs.

More than a century ago, Sir William Ashley made a case for the inclusion of economic history in the curriculum. He eloquently argued that the mere gratification of natural curiosity, of a desire to know about our past, what created it, and what led us to our present, was motivation enough to study it. If for no other reason, economic history was needed to "widen [the] sympathies [of its students], enlarge [their] conceptions of the possible, and save [them] from the Philistinism of the market-place. … and finally, there may be some who will be drawn to this field of inquiry by a hope … that they may thereby arrive at a more satisfying and intelligible conception of the evolution of human society" (Ashley 1893, p. 134).

Rondo Cameron (1965, p. 114) argued that because the fundamental role of the economic historian is to describe, analyze, and explain change, "any theory of structural change must, in order to command respect, be tested against historical or long-term data. The symbiosis of history, theory, and policy in application to problems of economic development is therefore a natural consequence." And in the 1960s, Hugh

Aitken (1960) and Robert Gallman (1965) emphasized this link while making the case for economic history in the curriculum. They argued that economic historians require a theory of economic development, and as a result needed to consider variables such as time and institutions that theorists normally exclude from their models. Economic history has a definite role to play in the education of all economists, and it can best do this if it speaks explicitly of economic development.

Richard Tawney (1933) identified the role of economic history by focusing more broadly on the role of historians as chroniclers of social behavior under a variety of conditions and environments with the object of identifying the characteristics of different types of civilization in order to discover the forces in which change has found its dynamic, and to critically examine those doctrines accepted in each epoch as self-evident truths. He claimed that the purpose of all history is to widen the range of observations from the experience of a single generation or society to that of mankind. John Nef (1944) argued that economic history was an inexhaustible subject, tasked with providing a framework for the collection and presentation of mass quantities of information of all kinds and values.

In the early 1960s, when Purdue was the center of the cliometric movement, it required a graduate course sequence in economic history because it was considered to be the empirical part of economics. The skills taught in the economic history courses were designed to provide students with a basic knowledge of the evolution of economic institutions and their impact on economic growth. And since economic history is by definition empirical, the courses served as an introduction to the techniques of empirically testing economic theory. Economic history courses introduce students to sources of economic data and, in connection with econometrics courses, the formulation of hypotheses in testable forms. On a different note, bemoaning the frequent misuse of history, Rondo Cameron (1965) cited a more basic role for economic history as the watchdog to assure that it is used properly.

The Evolution of the Economic History Discipline

Economic history emerged as a distinct discipline during the course of the revolt against the deductive theories of classical economics, led by the likes of Gustav Schmoller in Germany and Sir John Clapham in England. The original aim of the historical school was to replace what they believed to be the unrealistic theories of deductive (the gathering of facts leading to a certain conclusion) economics with theories developed inductively (the development of theories providing evidence of the truth) through the study of history. They held that history was the key source of knowledge about humans and human organizations, and because it was culture and time specific, it could not be generalized over time or space, hence general theories were useless. Their view was that economics was best approached from the vantage point of empirical and historical analysis, not abstract theory and deduction.

Economic history set its first serious footings in 1895 when the London School of Economics (LSE) opened its doors. It was founded in opposition to the tenets of orthodox economics. As a result, economic history was an important presence from the beginning. In 1901, LSE became the first British university to offer a degree in economics, and economic history was one of the possible fields of specialization in the degree.

Harvard was the incubator of economic history in the US. Charles Dunbar, founder of the Harvard economics department, along with his colleagues Frank Taussig, and J. Lawrence Laughlin, who later would found the University of Chicago economics department, offered courses in a variety of US economic history topics beginning in 1883. In 1892, Dunbar and Taussig were responsible for the hiring of William J. Ashley to the first chair of economic history in the world.

Ashley was strongly influenced by German scholarship, as was his Harvard successor, Edwin F. Gay. Gay imparted the standards and techniques of the German academy—the methodological principle of sticking to the facts, of telling history as it really was—on his colleagues and students. He used a multidisciplinary approach and stressed that a good hypothesis was multidisciplinary and reflected social, political, international, and psychological, as well as economic analysis.

Economic history spread across departments early in the twentieth century. Chairs in economic history were created at many leading institutions, but the discipline had difficulty gaining traction in graduate programs due to the lack of a dedicated journal or society to promote its research. Contributing to the problem was the growing fascination with the scientific method and its potential applications to economics, exemplified by the theoretical approach espoused by Marshall in the UK, but soundly rejected by economic historians. In the USA, this manifested itself in the growth of economic forecasting, which eventually led to the creation of the *National Bureau of Economic Research* (NBER).

During WWI, Edwin Gay and Wesley Mitchell headed the Central Bureau of Planning and Statistics, responsible for the gathering and reporting of statistical data. This experience convinced them of the importance of regular and reliable collecting of economic statistics. Together they helped found the NBER to stimulate the collection and interpretation of historical statistics of the United States. They made it the mission of the NBER to gather empirical information about the American economy in order to create a robust foundation for theoretical generalizations.

Mitchell served as research director at the NBER for its first quarter century. He dedicated his tenure at the bureau to gathering the economic data that would be needed to draw inductive generalizations about the US economy. He combined his historical approach to understanding business cycles, which he saw as a global phenomenon, with an urgent call for more data collection from around the world. The NBER was central to this data collection effort and served as a sort of haven for statistical economists.

After WWI the increased focus on data collection and increased proficiency in the use of statistical materials took attention, students, and resources away from economic history. Enrollment in economic history courses held steady since major universities required a semester of it in their graduate programs, but writing it as a field declined.

By 1941, Gay felt that the work of the historical economists had not been able to displace the "theoretical school," but did modify it. He felt the time was right for a reunification of economic history with theory, noting that the economic historians knew a great deal about the long-run trends of productive energies and social pressures leading to economic growth, which could be combined with the tools of the theorist to lend greater insight into the growth process. Far from incompatible, he felt that true philosophical objectives and the careful assembling of data were complementary.

Over time, economic history presented itself as empirical and multidisciplinary. Empirical because it dealt with the facts of the past. The facts could be quantitative, as the NBER emphasized, or qualitative, as the German school believed was the responsibility of economic historians. Economic historians saw history as a laboratory uniquely suited to the testing of economic theory.

The Cliometric Movement

After WWII, with the American economy booming, economists gained cachet. Economics with its rigorous models, tested from an abundance of quantitative data by use of advanced, mathematically expressed formulae, came to be regarded as the paradigm of the social sciences.

At the same time, economists were becoming more interested in the determinants of economic growth and what they saw as the widening gap between the so-called developed and underdeveloped regions of the world. They saw the study of economic history as a source of insight into the issues of economic growth and economic development, and the new quantitative methods as the ideal tools for analysis.

The timing of the cliometric movement corresponded to the success of the quantitative growth studies of Simon Kuznets, a reflection of the infatuation economists had developed for the national accounting approach. This predisposed them to view the past through this same lens and altered their definition of historical evidence. Robert Fogel credited his mentor Kuznets as the primary inspiration for the work espoused by the cliometric movement.

The main achievements of cliometrics have been to slowly but surely establish a solid set of economic analyses of historical evolution by means of measurement and theory, and following the path blazed by Douglass North, to recognize the limits of neoclassical theory and bring into economic models the important role of institutions. Nothing can now replace rigorous statistical and econometric analysis based on systematically ordered data.

The Decline of Economic History

Over time, cliometricians gravitated toward the econometricians. They turned to the collection and accumulation of historical data and their use in testing hypotheses about economic activity. In this way, cliometrics brought economic history into the mainstream of economics as it was developing. Economic history is now dominated by the cliometric method, so much so that it may be a contributing cause to the demise of economic history positions and courses. To non-historians, it appears that economic history is little more than the use of historical data to test economic theory. Departments facing declining resources feel they can do without a specialist in economic history, since any economist can apply theory to historic data.

Cliometrics, and by association, economic history, lost some of its significance with economists, who saw it as another application of economic theory. Applied economics is certainly not a bad thing, but cliometrics is certainly not the only applied field of economics. Today it is often perceived as merely the application of theory and the latest quantitative techniques to old data instead of contemporary data. In that world view, a cliometrician is just a theorist with a more limited repertoire. As early as 1986, William Parker foreshadowed this problem when he observed that what was lost in the move by cliometricians to theory and econometric emphasis was the humane interest of the old British political economy and social welfare and the idealistic German historical economist's concern for the whole society.

The Disappearing Economic History Course

As we will see in greater detail, economic history course requirements at leading PhD granting institutions are a rare breed. This was not always the case. A closer look at two specific examples will suffice to illustrate the problem.

Temin (2016) noted that when he first joined the MIT economics department in 1965, the approach to graduate education had long since been a three legged stool consisting of theory, econometrics, and economic history. Today, the three legs of the stool are micro theory, macro theory, and econometrics. Economic history is no longer required, nor is it listed as a subfield available to graduate students. In fact, among the 46 courses listed in the current graduate curriculum, six are statistics and econometrics courses, four are micro theory, and none are economic history.

Research by Haupert (2005) indicated that 7.1% of U.S. based economic historians had earned their PhD at the University of Chicago. This was second only to Harvard, which had produced 7.4% of economic historians, and just ahead of UC-Berkeley at 6.3%. Like MIT, the University of Chicago no longer requires a field course in economic history at the graduate level. Unlike MIT, it does at least still have one economic history course listed in the graduate course catalog. The three core areas of study at Chicago are price theory, quantitative methods, and the theory of income. David Mitch (2011) dates the decline of economic history at

Chicago to the elimination of the economic history requirement for the PhD in the early 1980s. Predictably, this led to a decline in doctoral dissertations written in the field after 1990. The shift of the two remaining economic historians into other fields and the termination of the economic history workshop were the final nails in the coffin.

MIT and Chicago are not unique among top programs. More than half of the 50 programs in this survey do not offer any economic history course, only 11 offer it as a field of emphasis, and eight require a course in economic history as part of the core curriculum. An additional three programs offer an economic history course as one of a number of restricted electives. Gone are the days when Rondo Cameron (1965) was able to boast that the vast majority of professional economists were trained in graduate schools that required courses in economic history. The view that economic history is a useful tool, and that the research of its practitioners is useful, has not translated into the belief that it is an integral part of the graduate curriculum.

While the decrease in economic history positions is discouraging, many young economic historians market themselves as specialists in other fields, but continue to publish in the economic history journals as well as other field journals. However, the drop in required economic history courses presents a grave concern for the future production of economic historians.

The disappearance of economic history from leading economics graduate programs is problematic. Without the tools being taught, without specific instruction in the methodology and approach, economic history risks extinction. Economic historians understand the difference between economists using historical data and true economic history research, but apparently economics departments don't care.

It is not just self-preservation that underlies this concern for the disappearance of economic history courses. The economics profession does not appear to share the view of economic history espoused by Ashley, that a desire to know about our past is reason enough to study it. Today the typical economist cares about the past "only to the extent that it sheds light on the present. This is unfortunate and we can (and should) keep arguing that this is a narrow view of social science" (Abramitzky 2015, p. 1242). Certainly, studying the past to understand the present is important, but we risk missing many important contributions, or worse, failing to investigate them in the first place if our scope is that narrow.

What makes economic historians unique is not their use of historical data or their focus on the past, but that they study the growth and evolution of economies over the long term. In this way, economic history's closest kin is development economics. In addition, the attention that economic historians give to noneconomic factors, such as legal and political systems, to say nothing of the contextual setting provided by their study of history, distinguishes them from economic theorists. Given the longer time span economic historians consider, doing so gives fuller attention to changes in institutions.

What Do Graduate Programs Do?

The training of an economist is something that is likely familiar to anyone reading this. According to the American Economic Association, there are 144 institutions in the United States that grant a Ph.D. in economics (https://www.aeaweb.org/resources/students/schools). This is the source of most of the academic economists in the country. There is a wide range of programs with a variety of requirements for those seeking the degree, and no doubt there are varying degrees of rigor across those institutions, but what are the similarities?

In an effort to discern these vital tools for economists, I looked at 50 of the top ranked U.S. doctoral programs (Table 1) with an eye toward finding the common elements in the programs. What I found is not particularly surprising, and for economic historians, not particularly encouraging. This is especially true when considering that the graduates of these 50 programs are a substantial share of those who will be teaching the next generation of economists, since they will disproportionately land jobs in the doctoral programs. And the concentration is especially heavy at the top, where 76% of the current faculty in top ten economics departments were hired from other schools in the top ten (Table 2).

All programs promote original research and promise faculty who are interested in training students to realize that goal and working with them to hone those skills. Many tout small enough class sizes to make that promise more doable. The use of AI to generate a mission statement from these programs would read: our doctoral program is designed to train students for careers in teaching and research in economics by providing strong backgrounds in economic theory and quantitative methods that can be applied to selected fields of specialization within the discipline.

The most common fields offered by these programs are microeconomic theory (offered by 92% of the surveyed programs), econometrics (84%), industrial organization (74%), labor (68%), and international economics (66%), followed by public

Table 1 Top Fifty U.S. Economics Graduate Programs

Arizona	Cornell	Michigan	Princeton	UCLA
Arizona St	Duke	Minnesota	Purdue	UCSD
Berkeley	Georgetown	Mississippi	Rice	UNC
Boston College	Harvard	MIT	Rochester	USC
Brown	Illinois	Northwestern	Rutgers	Vanderbilt
BU	Indiana	NYU	Stanford	Virginia
Cal Tech	Iowa	Ohio State	Texas	Wash U
Carnegie Mellon	Iowa St	Penn	Texas A&M	Washington
Chicago	Johns Hopkins	Penn State	UC Davis	Wisconsin
Columbia	Mich State	Pitt	UC Irvine	Yale

Note: https://www.aeaweb.org/resources/students/grad-prep/program-rankings. The list was compiled from the AEA website at aeaweb.org. I looked at the top 50 graduate programs in economics that appeared on both the Ideas RePEc ranking and the Econphd.net ranking of top economics programs and top economic history programs

Table 2 Origin of faculty at top ten programs

	Program									
Source of PhD	Berkeley (%)	Brown (%)	Chicago (%)	Columbia (%)	Harvard (%)	MIT (%)	NYU (%)	Princeton (%)	Stanford (%)	Yale (%)
[a]Berkeley	10.1	10.0	3.5	13.7	8.6	0.0	5.3	5.3	4.9	4.3
Brown	0.0	5.0	0.0	0.0	0.0	0.0	0.0	0.0	2.4	0.0
Chicago	0.0	2.5	10.4	3.9	3.4	5.1	7.9	8.8	2.4	4.3
Columbia	1.4	10.0	1.7	3.9	0.0	0.0	6.6	0.0	2.4	2.2
Harvard	20.3	22.5	17.4	15.7	29.3	30.8	13.2	26.3	19.5	6.5
MIT	17.4	7.5	3.5	11.8	29.3	28.2	7.9	12.3	22.0	19.6
NYU	2.9	2.5	3.5	5.9	0.0	2.6	1.3	1.8	0.0	0.0
Princeton	4.3	7.5	6.1	3.9	3.4	7.7	6.6	12.3	0.0	2.2
[a]Stanford	11.6	2.5	8.7	9.8	3.4	10.3	7.9	0.0	24.4	8.7
[a]Yale	5.8	2.5	5.2	3.9	3.4	0.0	6.6	5.3	4.9	8.7
TOP TEN	73.9	72.5	60.0	72.5	81.0	84.6	63.2	71.9	82.9	56.5
PhD from [a]Program	27.5	15.0	17.4	27.4	15.4	10.3	19.8	10.6	34.2	21.7

Note: [a] Required course in economic history. The final row is % of hires from top ten programs that require economic history. It does not count faculty from any programs outside of top ten finance, macro theory, development, and finance/financial economics. Economic history is 11th on the list of most popular fields, offered by 32% of the programs surveyed, the same as environmental/natural resources/energy and monetary theory.

The top graduate programs in economics all have a strong quantitative and analytical orientation. They are clearly designed to provide a working knowledge of cutting-edge research skills and economic theory. All require some breadth to this theoretical foundation, and some go further to broaden each student's understanding of economic institutions. The one bright spot for economic history is that the single most common course among other required courses is economic history, which 16% of the programs require outright and another 6% offer as a restricted elective. This is followed by an advanced methods course (technical methodology) in 16% of the programs, advanced micro or macro theory (14%), research methods (12%), and game theory (8%). Two programs require courses on teaching and two others on writing.

The prevailing curriculum stresses the grounding of models in theory, thus ensuring that, even in applied work, theoretical assumptions are clearly specified in place of intuition. This approach promotes an open discussion of the implications of the results and the fit of the model. Most of these 50 PhD programs are organized in a way to provide students with a rigorous training in economic theory and econometrics, which they can then use to produce original research in a variety of applied, theoretical, and empirical settings. The intense focus on theory and technique allows for the application of rigorous theory enhanced with the latest techniques to carefully study "real world" issues and institutions.

Regardless of the final landing spot—be it academia, government, or the private sector, a PhD in economics arms students with research skills, data modeling, and oral and written communication skills that make economists relevant far beyond the classroom. A graduate of one of these programs should be able to successfully apply the knowledge and skills gained to a wide range of economic problems in a broad array of institutional settings.

Some programs have a unique spin, or at least a good catch phrase. For example, the stated goal of the program at the University of Wisconsin is fundamental and simple: "To train top notch economists." On the other hand, CalTech promises "the opportunity for highly motivated and quantitatively oriented students to pursue interdisciplinary research in areas common to economics, political science, political economy, history, psychology, anthropology, law, and public policy … [because] a wide variety of social phenomena are best understood as the consequence of intelligent decisions by individuals pursuing their own ends."

The Three-Pronged Core

Regardless of the mission statement each program may have, most of which are generically similar, the foundation courses are de rigueur: two semesters (or the quarter equivalent) of microeconomic theory, two semesters of macroeconomic theory, two semesters of econometrics, and a semester of quantitative methods. It is clear that an economist receives a strong theoretical and technical foundation (Table 3).

The typical core is 2 years, consisting of a first year sequence of two semesters of micro and macro theory, two of econometrics or quantitative methods, with the remaining econometrics or methods courses in the second year, along with any other required courses, and a start on the field courses. Theory exams in macro and micro, and in some cases quantitative methods as well, are taken between the first and second year. And all programs require participation in workshops where students will be exposed to a wide range of original research and present their own work in progress.

Two semesters (or the quarter equivalent) of micro theory are required by 74% of the programs, with 23% requiring three or more. The numbers are nearly identical for macro theory (74% and 20%). One program requires no specific microeconomic theory and only one semester of macroeconomic theory. Seven programs require one additional theory course beyond the required core.

The typical sequence of microeconomic theory courses covers models of equilibrium, utility, and duality including general and partial equilibrium, and core concepts and methods such as optimality, comparative statics, and envelope theorems. Game theory is used to study strategic interactions in economic organizations, including imperfectly competitive markets and economies with public goods and externalities.

Microeconomics makes use of data on the behavior of economic agents, markets, and institutions to understand issues in industrial organization, public finance, political institutions, labor markets, and the household, to name but a few. The micro courses prepare students to leverage the empirical implications of theoretical economic models, so they can test and estimate those models using the latest econometric and statistical techniques.

Table 3 Characteristics of fifty leading graduate programs in economics

Count	Math camp	Stats/Math courses	Micro courses	Macro courses	Econometrics courses	Number of economic history courses
0	38	18	0	1	2	27
1	11	24	1	2	6	7
2	1	6	37	37	30	8
3 or more	0	2	12	10	12	7
max	2	6	4	4	6	4
mean	1.1	1.4	2.2	2.2	2.2	0.9
min	1	1	1	1	1	0

Note: Courses are semester equivalents

Almost universally, the sequence is designed to provide a thorough overview of microeconomic tools that will be used by Ph.D. students in all fields. The broad topics of the theory of firms and consumers, market structure and innovation, firm dynamics, product markets, and business networks form the bedrock of the education of an economist.

The topics appearing most frequently on macroeconomics course syllabi include growth theory, dynamic equilibrium, business cycles, monetary and fiscal policy, and Keynesian, Classical, and neo-Keynesian models of the economy. Intertemporal models of consumption and labor supply, implications of these models for the behavior of macroeconomic aggregates, fiscal policy, monetary policy, money demand, and inflation are common topics as well. Economic growth appears on several syllabi. This connects macro theory to the common tenet of economic history, but there is no link between the programs that highlight economic growth and those that offer economic history courses.

The core courses are designed to train students in the methodology of modern dynamic economics, including dynamic programming, vector autoregressions, equilibrium concepts, and computational methods. Advanced courses required in some programs are topical and track frontier research in macroeconomics, including heterogeneous agent economics with adjustment costs to capital and labor, wealth inequality in incomplete market economies with financial market imperfections, optimal taxation, and search theories of unemployment.

A quarter of the programs surveyed require a "math camp" prior to the beginning of the first semester of the program and two thirds of them require at least one additional math, quantitative methods, or statistics class. 94% of the programs require a minimum of two semesters of econometrics and 20% require three or more semesters. In addition, 16% of the programs require an elective in an advanced technical methods course, and four require a course in game theory.

The purpose of the quantitative methods courses is to build a sound background in statistical inferential procedures that are used in economic data analysis. While verbal and graphical analyses are often helpful, economists can truly achieve precise and powerful results by setting up and solving constrained optimization problems.

Sampling theory and Bayesian viewpoints form the bedrock of statistics courses. Courses usually cover probability, random variables and distributions, estimation, testing hypotheses, and sampling distribution of estimators. The math portion of the curriculum covers basic mathematical tools for consumer and producer theory, such as compact sets, differentiability, constrained optimization, linear algebra, and quadratic forms. Dynamic models of macroeconomics, growth, and human capital round out the common syllabus topics. The emphasis is generally not on proving theorems, but rather using the tools of mathematics to develop an understanding of how and why each method works in order to determine which approach is best to address the problem at hand.

The econometrics core of the graduate curriculum is designed to equip students with the tools they will need to ply their trade. Most of the programs build an empirical portion into these courses, particularly the econometrics sequences, requiring students to produce a paper highlighting a technique or model from the course. This requirement helps students acquire experience in applied econometric work, including the use of econometric software packages and programming techniques. These skills, unknown a generation ago, are now indispensable for all practicing economists, regardless of their fields of specialization.

A standard first year course in econometric theory and methods provides an understanding of econometric theory that underlies common econometric models, with a focus on regression models and their many extensions. It covers estimation techniques such as least squares, maximum likelihood, and generalized methods of moments, as well as inference techniques including standard asymptotics, unit root asymptotics, and bootstrapping. The econometrics course sequence covers the foundational material in probability theory and econometric methods, preparing students to construct, estimate, and test econometric models as a process, bridging the gap between theory and applied work.

Teaching Experience (Sometimes) Required

An essential skill of any successful researcher is the ability to communicate effectively in both written and oral presentations. Research presentations are one obvious example of oral communication, but teaching is certainly another, and arguably a more important one, since most Ph.D. economists work in academia. To that end, many of the top graduate programs (but not all) require a workshop, if not an entire semester course, in teaching.

Teaching has certainly evolved over time, and no longer resembles what those of us from an earlier generation remember as the standard lecture format. Note that here I am not referring so much to graduate education, which has long resembled more of a seminar format featuring the development and exchange of scholarly information, often in a small group setting. Rather, I am referring to undergraduate teaching. It is undergraduate teaching that will occupy the lion's share of the workload of most academic economists. Most academic economists don't work at Ph.D. granting institutions, and even those that do will seldom be tasked exclusively with teaching graduate students.

Teaching experience is an essential part of graduate training. The task of teaching economics then is one of the practical applications of theoretical learning within a group setting, which ideally involves the introduction of ideas and methodology, the practice of skills, and beyond the most basic introductory levels, an exchange of ideas. Teaching courses are designed to introduce students to the art of planning, presenting, evaluating, and assessing course content, delivery, and comprehension.

In the belief that practice makes perfect, and because it is cheap labor, most programs require, or at least offer the opportunity (or encouragement) to students to become teaching assistants and eventually take responsibility for their own courses. Most programs state as a goal that their graduates will have taught at least one course completely on their own before graduating.

Some programs also offer an introduction to research, or a research methods course. The object of this course is to teach students how to do research. It often takes the form of a workshop where students discuss and analyze in detail recent papers drawn from literature relevant to various areas of economics. It serves as a formal environment in which the students present and evaluate their research on a regular basis.

Economic History Courses

The economic history courses at the schools in this survey tend to focus either on European or American economies. The typical European course will focus on the evolution of the economy from the industrial revolution forward, and the typical American course begins with the colonial economy. While the overarching theme tends to be economic growth, coverage of specialized topics is prevalent on the syllabi. For the European courses, topics include mercantilism, industrialization, the standard of living debate, international trade, the gold standard, war, and the European Union.

The growth and development of the economy forms the backbone of the American courses. Certain topics receive special attention there as well: agriculture, banking, slavery, westward migration, the Great Depression, and postwar growth.

In either case, the tools learned in the core courses are applied here as well as in other field courses. In economic history courses, the focus is on the use of theory and econometric techniques to research long-term factors in the development of the economy. While any country could be the focus of such examination, Europe and North America are most likely to be the focus of an economic history course in a U.S. college or university. None of the programs surveyed has a regularly scheduled economic history course dedicated to a region other than America or Western Europe.

Berkeley offers a unique course entitled Macroeconomic History. The course focuses on the study of research intersecting empirical macroeconomics and American economic history. Its stated purpose is to provide a firm grounding in the areas of economic policy, with a special focus on credit market disruptions, financial crises, and short-run fluctuations in the American economy. In other words, a historical analysis of the successes and failures of monetary and fiscal policy. Its main focus is on innovative approaches to identifying causation, empirical estimation of macroeconomic relationships, and overcoming the problems of data limitations. The desired outcome of the course is to guide students as they transition from reading research to undertaking their own.

We can take a broader look at economic history course syllabi, beyond just our 50 school sample by looking at the economic history course syllabus database available on the EHA website. Focusing only on graduate programs, we find a bit more variety in topics, but the same overall theme of the course being economic growth and development. The general orientation of the courses are much more macro (80%) than micro (20%). A very few courses are defined as an introduction to applied empirical research in economics mixing applications and policy with history. More or less all the other courses deal with the sources of growth faithful to the founding fathers of economic history and cliometrics. Emphasis is given to the use of economic theory, quantitative methods and the insights that profound historical knowledge can provide to the practice of economics. The US economy continues to serve as the central experimental lab. This is no surprise, given that this survey was restricted to American universities. Courses focused on international comparisons and Europe predominantly start with the Industrial Revolution. Very few deal with earlier periods. The topics appearing most frequently on syllabi include long-run trends in economic history and development, including globalization, growth theories, the role of institutions, agriculture, demography, and transportation.

The overall themes that pervade these courses focus on big questions such as the sources and determinants of sustainable economic growth. In particular, can technical progress alone increase social welfare or can capital accumulation also lead to a permanent increase in per capita income? What factors of production engender sustainable growth: physical, environmental, human, social, or technological knowledge? What mechanisms guarantee long-term growth in a market economy? What are the market structures within which such growth can be achieved? And above all, why isn't the whole world developed?

The primary skills emphasized in these courses include modeling, a strong focus on quantitative and empirical methods in economic history, the application of appropriate analytical tools, constructing datasets, putting economics in context (in a non-mathematical style) and deep sources analysis, and written and oral communication, group work, computer skills, and academic integrity. This long run, big picture focus is common among all the economic history courses surveyed, and indeed, is central to our argument that economic history does provide added value to the education of an economist.

What Do Economic Historians Have to Offer?

Economic historians ask the most compelling questions, but research that makes use of historic data is not necessarily economic history. Robert Solow (1985, p. 330) complained that data without historical context "gives back to the theorist the same routine gruel that the economic theorist gives to the historian. Why should [one] believe, when it is applied to thin eighteenth-century data, something that carries no conviction when it is done with more ample twentieth-century data?"

Solow verbalizes the problem that occurs when the use of old data is considered economic history. Without proper context, we run the danger of misinterpreting the meaning of our analysis of the model we test using "old data." Data are not generated in a vacuum. Failure to appreciate the historical setting of the era from which data were gathered will result in unreliable results. It is imperative to be cognizant of how the data were collected, from what source, by whom, and for what purpose. Such knowledge is critical if one is to avoid errors caused by non-random data that can introduce biases to conclusions drawn from it. Without history, it is just theory applied to old data.

The story (historical background), which provides context, is important. There is no vacuum in which we can analyze data. Economic history is an observational discipline, making use of a wide variety of explanations and weighing the importance of each. The focus on one explanation is too narrow and ignores too much of what is going on in the world. Economic historians are trained to look beyond the field of economics. To do otherwise is to lose sight of the forest by focusing too much on the trees.

Economic historians are trained to look around themselves and beyond economic theory for explanations. They are trained to consider the source of their data, how it was compiled, by whom, at what time, and under what circumstances. History done right can provide valuable insight into current policy debate. History without context will more likely lead us astray. History links events over time and across disciplines, and economic historians are uniquely prepared to bring their tools of analysis to do just that.

Robert Fogel (1964) long argued that data, not relevant theory, was the scarce resource that hampered historical research. The lack of data was the greatest hurdle to our ability to analyze economic growth. Without data we have nothing to measure, and if we cannot measure change, we cannot be certain that it occurred. Some of the greatest contributions to the fields of economics and history by economic historians have been the discovery and compilation of new datasets that allow us to analyze economic theory.

Economic historians have always been known for their work in building databases by collecting data from archival sources and gathering it into useful forms for analysis. Before the advent of the computer and digitization this was done by hand, painstakingly and slowly. With the evolution of advances in technology including the computer, scanning, and digital photography, the task was not eliminated, but sped up, allowing for the building of larger and richer datasets.

Economic historians emphasize the relationship between data and its historical origins. Cliometrics is often associated with technique. Economic theory requires that we be able to measure the impact of one variable on another. Without good data, the best technique is limited in its ability to illuminate these relationships. The application of sound theory to solid, unbiased data is the essence of cliometrics. The collection, collation, and careful vetting of the data to clean it of errors are necessary prerequisites to the measurement of economic change. Understanding the source of the data is key.

Diebolt (2016) encapsulates the need to bridge the gap between the *Geisteswissenschaften* (human sciences) and *Naturwissenschaften* (natural sciences). His perspective advocates for a synthesis of qualitative understanding (*Verstehen*) and quantitative explanation (*Erklären*), blending historical narrative with empirical validation. By integrating facts and stylized facts with rigorous data-driven methodologies, cliometrics achieves a more holistic analysis of economic history—one that explains past economic experiences while elucidating the intricate ways economic factors shape social and political developments. This interdisciplinary approach fosters a unified framework within the social sciences, enhancing our ability to comprehend and forecast economic and societal transformations across both developed and developing economies.

The oft unheralded but important role of dataset creation is one of the pillars of the training of an economic historian. It is less sexy than its brethren, economic theory and econometric techniques, but it has grown in prominence and value as a result of the computer revolution, as has the ability to conduct cutting-edge econometric tests on said data. Simply put, without the data, there would be no theory to empirically test.

The use of newly created datasets is common in economic history research. A survey of articles published in four leading economic history journals shows the reliance on measurement or exploitation of newly discovered or created databases for new research. Looking at the 2018 volume of the *Journal of Economic History*, *Explorations in Economic History*, *Cliometrica*, and the *Economic History Review*, 58% of articles relied on newly created or discovered data for their analysis (Diebolt and Haupert 2019b).

Matt Jaremski (2019) makes a case for the value of database creation in the education of graduate students. Graduate school is the most likely environment when young scholars will have support and time to collect and build a new dataset that has the potential to advance the frontiers of knowledge. Economic history classes must cover how data are collected and what to do when data are not available. Research in economic history is more often than not built on archival work. Therefore, to understand that research, we must understand how and why the data were gathered or created. He argues that young scholars tend to gravitate toward the same publically available data, and because of its heavy use, they are forced to make more marginal contributions rather than opening new areas of study.

Economic historians have contributed large and expansive datasets for researchers. The accumulation of the data is in itself monumental in many respects, but its usefulness has been expanded by the rapid growth of computing power. The ability to handle "big data" is not an economic issue by itself, but the construction of significant, important historical datasets, which can then be analyzed using the latest econometric techniques and computer programs, is very much a contribution of economic historians.

Demography has benefitted from technology and techniques that have allowed for the explosion of individual-level microdata. The digitization of marriage, birth, and death records, state censuses, immigration records, and the federal census has made it possible to gather large amounts of data on individuals by linking these databases in order to follow them across generations in an effort to better understand behavior, causality, and intergenerational mobility.

Finally, economic historians have spawned entire new approaches to the study of economics. At the forefront are the new institutional economics, pioneered by Douglass North, and anthropometrics, which counts among its initial practitioners Robert Fogel. It is no coincidence that these two were recognized with the Nobel Prize in Economic Science in 1993.

Conclusion

Theory and technique are the building blocks in the training of American PhD economists. The addition of history in that training is what separates economic historians from other economists. All three are necessary to the success of the discipline, and historically, all three were part of the training. The training of economists in the United States is extensive and rigorous, but it could be even better. Reviving economic history as an integral part of that training would accomplish that.

Economic History plays an important role in the training of economists: Milton Friedman's classic treatise on money, as well as Simon Kuznets's path-breaking work on economic development, for example, was, to a considerable degree, based on historical analysis. Economic historians analyze the dynamic processes of development over time by formulating explicit formal models and econometric methods. They test hypotheses formally in order to enhance our understanding of how major determinants such as the industrial revolution, industrialization, and the information revolution have impacted our lives today. And they use historical (often archival) data to test the extent to which economic theory can be validated or improved upon in a wide array of ways, spawning totally new perspectives, such as counterfactual history. The granting of Nobel Prizes in Economics to economic historians Douglass North, Robert Fogel, Claudia Goldin, and Daron Acemoglu is a clear recognition of the unique scientific contribution economic history makes to the larger economics discipline.

But should we even have to argue for a place for economic history? George Santayana (1905) tells us that at the least pragmatic level, the worth of economic history is that of general intellectual activity, and nothing should be easier than convincing professional intellectuals that such activity is worthwhile. Economic history provides more and better economic facts, better economic theory, better economic policy, and does so over a longer period of time and greater variety of institutional settings than any other field of economic study can provide. The practical value of historical scholarship is not necessarily in its direct or immediate application. It is, rather, an indispensable part of the combined labor of the social sciences.

So in the end, what is the place of economic history in the training of economists? Robert Fogel defined the methodological features of cliometrics, which is the current de facto training of economic historians. He considered it fundamental that cliometrics should lay stress on measurements and that it should recognize the existence of close links between measurement and theory. Indeed, unless accompanied by statistical and/or econometric processing and systematic quantitative analysis, measurement is just another form of narrative history. It is true that it replaces words with figures, but it does not bring in any new factors.

But quantitative does not displace qualitative. Dropping history in favor of technique does not make the toolkit of the economist more robust. Rather, the two complement one another. History is a discipline of synthesis. The main contribution of economic history is to mobilize all the relevant information that can be gathered from history, including cultural and institutional development, so as to enrich and challenge economic theories. It has performed this task admirably, and in combination with training in the use of cutting-edge techniques, access to bigger and better databases, and advanced computing power, it shows no signs of slowing down, nor of letting either the disciplines of history or economics down.

Finally, to address the marginalization of economic history in graduate training, several concrete steps can be taken. First and foremost, departments should consider reintroducing economic history as a required core course, or at the very least, as one of the standard field options in the PhD curriculum, signaling its foundational role alongside theory and econometrics. The usefulness of economic history to graduate students has already been discussed, so even if students do not select it as a field of study, the course would be beneficial. Second, pedagogical approaches in any courses that require research as an output should blend narrative and quantitative methods—encouraging students to engage with both primary historical sources and formal empirical techniques. Third, economic history can be woven into existing courses. For example, macroeconomics modules might incorporate long-run growth case studies, while institutional economics could benefit from historical perspectives on state capacity, banking, or inequality.

In an ideal world, the education of economists would expand beyond the economics department and become more interdisciplinary. Collaboration should be encouraged, particularly with historians, sociologists, or political scientists who share empirical interests. Funding for historical data collection, digitization, and replication studies could also be prioritized, giving students hands-on research experience. Graduate seminars and workshops in economic history—involving students across fields—can foster intellectual exchange and reinforce the relevance of historical thinking in contemporary economic research. These changes would not only enrich students' training, but would strengthen the discipline's capacity to address deep-rooted and long-term economic questions.

References

Abramitzky, Ran. 2015. Economics and the Modern Economic Historian. *The Journal of Economic History* 74 (4): 105–147.

Acemoglu, Daron, Simon Johnson, and James A. Robinson. 2001. The Colonial Origins of Comparative Development: An Empirical Investigation. *American Economic Review* 91 (5): 1369–1401.

Acemoglu, Daron, Simon Johnson, and James A. Robinson. 2002. Reversal of Fortune: Geography and Institutions in the Making of the Modern World Income Distribution. *Quarterly Journal of Economics* 117 (4): 1231–1294.

Aitken, Hugh G. J. 1960. On the Present State of Economic History. *The Canadian Journal of Econmics and Politic Science / Revue canadienne d'Economique et de Science politique* 26 (1): 87–95.

Arrow, Kenneth J. 1985. Maine and Texas. *American Economic Review* 75 (2): 320–323.

Ashley, William J. 1893. On the Study of Economic History. *The Quarterly Journal of Economics* 7 (2): 115–136.

Ashley, William. 1927. The Place of Economic History in University Studies. *The Economic History Review* 1 (1): 1–11.
Cameron, Rondo. Mar 1, 1965. Has Economic History A Role in an Economist's Education? *The American Economic Review* 55 (1/2): 112–115.
Clark, G. N. 1932. The Study of Economic History. *History, New Series* 17 (66): 97–110.
Clarke, Conor. 2009. A two part interview with Paul Samuelson. *The Atlantic*, June 17–18. https://www.theatlantic.com/politics/archive/2009/06/an-interview-with-paul-samuelson-part-one/19572/, downloaded December 2017
Coclanis, Peter, and David Carlton. 2001. The Crisis in Economic History. *Challenge* 44 (6): 93–103.
Collins, William J. 2015. Looking Forward: Positive and Normative Views of Economic History's Future. *Journal of Economic History* 75 (4): 1228–1233.
Diebolt, C. 2016. Cliometrica after 10 years: Definition and principles of cliometric research. *Cliometrica* 10 (1): 1-4.
Diebolt, Claude, and Michael Haupert. 2016a. Clio's Contributions to Economics and History. *Revue d'Economie Politique* 126 (5): 971–989.
Diebolt, Claude, and Michael Haupert. 2016b. An Introduction to the Handbook of Cliometrics. In *Handbook of Cliometrics*, ed. Claude Diebolt and Michael Haupert, v–xiv. Berlin: Springer.
Diebolt, Claude, and Michael Haupert. 2019a. We Are All Ninjas: How Economic History Has Infiltrated the Economics Discipline. *Sartoniana* 32:197–221.
Diebolt, Claude, and Michael Haupert. 2019b. Measuring Success: Clio and the Value of Database Creation. *Annals of the Fondazione Luigi Einaudi: An Interdisciplinary Journal of Economics, History, and Political Science* LIII (2): 59–80.
Drobak, John N., and Douglass C. North. 2005. Legal Change in Economic Analysis. In *The Elgar Companion to Law and Economics*, ed. Jürgen G. Backhaus, 2nd ed., 53–57. Edward Elgar Publishing.
Ellison, Glenn. 2013. How Does the Market Use Citation Data? The Hirsch Index in Economics. *American Economic Journal: Applied Economics* 5 (3): 63–90.
Fogel, Robert. 1964. Discussion. *American Economic Review* 54 (3): 377–389.
Gallman, Robert E. 1965. The Role of Economic History in the Education of the Economist. *American Economic Review* 55 (1/2): 109–111.
Goldin, Claudia, and Marcella Alsan. Watersheds in Child Mortality: The Role of Effective Water and Sewerage Infrastructure, 1880 to 1920. *Journal of Political Economy* 127 (2): 586–638.
Goodrich, Carter. 1960. Economic History: One Field or Two? *Journal of Economic History* 20 (4): 531–538.
Gras, N. S. B. 1920. The Present Condition of Economic History. *Quarterly Journal of Economics* 34 (2): 209–224.
Haupert, Michael. 2005. Economic Historians: A Preliminary Review of Society Responses. *Newsletter of the Cliometric Society* 20 (2): 56–59.
Haupert, Michael. 2024. History of Cliometrics. In *Handbook of Cliometrics*, ed. Claude Diebolt and Michael Haupert, vol. II, 3–32. Berlin: Springer.
Hohenberg, Paul M. 2008. Toward a More Useful Economic History. *Journal of Economic History* 68 (2): 339–354.
Jaremski, Matt. Today's Economic History and Tomorrow's Scholars. *Cliometrica* online first. Accessed June 2019.
Knight, Frank. 2014. The Limitations of Scientific Method in Economics. In *The Ethics of Competition and Other Essays*, 105–147. Mansfield Centre, CT: Martino Publishing [1924].
Knight, Jack, and Douglass North. 1997. Explaining Economic Change: The Interplay Between Cognition and Institutions. In *The Political Economy of Property Rights*, ed. David L. Weimer, 349–354. Cambridge University Press.
Lamoreaux, Naomi. 2015. The Future of Economic History Must Be Interdisciplinary. *Journal of Economic History* 75 (4): 1252–1256.

Liebowitz, S. J., and J. P. Palmer. 1983. *Assessing the Relative Impacts of Economics Journals*. Centre for the Economic Analysis of Property Rights, Working Paper 83-01, U. of Western Ontario.
Liebowitz, S. J., and J. P. Palmer. 1984. Assessing the Relative Impacts of Economics Journals. *Journal of Economic Literature* 22 (1): 77–88.
Lyon, E. B. 1926. Economic History and Its Place in the College Course. *Social Science* 1 (3): 238–242.
Magnusson, Lars. 2003. Review of *The Problems and Methods of Economic History* by Wittold Kula. *Journal of Economic History*928.
Mantzavinos, Christopher, Douglass C. North, and Syed Shariq. 2004. Learning, Institutions, and Economic Performance. *Perspectives on Politics* 2 (1): 75–84.
McCloskey, Deirdre N. 1976. Does the Past Have Useful Economics? *Journal of Economic Literature* 14 (2): 434–461.
Mitch, David. 2011. Economic History in Departments of Economics: The Case of the University of Chicago, 1892 to the Present. *Social Science History* 35 (2): 237–271.
Mokyr, Joel. 2003. *The Oxford Encyclopedia of Economic History*. Vol. 1. New York: Oxford University Press.
Nef, John U. 1944. What is Economic History? *Journal of Economic History* 4 (Supplement: The Tasks of Economic History): 1–19.
North, Douglass C., and Barry R. Weingast. 2000. Introduction: Institutional Analysis and Economic History. *The Journal of Economic History* 60 (2): 414–417.
Price, L. L. 1906. The Study of Economic History. *The Economic Journal* 16 (61): 12–32.
Romer, Christina D. 1994. The End of Economic History? *Journal of Economic Education* 25 (1): 49–66.
Roy, Tirthankar. 2004. Economic History: An Endangered Discipline. *Economic and Political Weekly* 39 (29): 3238–3243.
Santayana, George. 1905. *The Life of Reason*. New York: Charles Scribner's Sons 1953.
Solow, Robert M. 1985. Economic History and Economics. *American Economic Review* 75 (2), Papers and Proceedings of the Ninety-Seventh Annual Meeting of the American Economic Association, 328–331.
Tawney, R. H. 1933. The Study of Economic History. *Economica* 39:1–21.
Temin, Peter. 2016. Economic History and Economic Development: New Economic History in Retrospect and Prospect. In *The Handbook of Cliometrics*, ed. Claude Diebolt and Michael Haupert, 33–51. Berlin: Springer Verlag.
Usher, Abbott Payson. 1933. Two Notable Contributions to Economic History. *Quarterly Journal of Economics* 48 (1): 171–180.
Whaples, Robert. Review of John Black *A Dictionary of Economics*. Economic History Services, March, 2004. https://eh.net/book_reviews/a-dictionary-of-economics/

Economic History in Western Europe: Bridging *Verstehen* and *Erklären*

Claude Diebolt

> *Like many children of Clio, Economic History took shape even before it was born. ("Flexibility and Growth: the Discipline of Economic History in the Mirror of the Past", Professor em. Herman Van der Wee, Leuven University, Belgium, Opening lecture at the XIIIth I.E.H.A.Congress, Buenos Aires, 22 July 2002.)*

Abstract In this chapter, *wie es eigentlich gewesen (ist)*—as it actually happened—and *zu den Sachen selbst*—to the things themselves—resonate particularly through the engagement with the concepts of *Verstehen*—understanding—and *Erklären*—explaining—, two methodological poles in dynamic tension that continue to shape research in economic history in Western Europe, and arguably at the global level.

Introduction

Economic history emerged at the end of the nineteenth century in response to a major methodological dispute—the *Methodenstreit*—which pitted economists favoring a historical, evolutionary, and institutionalist approach against those advocating a purely theoretical, neo-classical model. The latter ultimately prevailed, prompting economic history to carve out a new identity for itself—one marked by relative autonomy not only from economics but, perhaps paradoxically, from history as well.

C. Diebolt (✉)
BETA/CNRS, University of Strasbourg, Strasbourg, France
e-mail: cdiebolt@unistra.fr

C. Diebolt, M. Haupert (eds.), *The State of Economic History*, Frontiers in Economic History, https://doi.org/10.1007/978-3-032-01624-9_2

In Western Europe before 1914, history remained largely political. It followed the event-driven, Rankean tradition whose goal was to reconstruct the past "as it actually happened" (*wie es eigentlich gewesen* [ist][1]), through textual analysis using historical criticism and philological methods. Its institutional role was clear: to train secondary school teachers and, in the realm of research, to contribute to the construction of national identity. This did not preclude significant advances toward economic history—one need only to recall the work of Belgian historian Henri Pirenne, who, as recognized even by the *Annales* School (Lyon and Lyon 1991), helped open the way to a more global and integrated historical perspective. In its own way, *wie es eigentlich gewesen ist* also evokes Edmund Husserl's renowned formulation *zu den Sachen selbst* (Heidegger and Herrmann 1995) often understood as an appeal to return to immediate experience—direct engagement with phenomena prior to any conceptualization or theorization—with the aim of arriving at *Aussagen* (statements), which constitute the enduring core of scientific knowledge. Phenomenological analysis thereby becomes a tool for conceptual purification, wherein lived experience is mobilized to validate or refine the meaning of logical terms. This process may be seen as a form of mediation between intuitive experience and logical formalization—one that resists both the imprecision of subjective experience and the abstract detachment of law-like formulations devoid of experiential grounding.

In some European countries, economic history developed to the point of institutional independence, forming dedicated departments—as was the case with the London School of Economics. Yet in many other Western European nations, it struggled to gain similar footing.

In France, economic history was initially pioneered by economists such as Ernest Labrousse (1895–1988) and François Simiand (1873–1935), before being taken up by the *Annales* School, which came to dominate historical research after World War II. The 1960s and the 1970s were a golden age for economic history in many Western countries. The discipline emphasized long-term trends, cycles, and economic conditions. Quantification, computers, and deterministic, global approaches flourished. This was a period when economic history aligned closely with the social sciences and enjoyed high visibility. Yet this moment was short-lived.

By the late 1970s, enthusiasm for quantitative approaches began to fade. Historians turned toward the new human sciences, particularly anthropology. Cultural history and the history of mentalities gained prominence, often with little interest in quantification. Broad, sweeping syntheses gave way to micro-histories and more granular analyses. Business history and case studies of individual firms rose to prominence, perhaps echoing both the decline of Marxist frameworks and the resurgence of liberalism. At the same time, Keynesian economic paradigms—which had underpinned much of macroeconomic and quantitative economic history—began to lose ground.

[1] Man hat der Historie das Amt, die Vergangenheit zu richten, die Mitwelt zum Nutzen zukünftiger Jahre zu belehren, beigemessen: so hoher Aemter unterwindet sich gegenwärtiger Versuch nicht: er will bloß sagen, wie es eingentlich gewesen. (Ranke 1824, pp. 9–10)

As historical research became increasingly cultural, even postmodern, economic science evolved in the opposite direction: macroeconomics was increasingly built on microeconomic foundations and mathematical optimization models. In this bifurcated landscape, what place—and more pressingly, what future—remains for economic history?

This brings us to a fundamental question: What is economic history? I turned to a leading reference, *The New Palgrave Dictionary of Economics*, and found a definition by Alexander Field that would likely provoke irritation among many Western European historians:

> Economic history is a sub-discipline within economics and, to a lesser degree, within history, whose main focus is the study of economic growth and development over time.[2]

Field (2008) elaborates further:

> Studies in economic growth, whether historical or contemporary, develop and analyze quantitative measures of increases in output and output per capita, emphasizing in particular changes in saving rates and rates of technological innovations... Economic development is a larger and more encompassing rubric, also including considerations of the role of cultural changes and changes in formal institutions.

This is, of course, an economist's view. But it underscores how deeply definitions of economic history are shaped by institutional context, which in turn reflects the specific academic histories of different countries—and even individual universities, especially in more decentralized systems than France.

These institutional differences are far from trivial. They shape how economic historians are trained and influence the status of the field. In Western Europe, when economic history is housed within humanities faculties, it tends to be practiced by scholars with limited training in economics or statistics. Prior to the rise of the digital humanities, historians in these faculties—particularly in France—received little to no formal instruction in economic theory or quantitative methods. Their knowledge is often outdated and disconnected from modern economics, which has become a highly formalized, mathematically rigorous discipline.

The result is a profound disconnect. Many historians are unable to engage with the methods or language of their economist counterparts. They may struggle not just to interpret equations, but to grasp the epistemological foundations of economic models. Economists, for their part, generalize; they focus on the typical or average case. Even when they try to be precise, they often do so through empirical bias (e.g., the endogenous vs. exogenous debate), and use "theory" and "model" interchangeably. Historians, by contrast, prioritize the particular over the general, understanding over prediction. For them, causal explanations often emerge from analogy, intuition, and a deep engagement with sources.

This methodological divide has only widened since the late 1970s, with historians increasingly influenced by qualitative sociology and anthropology, and drawn toward cultural history and the study of representations. Their comparative

[2] Field, A.: "Economic History", in: Durlauf et al. (Eds.), *New Palgrave Dictionary of Economics*, Palgrave Macmillan, London, 2nd Edition, 2008, p. 694.

advantage lies in working with written documents, visual materials, and oral testimonies. As a result, economic history, when practiced by historians, often morphs into economic and social history with a culturalist orientation—a study of intermediaries, migrations, domestic labor, or biographies of entrepreneurs and policymakers. In this way, it becomes increasingly aligned with the current preoccupations of historical scholarship, which places greater value on cultural and intellectual history.

Conversely, when economists write economic history, they are shaped by their own intellectual training. Economics is modeled on the natural sciences: heavily mathematical, formal, and quantitative. From the undergraduate level, students encounter abstract modeling and statistical methods. There is little room for cultural or institutional context. Courses in economic history or the history of economic thought—once common—have virtually vanished from graduate programs. As a result, many economists today lack even a basic understanding of historical developments before 1945. The professional incentive structure—favoring formalized, short articles in high-ranked journals—discourages engagement with historical depth. Economic history thus appears increasingly irrelevant to young researchers, except in the abstract frameworks of growth theory or development economics.

In conclusion, since 1945, economic history departments in Western Europe have gradually disappeared. The growing professional divergence between history and economics has made hybrid training programs difficult to sustain—too quantitative for historians, yet not rigorous enough for economists. Economic history now finds itself in a liminal space: suspended between two disciplines that have grown apart, and struggling to speak both of their languages.

Economists: Modern-Day Platonists

Economic history occupies a unique position at the intersection of two firmly established academic disciplines: history and economics. Since the 1970s—marked by the decline of both Marxism and the *Annales* school (the two trends being not unrelated)—these disciplines have grown increasingly distant from one another. From the outset, they have pursued markedly different objectives.

Economics, despite ongoing internal debates, has long harbored the ambition to align itself with the natural sciences. While some economists view the discipline as akin to logic or pure mathematics—non-empirical and primarily concerned with the derivation of theorems rather than laws in the natural science sense—there has existed, since at least in the eighteenth century (notably in the works of Boisguillebert and Quesnay, and later in Smith and Ricardo), a clear intention to construct a political economy capable of uncovering the laws governing economic functioning.

After 1870, the neo-classical school continued along this path, albeit with some ambiguity: Is economics a non-empirical science like mathematics, or does it build models intended for empirical verification? In practice, before 1914, the empirical dimension remained marginal, with rare exceptions such as Juglar (1862) and Jevons (1884) and their early work on business cycles.

Neo-classical economics adopted a distinctly Platonic orientation, moving away from inductive reasoning based on historical observation or stylized facts—often the tools of economists-cum-historians. Instead, it favored a deductive approach grounded in axioms of instrumental rationality, in Max Weber's terms, and advanced through increasingly abstract mathematical models.

The Classical School of Political Economy (roughly 1776–1870) focused primarily on what drives growth—capital accumulation spurred by profit-seeking—and whether this growth would be sustainable (Ricardo was pessimistic, citing diminishing returns). The neo-classical turn sought instead to formalize Smith's "invisible hand" hypothesis: identifying the conditions under which markets generate optimal outcomes and efficient resource allocation. This was the central project of Walras and Pareto (general equilibrium theory), and also of English economists such as Edgeworth (1881) and Marshall (1890), who pursued more partial equilibrium analyses.

Such models of pure and perfect competition were far removed from the concerns of historians—and even from those of more empirically oriented or institutionalist economists. In a period of profound transformation linked to the Second Industrial Revolution, the emergence of new economic powers (Germany, Japan), the intensification of the "social question," and growing industrial concentration, many were dissatisfied with the course of economic science. While Marxist approaches existed, they had little academic presence.

Marx (1867), extending the tradition of classical economics, emphasized both the innovation-driving role of capitalist competition and its self-destructive tendencies—namely, capital concentration and class polarization. He envisioned capitalism's eventual replacement by a system that would distribute the gains from technological development more equitably. His evolutionary conception of history—structured in stages—also aligned him, to some extent, with the German Historical School.

Thinkers like Weber, and later Pareto, laid the foundations of sociology, while Weber and other heirs of the Historical School helped establish economic history as a distinct field in the late nineteenth century, particularly in Germany and the USA. The first chair in economic history was awarded to William Ashley at Harvard in 1892. From that point onward, economic history began to diverge institutionally from economic science—though the *Journal of Economic Literature* still categorizes it as a subfield of economics.

Economists increasingly turned toward measurement, business cycles, and sectoral analysis (as in the early work of the NBER and Mitchell in the 1920s). The Great Depression catalyzed the birth of macroeconomics, now clearly distinct from microeconomics. Keynes (1936) famously argued that economies do not naturally return to equilibrium, necessitating state intervention. This perspective, combined with Tinbergen's (1939) modeling efforts and Cowles' (1933) work on asset pricing, laid the groundwork for econometrics.

World War II further accelerated this process, spurring the development of tools like operations research and game theory (Von Neumann and Morgenstern 1944). These advances culminated in the postwar Keynesian consensus, with the

Hicks–Hansen synthesis and large-scale macroeconometric models promising to fine-tune economies for continuous growth.

The postwar boom (1945–1970) reinforced this belief. In 1969, economics was formally honored alongside the Nobel sciences with the Bank of Sweden Prize. The 1950s also saw the institutionalization of national accounting, a cornerstone for economic policy and international comparisons. This methodological coherence had a major impact on quantitative economic history (Marczewski 1965), particularly in France (Perroux, Marczewski, Toutain, and Lévy-Leboyer), Germany (Hoffmann in Münster), and the UK (Deane and Cole).

Simultaneously, microeconomics and general equilibrium theory expanded rapidly. The 1950s and the 1960s witnessed landmark work in growth and development theory: Solow's (1956, 1957) growth accounting, Kuznets' (1966) sectoral analyses, and Rostow's (1960) developmental stages. From these threads emerged *cliometrics* in the USA—a new, model-driven economic history deeply embedded within economics and employing its formal language and tools almost exclusively.

However, the 1970s ushered in major shocks—the oil crisis, the end of Bretton Woods, the rise of emerging economies, deindustrialization in Europe—that undermined faith in Keynesianism and macroeconomic modeling. Lucas' critique (1976) argued that models ignoring microfoundations lacked predictive power. While Friedman and Schwarz (1963, 1982) still worked within macroeconomics and engaged with economic history, his successors—new classical macroeconomists—developed fully micro-founded models, assuming rational expectations and permanent equilibrium.

The new supply-side economics emphasized low inflation, budgetary discipline, open markets, and investor-friendly environments. The state's role was reimagined as long-term and structural—focused on infrastructure, education, and research.

In the 1980s, endogenous growth theory emerged (Lucas 1988; Romer 1986, 1990), incorporating R&D and human capital as internal drivers of growth. The 1990s then witnessed the expansion of industrial organization and game theory (Tirole 1988), alongside international trade theory (Helpman and Krugman 1987; Krugman 1994). Much of this work was highly theoretical and abstract, with limited empirical grounding—though econometrics regained prominence in the late 1990s and the 2000s, particularly in labor economics and development studies.

Despite internal diversity, the dominant neo-classical paradigm has fostered a consensus around a "hard science" vision of economics. Mathematics is now the discipline's lingua franca. Economists communicate through models—often untested empirically—and rely on quantitative data as the only acceptable representation of reality. Historical processes, institutions, and context are either ignored or reduced to variables. Econometric studies are frequently applied to wildly heterogeneous country samples, absent meaningful contextualization. This methodological stance could be described as a *Pythagorean bias*.

There are exceptions. Douglass North (1990), for example, reintroduced case studies and emphasized the importance of institutions and historical context. But overall, economists in Western Europe have embraced the idea that "there is no science but the general," largely excluding values, culture, and history. When such factors are acknowledged, they are typically quantified and plugged into models without questioning the models' theoretical architecture.

In short, prior to the empirical, behavioral, and experimental turns of the twenty-first century, economists became both *Platonists* and *Pythagoreans*: pursuing timeless theorems through deductive logic, with minimal concern for empirical nuance or historical specificity. This epistemological stance—deeply modernist in the philosophical sense—now stands in stark contrast to the historical discipline, which increasingly values contingency, subjectivity, and cultural embeddedness.

Historians: From Modernity to Postmodernity?

Historians in Western Europe have traditionally not sought to establish a nomothetic discipline. For a long time, their principal concern has been to reconstruct sequences of facts and events as precisely as possible, through meticulous source criticism. Some historians also aim to interpret these facts—assigning them meaning within broader contexts—or even to identify their causes and consequences. Yet on this last point, historians are generally cautious. Their skepticism toward cliometrics, for instance, is rooted in a deep distrust of the concept of causality, particularly when framed in deterministic terms.

As Floud[3] (1987) observed in his entry on cliometrics in the first edition of the *New Palgrave Dictionary of Economics*:

> More fundamentally, many historians rejected the concepts of causation which they judged to be implied in the closed and deterministic models of the economists; they argued, instead, that historical statements of causation were much weaker, multi-factorial and unsuitable to be tested by the economist's method of removing one possible cause and assessing the outcome, *ceteris paribus*.

This highlights that historians are fundamentally concerned with the specificity, contextuality, and empirical reality of events. Their orientation contrasts sharply with the economist's tendency toward abstraction and generalization. Indeed, historians stand in opposition not only to economists but also, at times, to philosophers—though they may not align fully with either (Kolm 1986). They hold that the past is unique and strive to understand (*Verstehen*, in the German sense) historical actors in terms of their values, representations, and cultures, carefully avoiding anachronism. Applying the categories of neo-classical economics to ancient economies, for example, is considered heretical. Economic behavior in antiquity was embedded in a world governed by status hierarchies, the primacy of politics over markets, and minimal market exchange—conditions incompatible with the assumptions of *homo oeconomicus*. This is the essence of Finley's (1973; 1999 edition) famous thesis on the contrast between primitivism and modernism.

[3] Floud, R.: "Cliometrics", in: Eatwell J. et al. (Eds.), *The New Palgrave. A Dictionary of Economics*, Macmillan, London, 1987, p. 452.

From the 1930s onward—and especially after World War II—the dominance of positivist, event-centered political history in Western Europe began to give way to the *Annales* School, with figures like Marc Bloch (executed in 1944) and Lucien Febvre (d. 1956). This *Nouvelle Histoire*, influenced by the German Historical School and, tacitly, by Marxism, aspired to a *total history* of human societies. It aimed to synthesize insights from across the social sciences and focused on long-term structures—especially economic and social ones—rather than isolated events. It pursued a comprehensive understanding of historical dynamics, favoring mass phenomena over individual actions.

Within this framework, the study of prices, demographics, production, and archival corpora—often requiring quantitative methods—gained prominence. The investigation of economic cycles, paralleling work by the NBER in the USA and Kondratieff in the USSR, demanded long-term historical perspective. French scholars like Labrousse (1933) and Simiand (1932) emphasized that understanding deep economic trends was crucial to interpreting major events such as the French Revolution. While not deterministic, their approach—like that of the Marxists—saw economic structures as decisive. This was the golden age of economic history in Western Europe, epitomized by Braudel (1902–1985), Le Roy Ladurie (1929–2023), and others.

Simultaneously, economic historians began to develop measures of historical wealth in collaboration with national accounting researchers—Hoffmann in Germany, Deane and Cole in the UK, among others. In France, particularly between 1945 and the early 1970s, a convergence emerged between history (focused on demographic, economic, and social developments) and economics (heavily influenced by Marxist and heterodox approaches, such as Perroux's center–periphery model). However, from the mid-1970s, this quantitatively oriented economic history began to lose traction. Long-term, mathematically sophisticated methods, though still used, began to clash with the ethos and training of traditional historians. A shifting intellectual climate—less ideologically Marxist and more attuned to individual agency and cultural meaning—further weakened interest in what were increasingly seen as arid and low-reward topics.

Cultural history, the study of mentalities, and symbolic representations began to dominate. In the 1980s, political history and international relations also re-emerged. Influences from critical sociology (Bourdieu), Foucault's discourse analysis, anthropology, and U.S.-born cultural and gender studies further reshaped historical practice. Historians increasingly adopted the perspective of the marginalized and dominated—no longer writing from the top-down vantage of states or elites, which critics associated with the economist's outlook. Biography and microhistory flourished. The *Annales* approach did not vanish, but it evolved, slowly diverging from economics.

By the late 1970s, Jacques Le Goff et al. (1978) declared that history had more in common with anthropology than with economics. There was a renewed focus on *Verstehen* rather than *Erklären*. Accordingly, history continued to drift from economic theory. It is telling that in several Western European countries, economic history courses were renamed "economic and social history" or "business history."

Even the grand *Annales*-style syntheses—such as Braudel's *La Méditerranée* (1949; 1966 edition)—were not theoretically modeled. Quantitative data served as scaffolding for rich narrative accounts, often focused on capitalism's evolution. This echoed Weber's project on the origins of Western modernity and was later extended by figures like Wallerstein (1992) with his world-systems theory.

In recent decades, history has returned to the particular, the qualitative, and even the event-centered. Yet even during its quantitative heyday, economic history sought to *understand* the past as it happened—contextually, inductively—not to model it in abstract terms. Quantification was embraced to ground analysis in historical reality—say, to assess the standard of living of French peasants under Louis XIV—not to build general models. *Verstehen* prevailed over *Erklären*, and natural language over formal mathematics. Economics, statistics, and demography remained auxiliary tools; the historian's ultimate goal remained a narrative, ideally culminating in a book.

Even the *Annales* historians, with their serial methods, resisted ahistorical theorizing. This helps explain why cliometrics met resistance in Western Europe during the 1970s. Historians accepted quantitative data, but only if derived from archival sources, not from statistical interpolation or econometric modeling. Recent techniques from sociology—data analysis, graph theory, regression, even some causal inference—are tolerated as ways of organizing archival corpora, not for replacing narrative argumentation. The goal remains interpretative synthesis rather than theoretical generalization.

Ultimately, the debate turns on legitimacy. Some historians cling to figures as they appear in archives; others accept statistical methods—but even then, the work remains descriptive and context-sensitive, far from the abstract theorizing economists favor. It is worth noting that quantified description persisted even among economists after the decline of the German Historical School. Scholars like Van Gelderen (1913), Kondratieff (1926), Labrousse (1933), and Simiand (1932) sought to identify real historical cycles and shocks, not just theoretical constructs.

Traditional historians may not fully grasp the abstract nature of modern economic growth or business cycle theory. Yet many could accept econometrics (e.g., Grenier 1995) as a useful auxiliary—provided it supports a holistic, interpretive, and ultimately narrative historical analysis.

Within this philosophy, the methods of traditional history and descriptive quantification are clearly complementary. This style of economic history—rooted in the *Annales* tradition but updated with modern tools—remains faithful to the historian's craft. It has simply become less dominant, as attention has shifted to cultural history, the history of minorities, and so on.

However, we remain far removed from cliometrics. That approach involves embedding causal explanations within formal economic models, often with counterfactual scenarios, to assess the relative strength of different factors—akin to forces in the natural sciences. Evaluating cliometrics thus hinges on methodological questions—about causality and explanation—that are foreign to many historians (Diebolt 2016).

Nonetheless, since 1993 (see the Nobel Prize announcement by the Royal Swedish Academy of Sciences[4]), cliometrics has significantly influenced economic history in Western Europe (Diebolt and Haupert 2024). It transformed the field from a narrative-based discipline to one grounded in quantitative analysis, integrating theory with statistics and new datasets to deepen our understanding of long-term economic growth.

More broadly, since the turn of the century, economic historians and cliometricians have helped bridge the epistemological gap between *Verstehen* and *Erklären*. They have combined theory with quantification, revised historical databases, and integrated the variable of time into economic models. As Diebolt (2016, pp. 3–4) puts it:

> […] to close the gap between the *Geisteswissenschaften* and the *Naturwissenschaften*, i.e., to move from the historical *Verstehen* or understanding side to the economic *Erklären* or explaining side or, much better, mixing both approaches, facts and stylized facts, explaining the economic experience of the past and understanding the ways in which economic factors influence social and political developments, for an increased knowledge of the past, present, and future economic and social development of developed and developing economies, for the achievement of a unified approach to the social sciences.

Conclusion

The long-standing tension between *Verstehen* and *Erklären*—understanding and explaining—remains central to the epistemological foundations of economic history in Western Europe. At its core lies the problem of causality: Is it reducible to efficient causation, to the mere observation of consistent regularities between cause and effect? Or must we account for a plurality of causes—formal, material, final—as integral components of historical explanation?

Within both history and economics, the act of causal explanation is never neutral. It is shaped not only by the data at hand but by the conceptual apparatus, mental heuristics, and interpretive frameworks employed by the observer. Thus, causality is always constructed—never simply discovered. The distinction between correlation and causation, between statistical regularity and explanatory mechanism, is neither trivial nor universally resolved. Causal generalizations remain vulnerable to omitted variables, unobservable contingencies, and subjective selection criteria—problems that no amount of statistical sophistication can fully eliminate.

Historians approach causation with an eye for complexity, singularity, and narrative coherence. Their causal claims are rooted in interpretive judgment, often guided by analogical reasoning, intuition, or contextual insight. The historian "selects and sorts" not only facts but meanings, crafting explanations that resonate with human experience and collective memory. Conversely, economists seek generalizable patterns, abstracting from historical specificities through formal models and

[4] See URL = https://www.nobelprize.org/prizes/economic-sciences/1993/press-release/

assumptions of rationality. Yet their reliance on ceteris paribus and *homo oeconomicus* underscores the tension between theoretical elegance and empirical validity.

Cliometricians—at the crossroads of these traditions—have attempted to bridge the gap. By embedding historical inquiry within formal economic models and supplementing them with counterfactual analysis, cliometrics has introduced a new methodological rigor to the study of the past. Yet this approach is not without limitations. The quality of data, the selection of variables, the framing of models—all remain subject to the same epistemological constraints that affect other social sciences. Moreover, the increasing mathematization of economic history raises concerns about the loss of nuance, context, and interpretive depth.

Despite these challenges, cliometrics offers a compelling case for methodological pluralism. Its strength lies not in providing definitive answers but in expanding the range of questions that can be asked—and answered—about the past. It brings quantification into dialogue with historical narrative, statistical inference with humanistic insight. Rather than replacing traditional historical methods, it enriches them by offering tools for sharper conceptualization, systematic comparison, and probabilistic reasoning.

Ultimately, the pursuit of causal explanation in economic history must remain open to multiple epistemic logics. It requires a recognition that both *Verstehen* and *Erklären* have their place—that understanding the motives and meanings of historical actors is as essential as identifying structural regularities and economic incentives. In embracing this dual heritage, we move closer to a unified, integrative vision of the social sciences: one that is at once rigorous and reflexive, analytical and interpretive, explanatory and meaningful. As Carlo Cipolla (1991) once reminded us, economic history thrives not by choosing sides, but by embracing its position "between two cultures." Reconciling *Verstehen* and *Erklären*, in this view, is less a dilemma than a disciplinary strength—a bridge (Diebolt 2016) rather than a border.[5]

References

Braudel, F. 1949, 1966 for the 2nd ed. *La Méditerranée et le monde méditerranéen à l'époque de Philippe II*. Paris: Armand Colin.

Cipolla, C. M. 1991. *Between Two Cultures. An Introduction to Economic History*. New York and London: W.W. Norton & Company.

Cowles, A. 1933. Can Stock Market Forecasters Forecast? *Econometrica* 1:309–324.

Diebolt, C. 2016. Cliometrica after 10 Years: Definition and Principles of Cliometric Research. *Cliometrica* 10:1–4.

[5] Diebolt, C.: "Building a bridge between theoretical models and history": https://www.springernature.com/gp/researchers/the-source/blog/blogposts-life-in-research/claude-diebolt/17744496, Springer Nature Interview, 27 February 2020.

Diebolt, C. 2020. *Building a Bridge Between Theoretical Models and History*. https://www.springernature.com/gp/researchers/the-source/blog/blogposts-life-in-research/claude-diebolt/17744496, Springer Nature Interview, 27 February 2020.

Diebolt, C., and M. Haupert, eds. 2024. *Handbook of Cliometrics*. 3rd ed. Berlin: Springer Nature.

Edgeworth, F. Y. 1881. *Mathematical Psychics. An Essay on the Application of Mathematics to the Moral Sciences*. London: Kegan Paul & Co.

Field, A. 2008. Economic History. In *New Palgrave Dictionary of Economics*, ed. Durlauf et al. London: Palgrave Macmillan.

Finley, M.I. 1999. *The Ancient Economy*, Updated Edition with a Foreword by Ian Morris (1st ed. in 1973). Berkeley: University of California Press.

Floud, R. 1987. Cliometrics. In *The New Palgrave. A Dictionary of Economics*, ed. J. Eatwell et al. London: Macmillan.

Friedman, M., and A. J. Schwarz. 1963. *A Monetary History of the United States, 1867-1960*. Princeton: Princeton University Press.

Friedman, M., and A. J. Schwartz. 1982. *Monetary Trends in the United States and the United Kingdom: Their Relation to Income, Prices and Interest Rates, 1867-1975*. Chicago: Chicago University Press.

Grenier, J.-Y. 1995. L'histoire quantitative est-elle encore nécessaire? In *Passés recomposés. Champs et chantiers de l'histoire*, ed. J. Boutier and D. Julia, 173–183. Paris: Editions Autrement.

Heidegger, M., and F.-W. Herrmann. 1995. Über das Prinzip "Zu den Sachen selbst". *Heidegger Studies* 11:5–8.

Helpman, E., and P. Krugman. 1987. Market Structure and Foreign Trade. *Increasing Returns, Imperfect Competition, and the International Economy*. Cambridge (MA): MIT Press.

Jevons, W. S. 1884. *Investigations in Currency and Finance*. London: Macmillan.

Juglar, C. 1862. *Des crises commerciales et de leur retour périodique en France, en Angleterre et aux Etats-Unis*. Paris: Guillaumin et Cie.

Keynes, J. M. 1936. *The General Theory of Employment, Interest and Money*. London: Macmillan.

Kolm, S. C. 1986. *Philosophie de l'économie*. Paris: Seuil.

Kondratieff, N. D. 1926. Die langen Wellen der Konjunktur. *Archiv für Sozialwissenschaft und Sozialpolitik* 56:573–609.

Krugman, P. 1994. *Rethinking International Trade*. Cambridge (MA): MIT Press.

Kuznets, S. 1966. Modern Economic Growth: Rate, Structure and Spread. New Haven: Yale University Press.

Labrousse, E. 1933. *Esquisse du mouvement des prix et des revenus en France au XVIIIe siècle*. Paris: Librairie Dalloz.

Le Goff, J., R. Chartier, and J. Revel, eds. 1978. *La Nouvelle Histoire*. Paris: Retz.

Lucas, R. E. 1988. On the Mechanics of Economic Development. *Journal of Monetary Economics* 22:3–42.

Lyon, B., and M. Lyon. 1991. *The Birth of Annales History: The Letters of Lucien Febvre and Marc Bloch to Henri Pirenne (1921-1935)*. Bruxelles: Académie royale de Belgique, Commission royale d'Histoire.

Marczewski, J. 1965. *Introduction à l'histoire quantitative*. Genève: Droz.

Marshall, A. 1890, edition of 1920. *Principles of Economics*. London: Macmillan & Co.

Marx, K. 1867, Ed. of 1964. *Das Kapital*. Berlin: Dietz-Verlag.

North, D. 1990. *Institutions, Institutional Change and Economic Performance*. Cambridge: Cambridge University Press.

Ranke, L. 1824. *Geschichten der romanischen und germanischen Völker von 1494 bis 1535, Erster Band, G. Reimer, Leipzig und Berlin*. https://www.digitale-sammlungen.de/de/view/bsb10408217?page=5

Romer, P. 1986. Increasing Returns and Long Run Growth. *Journal of Political Economy* 94:S1002–S1037.

Romer, P. 1990. Endogenous Technical Change. *Journal of Political Economy* 98:S71–S102.

Rostow, W. W. 1960. *The Stages of Economic Growth: A Non-Communist Manifesto*. Cambridge: Cambridge University Press.
Simiand, F. 1932. *Recherches anciennes et nouvelles sur le mouvement général des prix du XVIème au XIXème siècles*. Paris: Loviton.
Solow, R. 1956. A Contribution to the Theory of Economic Growth. *Quarterly Journal of Economics* 70:65–94.
Solow, R. 1957. Technical Change and the Aggregate Production Function. *Review of Economics and Statistics* 39:312–320.
Tinbergen, J. 1939. *Statistical Testing of Business Cycle Theories*, 2 vol. Genève: Société des Nations.
Tirole, J. 1988. *The Theory of Industrial Organization*. Cambridge (MA): MIT Press.
Van Gelderen, J. (J. Fedder). 1913. Springvloed: beschouwingen over industrieleele ontwikkeling en prijsbeweging. *De Nieuwe Tijd* 18:253–277, 369–384, 445–464.
Von Neumann, J., and O. Morgenstern. 1944, edition of 2007. *Theory of Games and Economic Behavior*. Princeton: Princeton University Press.
Wallerstein, I. 1992. *Le système du monde, du 15ème siècle à nos jours. 1. Capitalisme et Économie-Monde 1450–1640*, Flammarion, Paris.

Cliometric Approaches to Central, East and South-East Europe, 2019–2022

Matthias Morys

Abstract We provide an overview of quantitative economic literature on Central, East and South-East Europe published between 2019 and 2022. We outline the content of 16 journal publications and monographs, and how it relates to longer-term trends in the cliometric research on this part of the world. We will also detail the main findings of Morys (ed.), The Economic History of Central, East and South-East Europe (2021) which constitutes the first-ever quantitative economic history of the region. Finally, we spell out what kind of research to expect on the CESEE region in the years to come.

Introduction

Cliometric approaches to Central, East and South-East Europe[1] (CESEE) are of recent vintage. Their emergence went hand in hand with the political and economic transformation in the region after the fall of the Berlin Wall (1989) and the collapse

[1] Reflecting a long and well-established scholarly tradition, we will distinguish between Central Europe, East Europe and South-East Europe. Central Europe refers to the Czech Republic, Hungary, Poland and Slovakia. East Europe relates to the European successor states of the Soviet Union (Belarus, Estonia, Latvia, Lithuania, Moldova, Russia and Ukraine). South-East Europe (also referred to as the Balkans) encompasses the successor states of the Ottoman Empire on the Balkan Peninsula (Albania, Bosnia and Herzegovina, Bulgaria, Croatia, Greece, Kosovo, Montenegro, North Macedonia, Romania, Serbia and Slovenia). The number of independent countries on this territory has increased from four (Austria, Prussia, Russia, Ottoman Empire) to 22 over the past two centuries, and the sharp distinction between the three sub-regions has become blurred in the process. We will occasionally refer to "Eastern Europe" to avoid repetition of the acronym CESEE; in this case ("Eastern" as adjective), we mean CESEE as a whole.

M. Morys (✉)
University of York (UK) and Leibniz Institute for East and South-East European Studies, Regensburg, Germany
e-mail: matthias.morys@york.ac.uk

C. Diebolt, M. Haupert (eds.), *The State of Economic History*, Frontiers in Economic History, https://doi.org/10.1007/978-3-032-01624-9_3

of the Soviet Union (1991). Only then could the modern economic history approach make its way into Eastern lands and bear academic fruit.

In this survey, we are concerned with an even shorter timeframe, namely, publications on the region between 2019 and 2022. We build on earlier literature overviews provided by Morys (2020, 2022) for CESEE as a whole and by Zhuravskaya et al. (2024) for Russia and the Soviet Union. All three provide a good structure for the main areas of research. They suggest three main areas that have dominated quantitative economic history research on the region:

- *What were the long-term factors impeding economic growth in CESEE?* Serfdom was proposed as an early answer and still enjoys wide currency including in the recent literature. All other explanations can typically be divided into three strands: demography, institutional weaknesses and market access and integration.
- *How backward was Eastern Europe by the time of the communist take-over?* For Russia, this question either relates to economic development until the 1917 October Revolution; or to where the economy stood at the end of the "New Economic Policy" (NEP) in 1928, when the introduction of the first five-year plan under Stalin completely changed the trajectory of the Soviet economy. For all other countries, the transition to the command economy occurred after World War II. This question is not confined to a narrow GDP per capita comparison, but involves a broad analysis of structural change and the preconditions for sustainable income per head growth. It addresses, implicitly or explicitly, the counterfactual question whether the CESEE countries could have prospered under a liberal political and economic regime.
- *How should we assess the state socialist period?* In the absence of political and civic liberties under communism, economic history from Gerschenkron (1962) onwards has focussed on an evaluation of the *economic* achievements of the state socialist period. Was central planning necessary to industrialise and develop the backward Eastern European economies, and how successful was it at that? This question is different from the previous one, though not unrelated: the more positive the assessment of the pre-communist economic situation, the less credit state socialism can take for overall economic development. The connection between the second and the third question will become particularly clear when discussing Russian economic development between 1917 and 1928. That is, after the political take-over by the Bolsheviks but before the transition to central planning. Was there only one way to socialism, or were there several paths (of which the wrong one was taken)?

We will use this structure for our detailed discussion of individual contributions in section "Literature Overview 2019–2022". Yet first, we will discuss the importance of the 2021-publication, edited by Matthias Morys and written by 24 researchers, titled "*The Economic History of Central, East and South-East Europe from 1800 to the Present Day*" (section "A Network Approach to the Economic History of Central, East and South-East Europe"). We conclude in section "Concluding Remarks" with an outlook for research ahead in this field.

A Network Approach to the Economic History of Central, East and South-East Europe

Matthias Morys conceptualised, organised and led a network of 21 academics and 3 researchers from the Organisation for Economic Cooperation and Development (OECD) and the Vienna Institute for International Economic Studies (WIIW). The network drew on researchers based in the USA, nine West European countries, three East European countries and Israel. The basic idea of the network was to write a first-ever quantitative economic history of Central, East and South-East Europe (Morys 2021a).

The inspiration was twofold: Economic history in North America and Western Europe had moved closer to mainstream economics since the 1960s under the influence of the cliometric revolution, but there was no equivalent to these methodological developments beyond the Iron Curtain. By the early 2000s, a "critical mass" of Eastern European Ph.D. students had emerged at leading U.S. and U.K. universities, who wanted to be introduced to quantitative economic history. Yet a clearer framework was needed if the field was to move forward.

The second inspiration stemmed from a growing realisation that the transition had not gone according to plan. The collapse of communism in 1989 had resulted in great hopes, yet a quarter century on the picture was mixed: economic catch-up took longer than anticipated and political backsliding became an issue in several countries. Russia's annexation of Crimea in 2014 was the final straw that convinced Morys of the need for an academic network and a book: if even military conflict could no longer be ruled out in Europe, we needed to better understand the long-term trajectories of the Central and Eastern European countries. Quo Vademus?

He set the network three objectives:

- To secure the vast knowledge of the older "qualitative" economic history of Eastern Europe. In moving to quantification (and switching to the English language), there was a great danger of losing touch with important strands of historiography.
- To provide a concise picture of how we view the nineteenth and the twentieth century Eastern European economic history based on the quantitative research produced since the early 2000s.
- To clearly establish what we knew but also what we did not know about Eastern Europe. The project was meant to provide inspiration for future research.

Achieving the second objective was best served by moving from country-based accounts to a thematic approach. The book follows four key themes (economic growth; economic policy; economic integration with other countries; population and living standards) and four distinct historical periods (long nineteenth century; interwar period; state socialism; transition period). This resulted in a structure of 16 chapters, complemented by an editor's introduction and a chapter on living standards in the Early Modern period.

Condensing a book of 500 pages into one paragraph would probably read: While Eastern Europe has undergone massive economic, demographic and social changes, a remarkable feature is that the relative gap to income levels in Britain, France and Germany (Western Europe's "big three") has remained large and surprisingly stable over the course of two centuries. Eastern Europe has experimented with multiple political frameworks (feudalism, liberal capitalism, state socialism, western liberal democracy), yet failed to narrow the gap. On the upside, this book also documents regions/countries (the Czech lands, Estonia, Latvia and Slovenia in particular) which have consistently been closer to the West European experience. This book closes by offering policy advice to the 22 governments in Central, East and South-East Europe on lessons from history and how to achieve higher living standards in the region.

The objective of this book was not to produce genuinely new research, but to preserve and systematise what has been researched so far. In some cases, chapter authors ventured beyond this remit, or offered interesting interpretations which account for new knowledge in themselves. We will make reference to these contributions in the section which follows.

Literature Overview 2019–2022

What Were the Long-Term Factors Impeding Economic Growth in CESEE?

From the four factors widely seen as decisive to explain the retardation of CESEE in a pan-European perspective (section "Introduction"), the discussion on institutional weaknesses and strengths has received by far the most attention in recent years. The allure of this hypothesis is that we know today that institutions in CESEE countries are weaker than in their Western European counterparts. But can we be sure the same was true for past periods?

Malinowski (2019) is a recent attempt to break free from such deficiencies of earlier research. He studies the relationship between state capacity and commodity market integration for the region's largest state in the Early Modern period, namely, Poland between 1505 and 1772 (First Polish Partition at the hands of Austria, Prussia and Russia). The basic idea is that a more active parliament will pass more legislation, including laws and regulations conducive to foster market integration; conversely, if legal capacity is low (as proxied by the number of days the Polish parliament, the Seym, was in session each year), there will be less regulatory activity of parliament (as measured by the laws relevant to the economy passed each year) and markets will fragment.

In the successful economies of North-Western Europe, all three quantitative indicators used by Malinowski—parliamentary activity, regulatory output of parliament and market integration—would probably grow over time, potentially resulting in spurious econometric results. This makes Poland a historically interesting and econometrically attractive case study, as parliamentary activity *did not* grow over time. Rather, an initially very active parliament was severely undermined by the introduction of the so-called *liberum veto* in 1652; a stipulation which gave a single member of the aristocratic parliament the right to suspend proceedings, effectively introducing unanimity into the Seym. Consequently, Malinowski can show econometrically that the introduction of the *liberum veto* reduced the regulatory output of the Seym and reversed the high levels of market integration that a more active Polish parliament had achieved initially.

An important consequence of the *liberum veto* was that it gave foreign powers an easy tool to intervene in the domestic affairs of the Polish aristocratic republic. By aligning themselves with a single Polish aristocrat represented in the Seym, foreign powers could undermine the Polish state; an easy tool of foreign interference, which ultimately contributed to the complete dissolution of the Polish state in the three partitions of 1772, 1793 and 1795. Poland is an extreme example, yet one that points to a broader regional pattern that has spurred institutionalist research in recent years: the role of West European countries in the economic development of the poorer, and often small, CESEE countries.

An older qualitative literature tended to highlight the negative role of foreign countries. This was the case in particular if written from a dependency theory perspective (Berend and Ránki 1974) or under residual influence from the nineteenth century nationalistic historiography. Yet the more recent literature has tended to focus on the positive role played by foreign countries. Clavin (2013) observes that the League of Nations, while global in name, in actual practice was an international body chiefly concerned with stabilising the political and economic conditions of the Eastern European countries in the interwar period. Some of this research has made an explicit institutionalist argument. Morys (2021b), for instance, argues that policy-makers in South-Eastern Europe acquiesced into foreign financial supervision not because they necessarily had to, but in an attempt to compensate for domestic institutional weaknesses. Recurring problems of Bulgaria, Greece, Romania and Serbia/Yugoslavia with large external debts before World War II led to the introduction of financial control by the countries' West European creditors on various occasions. From the perspective of the dependency theory, such arrangements are typical examples of how core countries control peripheral countries, undermining their sovereignty in the process. By contrast, the authors show that there were strong domestic constituencies in favour of these arrangements (in the same vein as Tuncer 2015, Chap. 7). Foreign creditors constrained monetary policy and, to a lesser extent, fiscal policy. Yet such constraints were appealing to a large part of the domestic constituency, which blamed a legacy of fiscal deficits and debt monetisations (known as "fiscal dominance" in the relevant literature) for the country's inability to follow the gold standard. In this view, foreign financial supervision acts as an external commitment mechanism in the presence of weak domestic institutions. Using a Granger causality analysis of time series for budget deficits and debt monetisations for all SEE countries between the nineteenth century political independence and World War II, Morys (2021c) shows that a prevailing pattern of fiscal dominance was broken only under financial supervision, when the treasury's influence on the central bank was scaled back. Only then were central banks able to stabilise their exchange-rates. An accompanying political economy analysis shows that financial supervision was politically acceptable as it made successfully adhering to gold more likely in the view of contemporaries.

The research by Malinowski (2019) and Morys (2021a, b, c) is primarily concerned with institutional weaknesses, what they led to and how CESEE countries tried to address them. They stand in a long tradition dating back to Gerschenkron (1962) and reflect the perception that institutions in the region were part of the problem, not the solution. Only the recent literature has seen a change of tact with a more balanced view on institutions in CESEE. An early example is Nafziger (2011), who analyses the functioning of the *zemstvo*, an institution of local government created as part of the emancipatory reforms of the 1860s. While the peasants were heavily underrepresented in this new institution, they did have, for the first time ever, some political voice in a decision-making body that was extensively involved in providing local public services, from school and medical care, to agronomy and road maintenance. Nafziger takes an intermediate position: despite the *zemstvo* being confined to the local level and despite the heavy underrepresentation of peasants, this was a step in the right direction with beneficial effects for the farming population.

Other contributions with a more positive assessment of institutions include the recent work of Gregg (2020) and Gregg and Nafziger (2019) on corporations and other business forms and the work by Chuchko (2022) on tariff policy. Not coincidentally, all three contributions relate to Russia and to the late Tsarist period in particular. Institutionalist research on Central Europe, by contrast, retains a decisively critical undertone while noting positive aspects more on the sidelines. The fine work of Cvrcek (2020) on public education in Austria is an excellent example for this (continued) historiographical trend. An intermediate position is taken by research such as Tuncer and Weller (2022). They acknowledge that the CESEE countries were more autocratic than their Western European counterparts, yet argue that bond markets rewarded the East European countries during the 1870–1914 period by lower bond yields, as investors viewed such countries as reliable tax collectors unimpeded by complicated political processes.

How Backward Was Eastern Europe by the Time of the Communist Take-Over?

The second main area of research has been to evaluate where the CESEE countries stood economically by the time the communist parties gained political power and imposed central planning. Central planning and "big push" industrialisation have been justified—by contemporaries and subsequent scholars alike—on the grounds that they were the only solution to overcome economic backwardness. As communism arrived earlier in the case of Russia, it is worth distinguishing between the

Soviet Union, on the one hand, and all other CESEE countries on the other. There have been, to the best of our knowledge (Zhuravskaya et al. 2024 for their overview), no notable contributions on the Soviet Union in recent years. In the case of all other CESEE countries, the communist take-over and the introduction of central planning occurred only after World War II. Consequently, research similar to the case of late Tsarist Russia and the early Soviet Union would need to focus on where the Central and South-East European economies stood in the late 1930s. Yet not much research has been conducted on this topic in recent years. For the most part, we have only the older research by Kaser and Radice (1985–1989), which gave a negative account of this period, indirectly justifying the "big push" industrialisation as it then happened in the Soviet bloc countries. Most recent research has instead focused on the pre-World War I experience, providing new national account data (Mijatović and Zavadjil 2023 on Serbia) and/or presenting the overall economic development and the structural change in particular in a more positive light (Ivanov and Kopsidis 2023 for Bulgaria).

This is one of the cases where the edited volume of Morys (2021a) proves very useful. The editor, in a chapter written by himself on growth in the interwar period and drawing on published articles and readily available statistics, shows that some of the economies had already achieved—or at least covered substantial ground towards—structural transformation that Soviet-style industrialisation was meant to achieve (Morys 2021c). Czechoslovakia, for instance, had more people working in industry than in agriculture by 1930; its sectoral composition was more "modern" than the Southern European countries, which then all industrialised after World War II under market-based systems. In the case of Czechoslovakia after 1948, central planning and the command economy were "rolled out" for a country that clearly did not need them, and can only be "justified" on political grounds.

The situation might look differently for more backward countries in CESEE, one of which was the 1930s Bulgaria, a country in which more than 80% of the labour force was still in agriculture. In such cases, the idea of communism as the only way towards industrialisation has maintained followership among serious academics, even after the political changes of 1989–1991 (Avramov 2001). Yet even here Morys (2021c) can point to important research or recent years by authors such Ivanov and Tooze (2007) who show a more nuanced picture of the Bulgarian achievements by the late 1930s. While population growth had consumed most of the GDP advances in the four decades between 1890 and 1930 and per capita income growth was insignificant as a result, the country had laid important preconditions for rapid growth thereafter. The authors highlight three achievements in particular. First, the agricultural sector had broken with decades of extensive development and begun to move decisively towards intensification. As agriculture became more productive, the preconditions for the resource transfer towards industry were in place. Second, starting from very low initial levels in 1900, Bulgaria achieved mass literacy by 1945, providing an urban workforce ready to work in the industries soon to be established. Third, the country underwent virtually complete demographic transition in the space of only three generations, allowing it to escape the Malthusian trap that had kept per capita income levels almost unchanged between the 1890s and the 1930s.

In sum, before the advent of a strategy of state-centred economic policy, three vital preconditions for accelerated growth had already been established.

How Should We Assess the State Socialist Period?

The third area of CESEE cliometric research is an assessment of the economic achievements of the state socialist period. Following an earlier Western literature during the late state socialist and early transition period, this strand of research has seen important additions and revisions in recent years. It remains narrowly interested in GDP and is typically analysed in an economic convergence framework similar in methodology to studies of the Western European growth experience after World War II. Consequently, this research relies on accurate GDP estimates for an economic system with a non-functioning price system; an issue widely discussed in the literature but not seen as invalidating the research (Vonyó and Markevich 2021).

Socialist economic development has been traditionally interpreted as investment driven. Centrally planned economies were seen as relatively successful in mobilising resources, but stifled innovation and creative entrepreneurship. They achieved a relatively satisfactory performance in the phase of extensive growth, but began to fall behind when capital accumulation reached diminishing returns and total factor productivity increases remained low (Bergson 1987; Ofer 1987; Easterly and Fischer 1995). The Soviet Union operated this system for the longest period (1928–1991) and has been analysed in detail by Allen (2003). He interprets Soviet industrialisation as "Feldman and Preobrazhensky" in action (the two economists behind Stalin's first Five-Year-Plan in 1928) and demonstrates that the capital-intensive growth model prevailed until the fall of communism, with noticeably diminishing returns towards the end of the period.

Recent research has been more critical of the achievements of the state socialist period, including for the 1950s and the 1960s, a period dominated by extensive growth. Vonyó and Klein (2019) show that communism allowed the CESEE countries to perform well against their own past (and the interwar period in particular), but not against capitalist economies in the post-World War II period. Convergence in GDP per capita occurred both in Western and Eastern Europe. Yet there were two "convergence clubs", with the Western economies enjoying more rapid growth at the same level of initial income (GDP per capita in 1950). They also show that a simple convergence framework better explains the actual growth performance of Western economies, suggesting that convergence forces in the East were more disturbed by frictions typically associated with command economies. Pars pro toto and choosing the one country of CESEE that remained capitalist after World War II, Greece grew faster, for four decades, by almost one percentage point per year than neighbouring Bulgaria, even though the two countries began at roughly the same income level after World War II.

These results, based on a standard convergence framework, are consistent with two more recent findings, which have further weakened the older perspective of the relative strengths of communism. They relate to the command economy's supposedly superior ability (1) to push structural change and (2) to enable fixed capital formation. In both cases, it was thought that the coercive nature of communist political regimes was conducive to achieving these results better than capitalist economies. Vonyó and Klein (2019) and Vonyó (2017) are critical of communist economic performance on both accounts. Vonyo and Klein demonstrate that structural change in the Western European periphery went further than in Eastern Europe. While structural change proceeded quickly in the East and in line with its initial income levels, it slowed down considerably starting in the 1970s—while it continued to proceed along expectations in the Western European periphery. The authors conclude that market forces generated the macroeconomically beneficial outcome of structural change better than the forces of command did.

Secondly, Vonyó (2017) throws doubt on the success of the CESEE economies in generating high levels of fixed capital formation. Recalculating the investment numbers for the period 1950–1989, he documents that fixed capital formation in CESEE was initially high (in line with earlier accounts from Western economists), but then declined and essentially collapsed in the 1980s (with the exception of the Soviet Union). As the political legitimacy of the communist regimes was increasingly challenged, the political need to support consumption increasingly clashed with the economic imperative to ensure high investment rates. In the authors' view, this (political economy) rationale also explains why the Soviet Union could continue along the old path of high investment rates. The country had retained more financial room for manoeuvre, as it was the only Soviet bloc country to benefit economically from the oil price shocks of the 1970s. As an oil exporting economy, it made financial gains, which it used to maintain high investment rates until the end of the state socialist period.

In sum, recent work is markedly more critical than earlier work, which tended to portray state socialism in a relatively benign light at least until the oil price shocks of the 1970s. A rare exception to this broad historiographical trend is the recent work by Bukowski and Novokmet (2021) on long-term trends on inequality in Poland. They attribute a substantial fall of inequality to the advent of state socialism in the late 1940s.

Concluding Remarks

The current conditions for quantitative economic history research into CESEE look good, but there are a number of particular challenges. While some of them will vanish over time, others are likely to persist. In particular, even three decades after the fall of the Berlin Wall, the number of publications—both the stock and the flow—on Eastern Europe remains far smaller than on Western Europe. Will these research imbalances persist?

To begin with, linguistic barriers are far higher in the Eastern European case. None of the East European languages is one of the prevalent languages in historical research (English, French, German and to a lesser extent Italian and Spanish), making market entry for outsiders more difficult. Slavic languages dominate, but are often not mutually understandable. Some regional languages even form their own linguistic groups, either within the Indo-European languages (Albanian, Greek) or outside of it (Estonian, Hungarian). It is worth substantiating the resulting impediments to research with two examples. John Lampe and Mervyn Jackson were able to transcend country-specific Balkan studies and write their magisterial "*Balkan Economic History, 1550–1950: From Imperial Borderlands to Developing Nations*" (1982) partly because they mastered three regional languages (Bulgarian, Romanian and Serbian) and found ways to cover the other two (Albanian and Greek). It is perhaps not surprising that no similar attempt to cover all SEE countries has been made. Likewise, while Hungary's economic history is far better-known in the West than that of any other East European country except Russia, almost all of this work has been carried out by Hungarian mother tongue speakers (Berend, Ránki, Komlos, Vonyo).

Second, the instability of borders, the emergence of new countries and the submergence of old ones are a mixed blessing for historical research. While many Western European countries have hardly changed their borders since the High and Late Middle Ages (England, Spain and Portugal in particular, to a lesser extent France), border changes were frequent (and often sizeable) in Eastern Europe. Russia's current attempts to redraw the map of Ukraine help illustrate this point in dramatic fashion. Even large countries could "disappear" altogether, Poland being the paradigmatic case. It only regained its independence after World War I.

In the best case, the historical challenges of the region are turned into exciting research today. As exemplified by recent work on the Polish experience between 1505 and 1772 (Malinowski 2019), the travails of state formation might even constitute one of the region's comparative advantages in cliometric research. Somewhat similar in spirit, Bukowski (2019) uses the Polish partitions of the late eighteenth century as a "natural experiment" to analyse the long-run effects of different education systems (namely, the Prussian, the Russian and the Austrian systems) on learning outcomes in Poland today. Likewise, the long and often complicated history of sizeable minorities in Eastern Europe has recently inspired research on the transfer and diffusion of skills and technology in host countries (Vasilenok and Natkhov 2021; Nikolic et al. 2022).

Yet such comparative advantages come with two important caveats. Late state foundation and weak bureaucracies imply poor historical records and statistical material. Balkan economic history is a good case in point, where our understanding of economic history after political independence in the nineteenth century is far greater than for the period before (Lampe and Jackson 1982; Palairet 1997; Morys and Ivanov 2015). Moreover, who "owns" the economic history of a particular stretch of land in Eastern Europe when borders changed and settlement patterns were mixed? Poland-Lithuania (1386–1795) was for centuries the largest state in Eastern Europe, covering at times (partly or fully) the territories of Poland, Lithuania, Ukraine, Latvia, Belarus and Russia in today's borders. Should we expect the historical experience to be of interest to all "successor states", or only to Poland

and Lithuania? In a world of Open Science, such considerations should not matter, yet in actual practice they do (funding by national research agencies, linguistic proximity, etc.). Latvia offers another good example. From the available economic, social and demographic evidence, we know that the Baltic countries—and the region around Riga in particular—were early developers in Eastern Europe (Morys 2021a). Yet tiny Latvia, a country with a population of less than two million inhabitants, lacks the resources, and neighbouring Russia (to which the territory belonged until 1991 with the exception of the interwar period) lacks the interest to conduct the necessary research.

Finally, future research on CESEE is likely to focus on the region as a whole, rather than separately on its three constituent parts, namely, Central Europe, Eastern Europe and South-East Europe. This new approach reflects current interest, but also recognises that four decades of state socialism created a shared historical experience for a set of countries previously thought of as only loosely connected. Traditionally, research divided Eastern Europe—that is, Europe to the East of the German- and Italian-speaking lands—into three distinct regions. South-Eastern Europe, that is the successor states of the Ottoman Empire on the Balkan Peninsula (initially Greece, Serbia, Romania, Bulgaria and Albania; today also including the six successor states of Yugoslavia other than Serbia); Central Europe, namely, the Visegrad countries of the Czech Republic, Hungary, Poland and Slovakia (in some sense, the successor states of Austria-Hungary, including all of Poland but excluding Austria itself); and East Europe, that is the European successor states of the Soviet Union (Russia, the three Baltic countries, Belarus, Ukraine and Moldova). This classification leaves some ambiguity, as Romania and the Baltic countries demonstrate. It might even seem archaic, as its starting point is the three long-defunct Austro-Hungarian, Russian and Ottoman Empires. Yet the historiographical weight of these three distinct traditions (see next section) is clear to anyone trying to escape them. Recent overview articles show that both approaches currently co-exist, e.g. Zhuravskaya et al. (2024) with their focus on Russia only as opposed to Morys (2022) who reviews evidence from the entire region. Only future research can show whether the three distinct research traditions are worth being kept alive and separate, or whether amalgamating them into something new is more promising.

Quo Vademus? Two of the three research areas discussed in this chapter are not only crucial to our academic understanding of the East European experience, but connect to everyday concerns in the region. The economic gap with Western Europe has never been closed; the percentage gap in income levels between the two halves of Europe has remained stubbornly stable over the past two centuries (at approximately one third of the West European level if based on GDP data not adjusted for purchasing power parity). Likewise, the controversial assessment of the achievements of state socialism is mirrored by a political discourse in the region between veneration for an idealised communist past, on the one hand, and a complete rejection of the state socialist experience, on the other.

The economic grievances in the region have been superseded recently by the full-scale invasion of Ukraine by Russia in February 2022. Yet the war itself might be partly driven by economics: Ukraine performed particularly poorly during the transition period 1991–2008 (Voskoboynikov 2021), making it easy prey in the view of Russia's leadership; and Russia fell on hard economic times after the Global Financial Crisis of 2008, possibly tempting President Putin into playing the nationalistic card more strongly than he would have if the benign 2000–2008 economic conditions had continued. Recent political events might therefore reinforce our need to understand better not only the political but also the economic history of Central, East and South-East Europe, including how they interact with each other.

References

Avramov, Rumen. 2001. *The Economic Twentieth Century of Bulgaria* (in Bulgarian). Sofia.

Allen, R. C. 2003. *Farm to Factory. A Reinterpretation of the Soviet Industrial Revolution.* Princeton: Princeton University Press.

Berend, I., and R. Ránki. 1974. *Economic Development in East-Central Europe in the 19th and 20th Centuries*, 1974. New York and London: Columbia University Press.

Bergson, A. 1987. Comparative Productivity: the USSR, Eastern Europe, and the West. *American Economic Review* 77 (3): 342–357.

Bukowski, P. 2019. How History Matters for Student Performance: Lessons from the Partitions of Poland. *Journal of Comparative Economics* 47 (1): 137–175.

Bukowski, P., and F. Novokmet. 2021. Between Communism and Capitalism: Long-Term Inequality in Poland, 1892-2015. *Journal of Economic Growth* 26:187–239.

Clavin, P. 2013. *Securing the World Economy: The Reinvention of the League of Nations, 1920-1946.* Oxford: Oxford University Press.

Chuchko, M. 2022. Business Representation in an Autocratic Regime: Tariff Policy and Exchange Committees in Late Tsarist Russia. *The Economic History Review* 75 (3): 801–829.

Cvrcek, Tomas. 2020. *Schooling Under Control. The Origins of Public Education in Austria 1769-1869.* Tuebingen: Mohr-Siebeck.

Easterly, W., and S. Fischer. 1995. The Soviet Economic Decline. *World Bank Economic Review* 9 (3): 341–371.

Gerschenkron, A. 1962. *Economic Backwardness in Historical Perspective. A Book of Essays.* Cambridge, MA: Belknap Press.

Gregg, A. 2020. Factory Productivity and the Concession System of Incorporation in Late Imperial Russia. *American Economic Review* 110 (2): 401–427.

Gregg, A., and S. Nafziger. 2019. Capital Structure and Corporate Performance in Late Imperial Russia. *European Review of Economic History* 23 (4): 446–481.

Ivanov, M., and A. Tooze. 2007. Convergence or Decline on Europe's Southeastern Periphery? Agriculture, Population, and GDP in Bulgaria, 1892-1945. *Journal of Economic History* 11:672–704.

Ivanov, M., and M. Kopsidis. 2023. Industrialisation in a Small Grain Economy During the First Globalisation: Bulgaria c. 1870-1910. *Economic History Review* 76 (1): 169–198.

Kaser, Michael Charles, and Edward Albert Radice (1985–1989). The Economic History of Eastern Europe 1919-1975, Oxford: Clarendon Press

Lampe, J. R., and M. R. Jackson. 1982. *Balkan Economic History, 1550-1950: From Imperial Borderlands to Developing Nations.* Bloomington: Indiana University Press.

Malinowski, M. 2019. Economic Consequences of State Failure. Legal Capacity, Regulatory Activity, and Market Integration in Poland, 1505-1772. *Journal of Economic History* 79 (3): 862–896.

Mijatović, B., and M. Zavadjil. 2023. Serbia on the Path to Modern Economic Growth. *The Economic History Review* 76 (1): 199–220.

Morys, Matthias. 2020. Cliometric approaches to Central, East, and South-East Europe. *Handbook of Cliometrics* (pp. 1-34). Berlin, Heidelberg: Springer.

Morys, M., ed. 2021a. *The Economic History of Central, East and South-East Europe, 1800 to the Present Day*. London: Routledge.

Morys, M. 2021b. The Gold Standard, Fiscal Dominance and Financial Supervision in Greece and South-East Europe, 1841-1939. *European Review of Economic History* 25 (1): 106–136.

Morys, M. 2021c. Economic Growth and Structural Change in Central, East and South-East Europe, 1918-1939. In *The Economic History of Central, East and South-East Europe*, ed. M. Morys, 277-302161-187. London: Routledge.

Morys, M. 2022. Has Eastern Europe Always Lagged Behind the West? Historical Evidence from Pre-1870. *The Review of Income and Wealth* 68 (S1): S3–S21.

Morys, M., and M. Ivanov. 2015. The Emergence of a European Region: Business Cycles in South-East Europe from Political Independence to World War II. *European Review of Economic History* 19:382–411.

Nafziger, S. 2011. Did Ivan's Vote Matter? The Political Economy of Local Democracy in Tsarist Russia. *European Review of Economic History* 15:393–441.

Nikolic, S., M. Blum, and T. Vonyo. 2022. *Immigration and Development. German-Speaking Agricultural Settlers in the Kingdom of Hungary*. CEPR Discussion Paper Number 17567.

Ofer, Gur. 1987. Soviet economic growth: 1928-1985. *Journal of Economic Literature* 25 (4): 1767-1833.

Palairet, M. R. 1997. *The Balkan economies* c. 1800–1914. Cambridge Books.

Tuncer, C. 2015. *Sovereign Debt and International Financial Control: The Middle East and the Balkans, 1870-194*. London: Palgrave Macmillan.

Tuncer, C., and L. Weller. 2022. Democracy, Autocracy, and Sovereign Debt: How Polity Influenced Country Risk on the Peripheries of the Global Economy, 1870-1913. *Explorations in Economic History* 85:101449.

Vasilenok, N., and T. Natkhov. 2021. Skilled Immigrants and Technology Adoption: Evidence from the German Settlements in the Russian Empire. *Explorations in Economic History* 81:101399.

Vonyó, T. 2017. War and Socialism: Why Eastern Europe Fell Behind Between 1950 and 1989. *Economic History Review* 70 (1): 248–270.

Vonyó, T., and A. Klein. 2019. Why Did Socialist Economies Fail: The Role of Factor Inputs Reconsidered. *Economic History Review* 72 (1): 317–345.

Vonyó, T., and A. Markevich. 2021. Economic Growth and Structural Developments, 1945-1989. In *The Economic History of Central, East and South-East Europe*, ed. M. Morys, 277–302. London: Routledge.

Voskoboynikov, I. 2021. Economic Growth and Sectoral Developments During the Transition Period, 1990-2008. In *The Economic History of Central, East and South-East Europe*, ed. M. Morys, 383–412. London: Routledge.

Zhuravskaya, Ekaterina, Sergei Guriev, and Andrei Markevich. 2024. New Russian economic history. *Journal of Economic Literature* 62 (1): 47-114.

The State of Economic History: Credible or Incredible?

Jane Humphries

Abstract Economic History is not the favoured child of its parent disciplines. Economics and history do not vie for their offspring's attention. Instead, she struggles for favour. Facing decreasing interest, the closure of independent departments, and the erosion of her separate intellectual identity, economic history has contemplated the future with trepidation. Recently, reflections have focussed on bibliometric evidence stimulated by Robert Margo's hypothesis of integration within economics (Margo, *The Integration of Economic History in Economics*, 2017; Fernández-de-Pinedo et al., *Cliometrica* 17:1–22, 2023; Cioni et al., *Cliometrica* 17:23–40, 2023). Although I summarize the bibliometrics, my aim is not to augment this literature but to dig deeper into the nature of integration. While economic history had little option but to fold itself into economics, I argue that attempted assimilation has exposed it to a methodological revolution involving research designs that ape experimental methods (Angrist and Pischke, *Journal of Economic Perspectives* 2 (2):3–30, 2010). Compliance with the 'credibility revolution' has become the gateway to amalgamation with economics. While integration may be desirable and many 'as if' natural experiments in economic history illuminating, fitting into the 'credibility revolution' might involve the neglect of important topics, and excision of other methods and perspectives. Alternatively, methodological diversity and the accommodation of different approaches to sequence, mechanism, and plausibility may provide the basis for a more robust and engaging economic history.

J. Humphries (✉)
University of Oxford, Oxford, UK

London School of Economics, London, UK
e-mail: jane.humphries@all-souls.ox.ac.uk; J.Humphries@lse.ox.ac.uk

C. Diebolt, M. Haupert (eds.), *The State of Economic History*, Frontiers in Economic History, https://doi.org/10.1007/978-3-032-01624-9_4

Introduction

Economic History is not the favoured child of its disciplinary parents. Economics and history do not vie for their offspring's attention. Instead, she struggles for favour. Facing decreasing interest, the closure of independent departments, and the erosion of her separate intellectual identity, economic history has contemplated the future with trepidation. Concern has prompted reflection on developments and their implications for the future (Diebolt and Haupert 2019; Margo 2017, 2018; Blum and Colvin 2018; Ó Gráda 2019; Fenoaltea 2019; Brownlow and Colvin 2022). Ruminations have recently focussed on bibliometric evidence stimulated by Robert Margo's hypothesis of integration within economics (Fernández-de-Pinedo et al. 2023; Cioni et al. 2023). Although I summarize the bibliometrics, my aim is not to augment this literature but to dig deeper into the nature of integration. I ask how this is progressing and think further about the costs and benefits.

Most histories of economic history see the 'Cliometrics revolution' as an important rupture. Defined as a 'self-conscious movement to revolutionize the study of economic history by incorporating quantitative methods and explicit economic analysis into the study of past economic phenomena', cliometrics allegedly swept to dominance in the 1960s and the 1970s (https://www.sciencedirect.com/topics/economics-econometrics-and-finance/cliometrics# accessed 6-1-25). While cliometrics kept economic history in step with an increasingly mathematical economics (Debreu 1991), it drove a wedge between our subject and history. Understanding cliometric contributions (let alone producing them) required investments in theory and econometrics, which many historians considered unjustified by the pay-off. Besides, history's 'cultural turn' with its new emphasis on meaning, cognition, affect, and symbols distracted historians (Geertz 1973; Foucault 1977; Bourdieu 1977). Grappling with 'critical theory' involved a huge time investment, leaving little space to investigate other demanding methodologies. History's embrace of postmodernism ruled out a positivist epistemology let alone cliometrics.

Struggling to maintain a foothold in history faculties and a separate institutional identity, economic history, in the USA particularly, sought shelter in economics departments.[1] However, ScienceDirect's claim that cliometrics 'swept to dominance' is excessive. After the first rush of excitement, a more considered position emerged with star pioneers distancing themselves (McCloskey 1976). Economic history remained more quantitative and theoretically alert, but in most academic settings, particularly beyond the USA, it co-existed with a more traditional methodology reliant on narrative and form, establishing a continuum within professional associations and academic personnel. Both the Economic History Society and the Economic History Association continued to reach out to historians via statements in journal frontpages, dedicated sessions at conferences, and methodologically diverse journals.

[1] For a less US focussed history of economic history, see Brownlow and Colvin (2022).

While individual economic historians whether in history or economics departments could still enjoy and benefit from interaction, interdisciplinary solidarity was difficult to maintain across institutional divisions within universities, especially as these involved differences between schools, that is between humanities and social sciences. Moreover, as a distinct specialism economic history struggled from the 1980s in the face of waning interest among undergraduates. In the UK, several independent departments closed and economic history as a requirement in undergraduate economics (and history) degrees was diluted, with knock-on effects for job opportunities (Brownlow and Colvin 2022). At the graduate level, economic history came to be seen as a specialized subject necessarily crowded out by increasingly demanding technical training in theory and econometrics. Diebolt and Haupert (2019) report that only about half of U.S. PhD programmes still offer an economic history course, and it is rarely a requirement. Graduate students who had worked hard to pass comprehensive examinations in ‘Micro, Macro and Metrics’ had little stomach for then becoming familiar with traditional economic history, archival research, voluminous historical literatures, unfamiliar languages, and even palaeography. Instead, they needed to focus on developments within economics and ensure their conformity even if this meant tailoring interests and approaches to fit a Procrustean bed carpentered by economists.

In a series of papers from 2017, Robert Margo argued that economic history has been successful in its assimilation, a process he called ‘the integration of economic history into economics’. He defined integration in terms of the convergence of professional behaviour as reflected in the use of econometric language in articles appearing in academic economic history journals and the publication strategies of successive cohorts of PhDs. His bibliometric evidence suggested that over time economic history became more like economics in its use of econometrics and in the likelihood of researchers publishing in economics, as opposed to economic history outlets, though the pace of change was slower in economic history than in other subdisciplines such as labour economics, and there was a structural break for post-2000 PhD cohorts, which he explained through an overlapping generations model of the academic labour market. Margo’s claim triggered responses, which also focussed on bibliometric evidence. These supported his main findings while clarifying the extent of integration and (importantly) beginning to worry about its implications.

While economic history, certainly in the USA, had little option but to fold itself into economics, attempted assimilation has exposed it to a methodological revolution involving the adoption of research designs that ape experimental methods (Angrist and Pischke 2010). Section “The Credibility Revolution in Economics” describes the origins of this ‘credibility revolution’ and introduces its importance for economic history. Section “Bibliometric Analysis of Integration” returns to the bibliometric evidence but broadens it to reflect an integration that involves the emulation of experimental research designs. The evidence suggests that economic history has been less enthusiastic about the application of this breakthrough methodology than other subdisciplines of economics, although this differs across generations and departmental affiliations. Section “‘Credible’ Economic History” looks in more detail at the ways in which economic historians have exploited the past in search of natural experiments and explores the roles that they might play in collaborations with economists. Section "Reasons for Circumspection" begins to explain economic historians' cautious embrace of experimental research designs by looking at the potential costs as well as the benefits. I cite existing criticisms of experimental and quasi-experimental research in the social sciences, specifically those that bite within economic history (Sims 2010; Deaton 2008; Ravallion 2012; Deaton and Cartwright 2018; Conley and Kelly 2025) but think further about the implications of fitting neatly into the 'credibility revolution' if it involves cutting out topics, approaches, and perspectives. Section "Conclusion" concludes. Integration may be desirable and many 'as if' natural experiments in economic history are illuminating but we should be wary about the pitfalls. Insistence on a single methodological gateway into economic history might prove regrettable.

The Credibility Revolution in Economics

In the past, working with observational data, economists (like other social scientists) estimated associations and then tried to work out the extent to which these associations captured *causality*. The issues are well known. Omitted variables, unobservable variables, and reverse causation haunt empirical work. Even if investigators could identify and measure all confounding factors, there is still the problem of controlling for them. Conventional quantitative methods, particularly multivariate regression was sold to generations of economists (mine included) as enabling control with often explicit parallels drawn between regression and experimental methodologies. But there was growing disillusionment with econometric standards of proof (Angrist and Pischke 2010). As early as 1983, Edward Leamer had claimed that econometricians' inferences were subject to data mining, whimsical assumptions, and subjective judgements (Leamer 1983). Leamer was not alone in his anxieties, and, in the 1980s, econometrics went through a process of self-examination (Backhouse and Cherrier 2017).

While Leamer had explicitly warned about projecting onto econometrics the false image of experimental science (Panhans and Singleton 2017), controlled experiments remained the gold standard in identifying and measuring causal relationships. Social scientists could not but be envious. There was growing interest in trying to adapt such methods to analyse observational data. Development economics, a sibling subdiscipline with which economic history has a natural affinity, set the pace by introducing *actual* experiments in the form of 'Randomized Control Trials' (RCTs) as a 'clean' way to measure the impact of an intervention and so 'identify' what really worked in development policy (Webber and Prouse 2017). Where actual experiments were impractical, expensive, or immoral, as was the case in most fields of economics, institutional or natural variation could sometimes be interpreted as a 'natural experiment' or observational data manipulated to create a 'quasi experiment'. Viewing observational data in this way, labour economics and public finance had pioneered new empirical methodologies designed to untangle causal effects: Matching, Instrumental Variables, Difference-in-Differences, and Regression Discontinuity (Angrist and Pischke 2010). These had spread rapidly to other sub-fields, so that when the *Journal of Economic Perspectives* hosted a symposium revisiting Leamer's provocative contribution in 2010, Angrist and Pischke presented applied economists' embrace of 'quasi-experimental' research design and associated econometric methods as providing a 'credibility revolution' that would take 'the con out of econometrics' (2020, p. 12), by nailing down causation. Pointing to examples from the economics of crime, education, and health, Angrist and Pischke claimed a swing within applied economics towards quasi-experimental methods, leaving behind only industrial organization and macroeconomics. Economic history though unmentioned probably also lagged behind.

According to Panhans and Singleton, by this date, Angrist and Pischke's paper was 'less an argument .... than a victory lap' (2017, p. 128). A paradigm shift was well underway. Practitioners were acclaimed. Of the nine economists awarded the John Bates Clark Medal in the previous 15 years, the research of at least five, most notably David Card and Steven Levitt, is 'quasi-experimental', a trend that has continued (Panhans and Singleton 2017, p. 128). Meanwhile the training of applied economists as reflected in courses, textbooks, and seminar presentations, increasingly emphasizes the importance of 'credible identification' with important effects on the ways in which economics engages with ancillary disciplines including economic history, a point to which I return below.

Bibliometric evidence traces the paradigm shift. In his *Natural Experiments in the Social Sciences* (2012), Thad Dunning reported that over 80 articles published in major economics journals from 2000 to 2009 contained the phrase 'natural experiment' in the title or abstract compared with only four in the 30 years from 1960 to 1989 (2012, pp. 1–2). My own recent search using the same engine located 87 such papers in 2000–2009 rising to 242 by 2010–2019 (Table 1, https://www.jstor.org/ accessed 13/1/2025).[2] This was a revolution beyond the cliometric scale and reveals

Table 1 Phrase 'natural experiment' in abstracts of papers published in economics and economic history journals

Dates (total)	AER	QJE	JPE	Econometrica	RESTUD	EJ	JEL	RESTAT	Other	Economic history
2000–9 (87)	7	8	3	3	0	4	0	4	57	1
2010–19 (242)	9	4	1	0	7	13	0	18	83	7
2020–24 (45)	4	0	0	0	2	0	0	0	39	0

[2] As Dunning does not say which economic journals he includes, I cannot be certain that my data is consistent, though our total papers for 2000–9 are close. I searched across all journals listed under economics in JSTOR, though the sample consulted is limited by the requirement that papers have an abstract.

the mere tip of the experimental iceberg as our searches only capture articles that have the phrase 'natural experiment' in their title or abstract. A full text search, especially one widened to include other identifiers such as 'identification strategy' would yield more hits.

Panhans and Singleton (2017), while concerned to locate quasi-experimental methods in the longer-run development of econometrics and particularly in a perceived shift from models to methods, provide additional bibliometric evidence. They count the number of articles with a quasi-experimental term (regression discontinuity, natural experiment, difference-in-differences, randomized control trials, and variants thereof) in either the title or abstract in several fields and top general interest journals according to the Web of Science online database. Beginning around 1990, they document a sharp uptick in the percentage of articles using such terms, an increase of about 400% between 2000 and 2010, the year of the *Journal of Economic Perspectives* symposium. Field journals and leading general interest journals (*American Economic Review*, *Econometrica*, *Quarterly Journal of Economics*, and *Journal of Political Economy*) share similar increases with predictable variation in the frequency of specific terms by sub-fields (e.g. diff-in-diff particularly popular in health economics, and RCT's in development) (Panhans and Singleton 2017, p. 132ff.).

Again, a focus on titles and abstracts underestimates the transition in the character of economic research. Moreover, such searches sometimes miss a particular kind of research that exploits 'as if' experiments and is important in understanding the relationship between economic history and economics: persistence studies. These relate present-day 'outcomes' to events in the past going back centuries, even millennia. Such studies aim to obtain quantitative and resilient insights into 'the significance of historical events for present economic development processes and their mechanisms with the assistance of new, mostly quasi-experimental identification methods' (Michalopoulos and Papaioannou 2017). The systematic inclusion of persistence studies would boost the counts further and uncover how integration is developing as we shall see.

Economics new gold standard of credibility with respect to causation encourages economic historians to seek out *historical* 'natural experiments' with truly randomly assigned subjects or where a case for random assignment could be made and, on this basis, estimate the impact of a 'treatment' or 'intervention'. The language borrowed from epidemiology or development economics is no accident. Presented in this way, economic history might prove more interesting to economists, perhaps inducing new respect. However, economists' attention is conditional on a specific methodological approach. This would often involve sophisticated econometrics when the assignment of observation units appears less than random, or excursions into technical rabbit holes like the plausibility of exclusion restrictions. These are likely to estrange those economic historians who remain unconverted and further alienate historians, which might prove unfortunate given their reborn interest in traditional areas of economic history such as capitalism, slavery, globalization, inequality, and discrimination.

Bibliometric Analysis of Integration

Bob Margo (2017) documented his early account of the 'integration' of economic history into economics with evidence on the use of econometrics in articles on historical topics appearing in economic history and economics journals and the publication records of successive cohorts of PhDs (see also, Abramitzky 2015). Margo found that the use of econometrics in economic history eventually converged with economics, and that over successive generations, economic historians who were employed in economics departments shifted their publication strategies away from books and field journals towards general interest economics outlets. Margo's analysis focussed on a limited number of North American academics and few journals (two in economic history, two in labour economics, and one top five general interest journal, the *American Economic Review*), and although his later (2018) contribution expanded the data set, it remained US oriented. Nonetheless, the number of economic history articles appearing in economics journals, particularly in the so-called top five, T5, (*American Economic Review, Econometrica, Journal of Political Economy, Quarterly Journal of Economics,* and *Review of Economic Studies*) was established as a key marker of integration (Abramitzky 2015; Margo 2018; Diebolt and Haupert 2019; Jaremski 2020). Since tenure and promotion in US, and increasingly top UK economics departments depend on publication in this golden group of outlets, their tyranny extends from economists to include ambitious economic historians (Heckman and Moktan 2020). The question then becomes the extent to which success with T5 requires a distinctive approach: selecting topics of interest to economists, connecting research questions with economic theory, providing extensive robustness checks, and, today, adopting quasi-experimental research methods. Integration comes at the cost of compliance, and we need to know how high this is.

Also focussing on where economic history was published, Cioni et al. (2021) document a recent (last 10 years) decline in the percentage of economic history articles published in top five economics journals and suggest that this indicates a pause in integration. Responding to this work, Fernández-de-Pinedo et al. (2023) worried that the coverage of economic outlets might be too narrow. They also point out that declining numbers of US economics graduates specialized in economic history (Margo 2021) means that the falling share of publications in general interest journals might simply reflect shrinking numbers of potential authors.

Fernández-de-Pinedo et al. (2023) provide their own bibliometric analysis using a dataset of 11,143 articles published between 1980 and 2019 in leading journals written by 919 economic historians identified by membership of a professional society. As the dataset includes biographical information, it enables publishing strategies to be related to authors' background. Using a probit regression, Fernández-de-Pinedo et al. find that since 1980, economic historians have become increasingly likely to publish in economics and finance journals, but that this tendency is more marked in North America than Europe. They relate this divergence to different training pathways. Americans were more likely to be educated as economists in economics departments, while many Europeans continued to be trained specifically as economic historians, even though there are few specialist departments (Lund and LSE). Network visualizations of cross citation confirm these regional differences. Citations to economics and finance journals are more central to US academics' research. These findings support Margo's claim that economic history is more integrated into economics in the USA than Europe.

Fernández-de-Pinedo et al. focus exclusively on journal articles ignoring monographs and short publications. Furthermore, the criterion for identification of economic historians (not a simple matter when they are distributed across potential departments, business, management, economics, history, area studies, labour economics, etc.) by membership of a professional association or attendance at an association's conferences is problematic. The authors acknowledge that this yardstick selects an activist group from the broader pool and imposes a regional filter since these associations and their meetings are European (2023, p. 5). Moreover, they apply the criterion inconsistently. Society membership selects differently than does conference participation and while the former is applied to the EHA and the Cliometric Society to identify practitioners, attendance at conferences is used in relation to the EHS and the EHES. A further concern is the categorization of PhD (Economics or Finance, Economic History, or History), especially as this plays a significant role in the US-Europe difference in integration. Given that few freestanding departments of economic history survive (even in Europe), how is an economic history PhD identified? Oxford, my own university, for example, does not categorize PhD's by training pathway or subject matter, and I suspect other European universities act similarly.

Attendees at Economic History Society annual conferences are significantly more likely to publish in history journals, unsurprising given that it is an explicitly umbrella organization existing 'to support research in economic and social history, broadly defined' (https://ehs.org.uk/about/ n. 23). However, it appears that members of the Cliometrics Society are also more likely to publish in history journals. What explains this? It might be possible to nuance the US-Europe divergence if the UK could be separately identified and compared with both the USA and Europe. The stronger influence of cliometrics on UK economic historians and their greater enthusiasm for the kinds of economics practised in US faculties suggests that UK experience of integration might stand between the USA and continental Europe. These issues aside the Fernández-de-Pinedo et al. dataset are impressive and its support for the integration hypothesis and its regional variation convincing.

In another bibliometric contribution, Cioni et al. (2023) agree that economic history is increasingly interesting to economists. In support, they cite several survey articles which stress the relevance of economic history to understanding economic development (Nunn 2009; Spolaore and Wacziarg 2013; Ashraf and Galor 2018), and two important collections which explore the opportunities as well as the challenges of interaction with economics (Diebolt and Haupert 2019; Bisin and Federico 2021). An investigation of these opportunities and challenges underpins their study, which is conventional in using bibliometric evidence but novel in categorizing articles not simply by publication outlet and their use of econometrics but also by other aspects of content. They identify economic history papers appearing in economics journals by looking at their abstracts and when available at the JEL codes of the American Economic Association. All articles are classified by topic, epoch, geographical area of interest, and extent and sophistication of the econometrics. Additionally, they isolate persistence studies, which they see as spearheading integration. These studies, as noted earlier, are distinctive in interpreting present-day outcomes as the result of something that happened many years (even centuries) earlier. Such studies are inherently both 'presentist' (i.e. interested in the past only for how it can inform understanding of the present) and econometric and so appeal to economists but deter economic historians interested in the past for its own sake or repelled by a methodology that often leaves the substance of history, the mechanisms through which persistence occurs, in a black box buried beneath the econometrics. If indeed persistence studies are the drivers of integration, it will divide economic historians with some embracing the approach and others harbouring serious reservations. Integration might leave many economic historians behind.

Cioni et al.'s attention to the content of publications enables them to link the outlet to the type of article and so investigate the important question whether publication in economics journals, particularly T5, requires a certain kind of economic history. Thus, Cioni et al. can uncover the extent to which economic history that conforms to the ideals of economics and so makes it through the reviewing procedures of these prestigious and competitive journals is different from economic history appearing in the top field journals. They also consider if it has more academic influence in terms of citations. Unfortunately, their categorization into persistence studies versus the rest is limiting. Persistence studies exploit institutional variation or the forces of nature in the framework of natural or quasi-experiments, but they form a specific group within a broader category of historical work marked by the credibility revolution. Cioni et al's fixation on persistence studies blinds them to the broader increasing role of natural experiments.

Cioni et al. compare papers appearing in top five economic history (field) journals, T5EH (*Cliometrica, Explorations in Economic History, Economic History Review, European Review of Economic History,* and *the Journal of Economic History*) with those appearing in T5 economics journals sometimes expanded to include three other respected general interest journals *(Economic Journal, Journal of Economic Literature*, and *Review of Economics and Statistics*), the T8.

The share of economic history articles appearing in economics journals is significantly higher after 2001 and increased even more for T5. However, the large year-to-year fluctuations and absence of any upward trend weakens support for integration (p. 30). The overall share of economic history papers was 4% higher for 'other economics journals' than T5 where it represented only 3.6% of papers overall, a mere 11 articles per year. There was a great variation in apparent receptiveness to economic history among T8 journals with the *QJE* appearing the most open. Persistence studies formed only a small minority of papers published, 0.5% exceeding 1% only in the *QJE*. If such papers represent the vanguard of economic history's thrust into economics, the process appears yet tentative.

Cioni et al. go on to explore the divide within economic history by looking at the characteristics of publications by where they appeared using multinomial regressions. These confirm the broad differences between articles published in economic history and economics journals detectable in the descriptive statistics. Most are predictable. The high share of twentieth-century articles published in T8 journals surely reflects, as the authors note, economists' greater interest in more recent and better-documented times. More interestingly, the relative emphasis of T8, and even more of T5, on 'institutions' suggests an emphasis on quasi-experimental research designs.

Turning to authors, again not surprisingly, two thirds of those authors publishing economic history in the T8 and four-fifths of those publishing in T5 were affiliated with American universities, reflecting the greater integration of economic history into economics in the USA with the associated need to publish in these outlets for career progression. Institutional representation documents similar differences. Eight European universities feature in the top ten for publishing in the field journals but only one in the top ten for the T8 and none in T5. Cioni et al. argue that these differences reflect a split within the economic history tribe, between researchers who publish in economics journals ('economists') and those who publish in field journals ('economic historians'). Most researchers publish exclusively in one or the other kind of journal with very few 'hybrid' authors able to command space in both. These rare beings are however very productive, providing almost a fifth of contributions to the economic history journals and a third of those to the T8.

The authors of persistence studies selected for particular attention by Cioni et al. turn out to be distinctive even among 'economists'. More than half of them have published *only* persistence studies, usually with a co-author, and no other economic history. Rather than the advance guard of integration they look more like a sub-caste (the Brahmins?) of economic history, only marginally contributing to a broader division between 'economists' publishing in economics journals and 'traditional economic historians' publishing in field journals. An analysis of citation patterns confirms this broader cleavage and the way it is created and maintained by the intellectual outlook of researchers who publish in economics journals, including but not limited to persistence studies. While, as Cormac Ó Gráda (2019) shows persistence papers have zero impact on historical scholarship and are little cited in economic history outlets, indifference is reciprocated in spades, for persistence authors pay less attention to the more general group of 'traditional economic historians' than they receive from them. The 'economists' are distancing themselves from the 'traditional economic historians' who struggle to remain relevant to their colleagues.

Citations also vary by outlet. Cioni et al. find that articles appearing in T8 journals garner more citations per year than do those in field journals, articles in T5 more than in other economics journals, and persistence studies more than other kinds of economic history, the greater impact of this last due partly to the heavy citation of three tremendously successful persistence studies (Acemoglu et al. 2001, 2002; La Porta et al. 2008). Adding controls to the baseline regression highlights other features: longer papers are cited more frequently (more content) as are co-authored papers. More unexpectedly, the controls halve the citation premium for publication in top five and eliminate any significant gain for publishing in other economic journals. Publishing in T5 yields citation dividends compared with economic history journals but nailing one of the other (albeit respected) economics journals reduces this bonus and it disappears if the comparison is with only the most cited (top decile) papers in economic history journals.

So, the integration thesis wilts in the face of Cioni et al.'s extensive and up-to-date bibliometric survey. Although economists superficially appear more interested in economic history today than in the late twentieth century, '...the impact of economic history in economics journals is still modest and has not been growing since 2001' (p. 45). Rather than showing integration with economics, their bibliometrics shows a cleavage within economic history according to whether it appears in economics or field journals. Articles in economics journals differ in terms of topics, periods, geographical areas, and use of econometrics compared with those published in economic history journals. Citation patterns reveal a bifurcated literature with economists citing economic historians less than the other way around. Authors comprise distinct groups, with individuals tending to publish exclusively in either economics or economic history journals. Few scholars overlap. We are really two separate tribes, three if we count the small but distinctive persistence economists, and our tribes inhabit different territories, with economists and persistence economists hanging out in the USA and economic historians in Europe including the UK.

Agnostic about the future, Cioni et al. think it premature to predict where these patterns will lead. If persistence studies are the drivers of integration, outcomes hinge on their future. If they break away to form a separate discipline, perhaps as a subsidiary of development economics, traditional economic history might then languish in interdisciplinary no-man's-land. Alternatively, authors of persistence studies could regroup with more traditional practitioners providing the basis for a new synthesis and possibly boosting the status of economic history within social science. Yet although Cioni et al. claim success for persistence studies, the bibliometric analysis suggests that it is only articles published in T5 economics journals that dominate the best articles published in field journals. Moreover, such studies are not without their critics coming from both mainstream economics and traditional economic history, as we shall see.

My argument is that while persistence studies are intrinsically different from conventional economic history, they are only a part of our subject's response to the credibility revolution that has taken economics by storm. The influence of experimental and quasi-experimental research designs extends well beyond persistence studies to cover other types of historical research. These are also intrinsically different from 'traditional economic history'. By specifically focussing on persistence studies and amalgamating all other types of papers into a 'traditional' category, Cioni et al. have misread the nature of economics' methodological turn and its impact on economic history and so perhaps underestimated the widening divide within our subject. Although bibliometric evidence documenting the extent and distribution of economic history articles which embrace a quasi-experimental frame is more difficult to establish, the latter surely represents the methodological revolution with which our subject will need to come to terms.

'Credible' Economic History

Angrist and Pischke (2010) begin their famous account of the credibility revolution with economists' growing disillusionment with econometric standards of proof (see above p. 4). In searching to establish causation, even if investigators could identify and measure all confounding factors, there remained the problem of controlling for them. Conventional quantitative methods, particularly multivariate regression analysis suggested the possibility of control with often explicit parallels drawn between regression and experimental methodologies. Thus, Wooldridge in his standard textbook says 'the power of multiple regression is that it allows us to do in non-experimental environments what natural scientists are able to do in a controlled laboratory setting' identifying the relationship between dependent and independent variables by holding all other things constant (2009, p. 77). In a textbook designed for economic historians, Feinstein and Thomas, explicitly contrast experimental research in plant science and medicine with historical studies in the social sciences where the ability to 'assess the influence of one particular variable while controlling for the influence of others' can normally only be achieved indirectly, by the application of appropriate statistical procedures 'of which multiple regression is the most powerful' (2002, p. 234–5).

As section "The Credibility Revolution in Economics" recalled, whether these methods replicated experimental conditions came to be questioned. There was dawning anxiety that if the assumptions about the model specification and functional form are incorrect, statistical manipulation can do little to bolster causal inference. In contrast, with random or as if random assignment unobserved or unmeasured, confounders are balanced up to random error (Dunning 2012, p. 25; but see Deaton and Cartwright's (2018) important discussion of 'random confounding'). Thus, and this must be a major advantage in a subject hoping to reach out to researchers in adjacent fields as well as engage with policy makers, if treatment assignment is truly random, or as good as random, a simple comparison of average outcomes in treatment and control is often enough to establish causal inference. The approach has potential benefits in terms of simplicity and transparency. If it heralds the future for economics, does it also provide a niche for economic historians? How can they contribute?

For one thing, they can be in on the ground floor. Natural experiments wait to be detected in observational data. Their discovery rests on awareness of both the methodology and the historical record. Economic historians can initiate projects for the past provides a storehouse of potential evidence. The idea that history provides a depot of economic facts at the service of applied economists is not new. Leading cliometrics revolutionaries, as Ó Gráda reminds us, tried to 'gain the respect of economists at the cost of reducing economic history to a testing ground for their hypotheses' (2019, p. 83). But if it would have been a 'Faustian bargain' in the 1970s, as Ó Gráda contends, it is equally hazardous today. Despite economic historians' comparative advantage in care with and understanding of original data, partnerships would likely collapse into master–servant relationships with economic historians supplying their economist masters with the data, and the latter doing the analytical work. Indeed, if reduced to assembling evidence, the economic historian encounters another threat for modern technology promises to deskill digitization and data collection. While this might open historical doors to natural experiments, as Ran Abramitzky suggests, it also brings data collection into the wheelhouse of '*general economists*' (2015, p. 1248, my emphasis). Even worse, modern technology often seems to do away altogether with human agency, prompting researchers who have toiled at the archival coal face to fetishize the process and celebrate its products to an irritating extent (Ó Gráda 2019). Nonetheless, old-fashioned historical familiarity with sources not only provides a better feel for the data's fragility but can also lead to the discovery of the kind of evidence that documents a credible natural experiment. Such discovery often arises serendipitously from what Cormac Ó Gráda describes as 'an interest in history for its own sake', rather than a pillaging of the past in a deliberate search for quasi-experiments. Overall, a deal which reduces economic historians to the quantitative donkey work for clever and innovative economists does not bode well. Fortunately, economic historians can be useful in other ways.

Thad Dunning's list of the features that make natural experiments convincing suggests how economic historians can contribute (2012, pp. 27–32; Dunning, 2008). First, and most obviously, their contextual knowledge can bolster the plausibility of the assumptions essential for a credible natural experiment. In rare cases, e.g., when a lottery is involved, researchers can claim true randomization, but even then, since the procedure is not under the control of the researchers (as in experimental work) the plausibility of randomization requires demonstration via detailed insight into the assignment process and procedural mechanisms. Where researchers claim 'as if' randomization even more effort must go into verification. Crucial supporting evidence comes from comparison of the 'treated' and 'control' groups before assignment to demonstrate their similarity and the likelihood that they were drawn from the same population, here playing to the historians' familiarity with comparative analysis. It is also important to be able to demonstrate that the units of observation themselves played no part in the selection into treatment and control, since self-selection rightly raises suspicion of non-randomness. Knowledge and understanding of the context, and an ability to look around the specific experiment at analogous or adjacent events, meat and drink to the economic historian, will help to demonstrate both *ex ante* balance and the absence of self-selection.

Second, the need to probe the credibility of the model of data generation is not removed by scrutiny of the randomization assumption but requires separate investigation to ensure that it is consistent with the statistical basis of experimental research. This too requires detailed knowledge and understanding but here internal to the postulated experiment. The researchers need to get inside the experiment to understand how it operated to generate the data, and ensure that there were no threats from attrition, or post random confounding or selection biases, creating another niche for the economic historian.

Third, there is the issue of the importance of the intervention and whether the findings can be generalized to make a theoretical point or have relevance for economic policy. As with RCT's in development economics, there are serious questions about whether any 'average treatment effects' can be generalized without more structure, prior information and ideas about what might make effects vary from place to place or time to time (Deaton and Cartwright 2018). The methodology might appear less seductive to economic historians who would then be less likely drawn to events enabling clever and creative research designs albeit with little bearing on important questions. However, if sufficiently integrated into economics, they will be just as prone to play 'small ball' (Angrist and Pischke 2010, p. 36), drawn to good answers rather than meaty questions. However, if related studies or other contextual evidence can support the claim to external validity, the economic historian's prior knowledge and greater familiarity with background and setting may again be helpful (or a related perspective on the optimal use of RCT findings, see Deaton and Cartwright (2018)).

Commentators cite labour economics and public finance as leading the exploitation of natural experiments (Angrist and Pischke 2010; Banerjee et al. 2019). In fact, one early (and beautiful) example of the use of a natural experiment that relates to the history of public health illustrates the points made above. John Snow, a Victorian doctor working in London during a horrendous cholera outbreak in 1853–4, doubted the prevailing 'miasmatic' view that foul air caused the disease. Snow suspected that cholera was waterborne, caused by Londoners use of sewage-contaminated water. For one affected district in Soho, Snow mapped where the victims of the outbreak lived, famously showing that their habitations clustered around the Broad Street pump. Contaminated water from this source contributed to the spread and intensity of the disease. However, Snow offered less well-known but even stronger evidence that cholera was waterborne. Two water companies, the Lambeth Company, and the Southwark & Vauxhall Company, supplied large areas of London. In 1852, the Lambeth Company had moved its intake pipe upstream on the Thames, so getting its supply before the river became inundated with the City's sewage. The Southwark & Vauxhall Company left its pipe in place. Snow had access to records of cholera deaths in houses throughout London according to their source of water supply. Simple cross-tabulation showed that for houses served by Southwark & Vauxhall, the death rate from cholera was 315 per 10,000 households, whereas for those supplied by Lambeth it was a mere 37 per 10,000 (Snow ([1855] 1965, table IX, p. 86; cited in Dunning 2012, p. 13).

Snow's account provides a good natural experiment according to the criteria sketched above. Although Snow did not systematically explore the similarity between households getting their water from the different companies nor test statistically for balance, he did note the qualitative similarities in terms of wealth, house size, and the conditions and occupations of the residents. His familiarity with context was vital to his claim that 'no experiment could have been devised which would more thoroughly test the effect of water supply on the progress of cholera…' (Snow, [1855], 1965, 74–75, Cited in Dunning 2012, p. 14). Snow's defence of his natural experiment went further with another lesson for would be modern mimics. Again, informed by his own familiarity with the context, he emphasized that an absentee landlord often made the decision as to which of the companies supplied their properties without the knowledge of the residents. There was no self-selection by householders confounding the assignment procedure. Moreover, the Lambeth water company made its decision to move its intake pipe to a less polluted stretch of the river before the epidemic and before the scientific community had accepted that cholera was waterborne. It had nothing to do with subsequent events: it was exogenous. Households were as if randomly assigned thereafter death rates were epidemiologically determined. And, of course, Snow's natural experiment was far from trivial since it demonstrated the nature of a deadly disease and how it could be controlled by a straightforward public health initiative, readily scaled up to deliver analogous benefits to those enjoyed by the Lambeth-supplied households to other areas of London. It had in today's parlance 'external validity' showing how to save thousands of lives.

The credibility and power of Snow's natural experiment rested not on clever econometrics, nor on thousands of robustness checks, but on his initial awareness of the potential of the variation in water supplies, his demonstration of both the similarity of treatment and control households, the absence of self-selection, and his simple and transparent comparison of outcomes, all mobilized by his intuition that cholera was communicated by bad water. These characteristics came from the knowledge of context that he had acquired as a firsthand medical practitioner in a filthy nineteenth century city.

The history of public health provides a depository of evidence amenable to quasi-experimental methods increasingly exploited by economic historians. Researchers can use such evidence to identify and measure causal relationships with powerful policy implications as well as to illustrate early use of the econometrics now associated with quasi-experiments. But evidence often requires excavation from obscure historical sources and extensive and painstaking contextualization. To illustrate from the most recent Economic History Society Conference, Jonathan James (2025) discovered that in 1900, thousands of people in England were accidentally poisoned by arsenic-contaminated sugar used in cheap beer production. James used an event study difference-in-differences design to estimate the drop in fertility caused by consuming the tainted beer. His paper also contributes to the history of economic ideas by demonstrating that Dr. James Niven, then Medical Officer of Health for Manchester, used a statistical procedure analogous to difference-in-differences to understand the data and claim causality.

If the credibility revolution offers opportunities to economic historians to use natural experimental research designs to smuggle themselves into the economics mainstream, is this detectible in the bibliometrics? First, although Table 1 shows an increase in economics journals publishing papers boasting a natural experiment in their abstracts, and this includes T5 journals, the group of other general interest journals (*EJ, JEL, and ReStat*), and all other economics journals, such papers remain in a minority. Nor does the bibliometrics suggest that the penetration of historical natural experimental research is gathering steam. What looks more apparent is the spread of the methodology, which might include historical experiences, into other subdisciplines of economics and their field journals. While labour and public finance were pioneers in the adoption of the new empirical methods for estimating causal

Table 2 Twenty-seven well-known persistence studies published in economics and economic history journals

Dates (total)	AER	QJE	JPE	Econometrica	RESTUD	EJ	JEL	RESTAT	Other	Economic history
2000–9 (87)	2	3		0	0		0	0	0	0
2010–19 (242)	5	4		2	0		0	1	2	0
2020–24 (45)	3	1	0	2	1	0	0	0	1	0

http://www.jstor.org/stable/25703496

effects (Banerjee et al. 2019), a survey of experiment-framed papers appearing in journals outside the T8 suggests that economic geography, population economics, health economics, and industrial organization, even the economics of sport are now involved (see section "The Credibility Revolution in Economics"; see also, Panhans and Singleton 2017). These subdisciplines, several of which have obvious purchase on natural experiments (e.g. economic geography) have seized the day. Economic history lags. Hardly any papers proclaiming a natural experimental research design have appeared in our leading field journals, which show the same reserve towards such research as they did to persistence studies where they published none of the 27 best known (Table 2; see also Ó Gráda 2019).

It may not be the journals but the authors who are behind this absence given the apparent success of such papers among the economics journals. Authors rationally seek to place their work where the academic payoff is greatest. Persistence studies are well known for nailing publication in top five journals (see Table 2) and garnering the associated career dividends. It appears that economic history papers based on a natural experiment fared similarly disproportionately well in T5 and T8 journals. For example, of the 9 papers published in the *AER* 2009–2010 with natural experiment in the abstract, four explored historical experiments, and while no similar papers appearing in the *JPE* or *ReSTUD* dealt with the past, 6 out of the 13 papers in this genre published in the *EJ* were historical. So not only persistence studies but economic history papers boasting natural experiments more generally appear to be able to overcome the hurdles to publication in highly regarded economics journals. What is mysterious is their absence from economic history journals when they have clearly spilled out from leading economics journals into field journals in other subdisciplines of economics. Authors of historical experiment papers with career progression in mind might well target top economics journals first but trickle down into the field journals should surely follow especially as the methodology grows in popularity.

So, papers which explore historical developments through an as-if experimental lens, can, like persistence studies, overcome the obstacles and appear in mainstream economics journals, even top five. But such papers are few. If the integration of economic history into economics involves piggybacking on the credibility revolution so far enthusiasm appears limited. What is more surprising is that economic history journals have not pushed from below, converging on economics by attracting articles with experimental designs. The limited showcasing of such papers in economic history field journals suggests a hesitant response to the opportunities afforded by 'the credibility revolution', a further detachment from mainstream economics, and a different and deeper cleavage within our subject than that represented by the separation of persistence studies and their authors.

The finding that economic historians and their journals have been hesitant in exploiting natural experiments is inconsistent with experience at seminars and conferences which frequently highlight research using quasi-experimental research designs. These events often feature younger scholars and recent research, suggesting a generational paradigm shift. For example, the last ten of the London School of Economics Epstein Lectures designed to 'showcase the work of up-and-coming academics in the field of economic history' have all used quasi-experimental research methods (https://www.lse.ac.uk/Economic-History/Seminars/The-Epstein-Lecture-Series). Similarly, papers delivered at the conference remembering Nick Crafts' contributions to economic history (Crafts Memorial Event, Warwick, November 2024) were almost all quasi-experimental whereas (to my knowledge) he never adopted this framing in his own research, though probably open to its use. Perhaps the credibility revolution in economic history will gather momentum. Alternatively, wariness may be real and suggest the need for caution.

Reasons for Circumspection

Economic historians have not jumped wholesale on the experiments bandwagon even though it promises to convey them to the cutting-edge of mainstream economics, showing more hesitation than researchers in other subdisciplines. Why?

First, experimental research itself is not without detractors. For example, critics have charged that the internal validity of Randomized Control Trials in development economics is rarely assured, while differences between 'treatment' and 'control' groups may not reflect the impact of the intervention if there is sampling error (Deaton and Cartwright 2018). More generally, we should not forget that natural experiments can give more biased estimators than multiple linear regression, usually when an IV is not actually random (even if the amount of endogeneity is small) as described in standard econometrics textbooks (Wooldridge 2009).

The 'streetlight effect' of insistence on quasi-experimental research design is also worrying (Deaton and Cartwright 2018; Ravallion 2019). The picture of 'graduate students and their teachers … wandering around looking for something they can randomly assign [and] if randomization is not feasible for the question being posed, … often drawn to ask other questions' (Ravallion 2019, p. 497) strikes a chord in economic history. Resisting the pressure towards amenable questions, we might lean away from the methodology. On the other hand, promoters have mounted a stout defence arguing that researchers have become adept at identifying and using natural experiments, and more cautious in interpreting the results with spillover effects on the standard of non-experimental research, and that this has been achieved without sacrificing attention to broad important questions (Banerjee et al. 2019; Cantoni and Yuchtman 2021).

Importantly too, economic historians might see causal identification as secondary to the verification of the chronology and meaning of historical events. The compulsory methodology course in Oxford is called 'What happened and Why'. Getting history right precedes understanding its causes. And getting history right is no simple matter. Researchers constantly excavate new evidence or develop alternative ways of looking at existing evidence, both of which can transform understanding of the past. Many articles in field and even general interest economics journals involve revisions to hitherto accepted accounts of 'what really happened'. Even ardent advocates of experimental framing acknowledge that important 'descriptive' historical work exists. Cantoni and Yuchtman (2021) cite as illustration work by Frydman and Saks (2010), Abramitzsky et al. (2012), and Piketty and Saez (2006), and readers might add to this list. Whether such research has no purchase on historical explanation is a moot point to which I will return. At any rate, the quality of 'description' matters since it forms the foundation of the most sophisticated natural historical experiments and the most famous persistence studies. The use of settler mortality as an instrument for expropriation risk so enabling the identification of the causal effects of institutions on the economic growth of previously colonialized countries was the clever core of Acemoglu, Johnson, and Robinson's celebrated study of the colonial origins of comparative development (2002). Doubts then about the historical reliability of their settler mortality series raise questions about the whole enterprise (Albouy 2012) or at least force further contemplation of what really happened in this case to cross-section settler death rates (Acemoglu et al. 2012). In the meantime, authors have gratefully used their series as an instrument for institutions without digging into or understanding its origins and potential weaknesses. Similarly, it really matters for persistence economists' claims that obligatory labour service had long-run adverse consequences whether the mining *mita* boundary in Dell's influential (2010) case study was as discrete as contended, a claim that historians have disputed (Abad and Maurer 2025). Concerns about the quality of evidence and its use in ways for which it might be ill-suited both give economic historians pause in their commitment to the methodology and provide them with a different task: improving the underlying data.

Although all experimental and quasi-experimental research leave transmission mechanisms underspecified, persistence studies are particularly vulnerable to this criticism. By linking long-ago events to recent outcomes with a lack of precision about the transmission process and insufficient attention to intermediate periods, they 'compress' history, ignoring the absence of direct evidence for the intervening eras and overlooking inconsistent developments (Austin 2008; Abad and Maurer 2021). Thus, Voitländer and Voth see fertility restriction emerging as an indirect consequence of the abundance of land in England created by the enormous mortality following the Black Death in1348–50 but persisting for centuries thereafter. They argue that the increased land-labour ratios that followed the demographic catastrophe of the Black Death raised wages … 'raising female employment opportunities outside the peasant household [which] increased the average age at first marriage in a Malthusian setting ….' (2013, p. 2229, 2260) and so reduced fertility. However, appealing these arguments, the evidence for both the dependent variable and its link to women's economic role is missing. There are no direct measures of English birth rates until parochial registration in 1540, nor is the effect of the Black Death on women's economic opportunities clearly documented, indeed it has been fiercely debated. Recent evidence on women's wages suggests that their gains in the post-Black Death labour market were subdued and that unmarried women in particular faced increased difficulties as the state sought through the Statute of Labourers to hold down wages and coerce workers (Humphries and Weisdorf 2015), offering little support for the mechanism cited as behind the persistence of fertility restraint.

Of course, such criticisms just suggest that studies need to be based on the best possible data, and its weaknesses acknowledged and (hopefully) offset within the research design. These points strengthen the case for the usefulness of economic historians, but even if persistence studies were to take history more seriously there might be other reasons to be wary.

The authority (the Oomph!) of many quasi-experiments lies in their impressive statistical results. But long ago McCloskey warned that statistical significance was not the same as economic significance or agronomic or psychological or medical significance (McCloskey and Ziliak, 2010). It is also not the same as historical significance. A variable can have a statistically significant causal effect, but that effect may be very small (even if persistent). There is danger too in putting too much weight on the size of a coefficient. Many quasi-experimental papers in economic history are attractive because they are clever, and their 'big' findings make us sit up! However, the effect may be large in one study and small in another, and findings from studies even dealing with similar times and places can be inconsistent as Cormac Ó Gráda demonstrates in his review of the effects of famines and epidemics (2019, pp. 89–94).[3] They can also fade quickly. In Jonathan James study of arsenic poisoning (cited above), while the effect was large as well as significant, an 11% drop in births, it was short-lived. After about 28 weeks, birth rates returned to pre-epidemic levels, so it is an entertaining example of public health history with additional insights into the development of statistics, but there is no demographic Oomph! Results that are both large and statistically significant attract attention, but as Ó Gráda reminds us, 'most useful knowledge is incremental and less sensational' (2019, p. 94).

Reliance on statistical authority is particularly true of persistence studies. As Conley and Kelly say objections 'crumble into irrelevance' in the face of the unusual explanatory power of the persistent variables with t-statistics of 5, 6 or even larger, unobtainable by 'massaging regressions' instead reflecting 'the enduring legacy of

[3] Historical knowledge can be useful in evaluating claims (and identifying when these might be oversold!). Thus, Beach et al. drew on their understanding of age heaping to qualify the role of selection bias in analyses of the 1918 influenza epidemic's effects on child health (see discussion in as Ó Gráda 2019, pp. 89–94).

the past' (2025, p. 1). What these authors go on to argue is that in studies where the underlying regressions are spatial, the spatial data is autocorrelated, and when corrected significance levels in many celebrated persistence studies are reduced and the unusual explanatory power of the persistent variables attenuated (see also, Betz et al. 2020). The response to this critique has been fiercely defensive, citing the standard set of tools that econometricians have at their command to deal with spatial error correlations (Voth 2021; Becker et al. 2025). As Ó Gráda says 'Whether the Emperor is stark naked remains to be seen but, for sure, he appears far less well-dressed than previously' (2019, p. 107).

It is also possible that the methodology faces diminishing returns. Research designs that were once fresh and exciting are increasingly applied in less convincing and meaningful contexts. For example, the interpretation of exogenously imposed borders as randomly assigning treatment, once clever and original has become humdrum, with the research design applied to cases where randomness is increasingly questionable and the findings of less and less interest. Similarly, the use of migrants to trace cultural embeddedness by linking their ongoing behaviour to distant individual and community experience, once so exciting, has become standard. Best practice is one thing but relentless conformity another. Presentations increasingly all following the same pattern from 'motivation' (surely demonstrated by the audience's presence) through to robustness checks, but often missing discussion of the generalizability and importance of the findings. Diversity of approach, methodology, and presentation might be worth preserving.

A more positive reason to resist any quasi-experimental methodological monopoly involves the claim that observational evidence can be organized to suggest (if not *prove*) causality. Chronology can provide guidance. Debates about technological or institutional pre-eminence in economic development have long involved investigation of whether changes in technology preceded or followed institutional change (Hodgson 2023). Similarly, Deidre McCloskey's claim that institutional inertia 'prior to the Great Enrichment' disqualifies institutions from any explanatory role in the English Industrial Revolution and supports her claim that ideas were the first mover (cited in Hodgson, p. 59). Of course, identifying causation by what happened first runs into exactly those same issues of omitted variable bias and simultaneity that prompted the credibility revolution. Moreover, accounts of the explanatory power of institutional structures often reverse the time structure of explanation. In what Karl Gunnar Persson, Paul Sharp, and Markus Lampe (2025) call a 'consequence explanation', institutions that prove functional for subsequent economic developments are preserved and those that are inconsistent are eliminated in a model of explanation resonant of evolutionary biology. An analogy between natural selection, 'the survival of the fittest', and the weeding out taking place in competitive markets might sometimes seem to fit but as Persson, Sharp, and Lampe emphasize institutional structures do not always have a rationale in efficiency. Historically as today, the politically and economically powerful can design institutions deliberately to serve their interests or their structure may be merely accidental.

Seeking causation in historical events is fraught with difficulty, yet traditional economic historians should not give up. Mary Morgan's (2017) argument that narrative itself can make sense of events provides inspiration. She presents narrative as a 'general purpose technology' not useful for 'finding out' but of value in making sense of accumulated pieces of evidence. '...[N]arrative making provides scientists with a means of making sense of the materials in their field ... of representing that knowledge and ... might even provide the site for scientific reasoning and knowledge claims' (Morgan 2022, p. 1). Translating this interpretation of 'scientific narratives' to historical research, she argues that historians 'pick out particular facts, particular events, particular relations, and order them to create a narrative account in answer to historical questions or problems'. For historians, narratives can 'explain how things happen and why things happen...' (Morgan 2017, p. 86).[4] The influential studies referred to earlier as 'descriptive' (p. 24) can be interpreted as using such a 'narrative strategy'. Thomas Piketty's *Capital in the twenty-first Century* (2014) drew on economic theory illustrated by graphs and tables, but these did not account for its phenomenal success. His claim that rising inequality was not an accident nor a temporary aberration, but an essential characteristic of capitalism was convincing because of the rich historical narrative that grounded both theory and evidence. Studies in this mould may not convince allcomers but can stand alongside quasi-experiments as providing interpretations of the past.

Conclusion

I have argued that the integration of economic history into economics has exposed it to a methodological revolution which involves research designs that ape experimental methods. To conform economic historians have exploited the past in search of natural experiments and been inventive about identification strategies. Some of us might harbour reservations, particularly about persistence studies, despite their quirky and clever findings and cutting-edge econometrics (not to mention their voluminous citations). That the regional spread of pogroms across Germany at the time of the Black Death portended the spatial support for National Socialism in the 1920s and 30s, or that the Spanish Inquisition looms large over attitudes in modern Spain, or that diffusion of the plough two millennia ago continues to influence the status of women today, or that folklore accounts for a significant proportion of international heterogeneity in female labour force participation are all intriguing ideas, securing publication in top journals, inviting headline summaries in popular presses and garnering astronomical numbers of citations. But the under-specification of the relevant transmission mechanisms and neglect of interim developments are worrying. It is possible to be less historically cavalier. For example, A'hearn et al. (2024) 'Mobility of the Innocent. Foundlings and their descendants in Florence, 1841–2005', traces the persistent burden of illegitimacy from the nineteenth century

[4] Harro Maas (2023) describes how Alfred Marshall moved from a chronology of events that covered a heterogeneous range of categories of phenomena, to an account that linked the events in these categories, to a causal ordering to show this 'narrative strategy' in action.

to the present day, by combining a convincing transmission mechanism in terms of the cultural stigma associated with a telling last name and tracing its effects over time. Moreover, away from persistence studies, on less contentious ground, I have argued that the use of quasi-experimental framing can bring economic historians and economists together (see also Cantoni and Yuchtman 2021). The skills and experience of economic historians can improve and strengthen such studies while throwing cold water on misguided attempts to apply the methodology where it is inappropriate.

Yet, there is danger in becoming the data management or contextual advice departments for economists ransacking the historical record for evidence of 'as if' experiments. Even without the additional problems of persistence studies, historical experiments or quasi-experiments have their critics, charged with prioritizing methodology, offering answers in search of questions, using low quality data, demonstrating ignorance of context, and lacking clear transmission mechanisms. Perhaps economists have become too dogmatic about the demonstration of causality. An activist role for economic historians is to argue against putting too much weight on completely implausible threats to causal inference, which might still be of value. Methodological diversity has often proved vital in advancing knowledge and we might want to preserve it within economic history by championing a variety of approaches to historical development paying attention to sequence, mechanism, and plausibility. Deaton and Cartwright's counsel that 'You cannot know how to use trial results without first understanding how the results from RCTs relate to the knowledge that you already possess about the world, and much of this knowledge by other methods' (2018). The same is surely true of historical experiments and quasi-experiments. Like Deaton and Cartwright, I am not 'against' RCTs or (in my case) historical experiments only opposed to 'magical thinking'.

It is useful to remember that the smoking–lung cancer link would not pass the current test for credible causality, since it consisted of observational studies from population data (potentially subject to omitted variables bias), and experimental studies performed on rodents and cells (potentially not externally valid in real-world settings). See: tobaccocontrol-2011-050338 87..91.[5] Yet if all cigarette smoking in the USA had ceased following the release of the first Surgeon General's report on smoking and health in 1964, a total of 2.5 million people would have been spared death from lung cancer in the following 36 years (Levy et al. 2013). It is well known that the tobacco industry responded with denialist propaganda particularly focussed on publicizing alternative diversionary hypotheses and spreading doubt about causal inference (https://pubmed.ncbi.nlm.nih.gov/22345227/). Not all evidence can 'cleanly' identify causality as defined in the credibility revolution, but probed, contextualized, compared, and accumulated it can still be informative.

[5] I thank Louis Henderson for alerting me to this illustration. A recent panel discussion of the pros and cons of randomized control trials and observational studies in medicine with useful crossover implications for social science is Fernainy et al. 2023.

Acknowledgements Comments on an earlier draft by and subsequent discussion with Lawrence Best, Christopher Colvin, Louis Henderson, and Mary Morgan improved the paper and I thank them for their help and collegiality. I also benefitted from (and much enjoyed reading) Cormac Ó Gráda's 'Economic History: "An Isthmus Joining Two Continents"'. Anybody interested in this topic should read his paper!

References

Abad, Leticia Arroya, and Noel Maurer. 2021. History Never Really Says Goodbye: A Critical Review of the Persistence Literature. *Journal of Historical Economics* 1 (1): 31–68.

Abad, Leticia Arroya, and Noel Maurer. 2025. The Long Shadow of History? The Impact of Colonial Labor Institutions on Economic Development in Peru. *Journal of Economic Growth.* https://doi.org/10.1007/s.10887-024-09249-9

Abramitzsky, Ran, Leah Boustan, and Katherine Eriksson. 2012. Europe's Tired, Poor, Huddled Masses: Self-Selection and Economic Outcomes in the Age of Mass Migration. *American Economic Review* 102 (5): 1832–1856.

Abramitzky, Ran. 2015. Economics and the Modern Economic Historian. *Journal of Economic History* 75 (4): 1240–1250.

Acemoglu, Daron, Simon Johnson, and James A. Robinson. 2001. The Colonial Origins of Comparative Development: An Empirical Investigation. *The American Economic Review* 91 (5): 1369–1401.

Acemoglu, Daron, Simon Johnson, and James A. Robinson. 2002. Reversal of Fortune: Geography and Institutions in the Making of the Modern World Income Distribution. *Quarterly Journal of Economics* 117 (4): 1231–1294.

Acemoglu, Daron, Simon Johnson, and James A. Robinson. 2012. The Colonial Origins of Comparative Development: An Empirical Investigation: Reply. *The American Economic Review* 102 (6): 3077–3110.

A'hearn, Brian, Giuliana Freschi, and Giacomo Gabbuti. 2024. *Mobility of the Innocents: The Social Mobility of Italian Foundlings and their Descendants*. Paper presented at the Economic History Society Conference, Newcastle.

Albouy, David. 2012. The Colonial Origins of Comparative Development: An Empirical Investigation: Comment. *The American Economic Review* 102 (6): 3059–3076.

Angrist, Joshua D., and Jörn-Steffen Pischke. 2010. The Credibility Revolution in Empirical Economics: How Better Research Design Is Taking the Con out of Econometrics. *Journal of Economic Perspectives* 2 (2): 3–30.

Ashraf, Quamrul H., and Oded Galor. 2018. The Macroeconomics of Comparative Development. *Journal of Economic Literature* 56 (3): 1119–1155.

Austin, Gareth. 2008. The 'Reversal of Fortunes' Thesis and the Compression of History: Perspectives from African and Comparative Economic History. *Economic History of Developing Regions* 27 (1): 996–1027.

Backhouse, Roger E., and Béatrice Cherrier. 2017. The Age of the Applied Economist: The Transformation of Economics since the 1970s. *History of Political Economy* 49 (Suppl): 1–33.

Banerjee, Abhijit Vinayak, Esther Duflo, and Michael Kremer. 2019. The Influence of Randomized Control Trials on Development Economics Research and on Development Policies. In *The State of Economics, The State of The World*, ed. Kaushik Basu, David Rosenblatt, and Claude Sepúlveda, 439–487. Cambridge: MIT Press.

Becker, Sascha O., P. David Boll, and Hans-Joachim Voth. *Spatial Unit Roots in Regressions: A Practitioners' Guide and a Stata Package*. Warwick Economics Working Paper, January 2025, No. 1541.

Betz, Timm, Scott J. Cook, and Florian Hollenbach. 2020. Spatial Interdependence and Instrumental Variable Models. *Political Science Research Methods* 8 (4): 646–661.
Bisin, Alberto, and Giovanni Federico. 2021. *The Handbook of Historical Economics*. Amsterdam: Elsevier.
Blum, Matthias, and Christopher L. Colvin, eds. 2018. *An Economist's Guide to Economic History*. Cham: Palgrave Macmillan.
Bourdieu, Pierre. 1977. *Outline of a Theory of Practice*. Cambridge: Cambridge University Press.
Brownlow, Graham, and Christopher L. Colvin. 2022. *Economic History and the Future of Pedagogy*. Queens University Centre for Economic History Working Paper 20-09.
Cantoni, Davide, and Noam Yuchtman. 2021. Historical Natural Experiments: Bridging Economics and Economic History. In *The Handbook of Historical Economics*, ed. Alberto Bisin and Giovanni Federico, 213–243. Amsterdam: Elsevier.
Cioni, Martina, Giovanni Federico, and Michelangelo Vasta. 2021. The Long-Term Evolution of Economic History: Evidence from the Top Five Field Journals (1927-2017). *Cliometrica* 14 (1): 1–39.
Cioni, Martina, Giovanni Federico, and Michelangelo Vasta. 2023. Is Economic History Changing its Nature? Evidence from Top Journals. *Cliometrica* 17:23–40.
Conley, Timothy G., and Morgan Kelly. 2025. The Standard Errors of Persistence. *Journal of International Economics* 153:104027.
Deaton, Angus. 2008. Instruments of Development : Randomisation in the Tropics, and the Search for the Elusive Keys to Economic Development. Keynes Lecture in Economics. *Proceedings of the British Academy* 162: 123–160.
Deaton, Angus, and Nancy Cartwright. 2018. Understanding and Misunderstanding Randomised Control Trials. *Social Science and Medicine* 210:2–21.
Debreu, Gerard. 1991. Presidential Address. *American Economic Review* 81 (1): 1–7.
Dell, Melissa. 2010. The Persistent Effects of Peru's Mining Mita. *Econometrica* 78 (6): 1863–1903.
Diebolt, Claude, and Michael Haupert. 2019. An Introduction to the Handbook of Cliometrics. In *Handbook of Cliometrics*, ed. Claude Diebolt and Michael Haupert, v–xvi. Berlin: Springer Verlag.
Dunning, Thad. 2008. Improving Causal Inference: Strengths and Limitations of Natural Experiments. *Political Research Quarterly* 61 (2): 282–293.
Dunning, Thad. 2012. *Natural Experiments in the Social Sciences*. Cambridge: Cambridge University Press.
Feinstein, Charles H., and Mark Thomas. 2002. *Making History Count*. Cambridge: Cambridge University Press.
Fenoaltea, Stefano. 2019. Spleen: The Failures of the Cliometric School. *Annals of the Fondazione Luigi Einaudi* 53 (2): 5–24.
Fernainy, Pamela et al. 2023. Rethinking the Pros and Cons of Randomized Control Trials and Observational Studies in the Era of Big Data and Advanced Methods: A Panel Discussion. *BMC Proceedings* 18 (1).
Fernández-de-Pinedo, Nadia, Alvaro La Parra-Perrez, and Félix-Fernando Muñoz. 2023. Recent Trends in Publications of Economic Historians in Europe and North America (1980-2019): An Empirical Analysis. *Cliometrica* 17:1–22.
Foucault, Michael. 1977. *Discipline and Punish*. New York: Pantheon.
Frydman, Carola, and Raven E. Saks. 2010. Executive Compensation: A New View from a Long-Term Perspective, 1936–2005. *Review of Financial Studies* 23 (5): 2099–2138.
Geertz, Clifford. 1973. *The Interpretation of Cultures: Selected Essays*. New York: Basic Books.
Heckman, J. J., and S. Moktan. 2020. Publishing and Promotion in Economics: The Tyranny of the Top Five. *Journal of Economic Literature* 58 (2): 419–470.
Hodgson, Geoffrey M. 2023. *The Wealth of a Nation: Institutional Foundations of English Capitalism*. Princeton: Princeton University Press.

Humphries, Jane and Jacob Weisdorf. 2015. The Wages of Women in England, 1260-1850. *Journal of Economic History* 75 (2): 405–447.
James, Jonathan. 2025. *Pick your Poison: Arsenic in Beer and Fertility*. Paper presented at the Economic History Society Conference, Glasgow.
Jaremski, Matthew S. 2020. Today's Economic History and Tomorrow's Scholars. *Cliometrica* 14 (1): 169–180.
La Porta, Rafael, Florencio Lopez-De-Silanes, and Andrei Shleifer. 2008. The Economic Consequences of Legal Origins. *Journal of Economic Literature* 46 (2): 285–332.
Leamer, Edward E. 1983. Let's Take the Con out of Econometrics. *American Economic Review* 73 (1): 31–43.
Levy, D., J. Ellis, and An-Tsun Huang. 2013. Smoking-Related Deaths Averted due to Three Years of Policy Progress. *Bulletin World Health Organization* 91:509–518.
Margo, Robert A. 2017. *The Integration of Economic History in Economics*. National Bureau of Economic Research, Working Paper 23538, Cambridge, MA.
Margo, Robert A. 2018. The Integration of Economic History into Economics. *Cliometrica* 12:377–406.
Margo, Robert A. 2021. The Economic History of Economic History: The Evolution of a Field in Economics. In *The Handbook of Historical Economics*, ed. Alberto Bisin and Giovanni Federico, x–16. Amsterdam: Elsevier.
Maas, Harro. 2023. Marking Time: Marshall's Search for Narrative Explanatory Coherence. *History of Political Economy* 55 (3): 434–446.
McCloskey, D. N. 1976. Does the Past Have Useful Economics? *Journal of Economic Literature* 14 (2): 434–461.
McCloskey, D. N. and Ziliak, S. T. 2010. *The Cult of Statistical Significance*. Ann Arbor: University of MichiganPress.
Michalopoulos, Stelios, and Elias Papaioannou. 2017. Series Introduction: Historical Legacies and Contemporary Development. In *The Long Economic and Political Shadow of History*, ed. Stelios Michalopoulos and Elias Papaioannou, vii–xxx. London: CEPR Press.
Morgan, Mary S. 2017. Narrative Ordering and Explanation. *Studies in History and Philosophy of Science* 62:86–97.
Morgan, Mary S. 2022. Narrative: A General-Purpose Technology for Science. In *Narrative Science. Reasoning, Representing and Knowing Since 1800*, ed. Mary S. Morgan, Kim M. Hajek, and Dominic J. Berry. Cambridge: Cambridge University Press.
Nunn, Nathan. 2009. The Importance of History for Economic Development. *Annual Review of Economics* 1 (1): 65–92.
Ó Gráda, Cormac. 2019. Economic History: "An Isthmus Joining Two Great Continents". *Rivista Di Storia Economics* 35 (1): 81–120.
Panhans, Matthew T., and John D. Singleton. 2017. The Empirical Economist's Toolkit: From Models to Methods. *History of Political Economy* 49 (Supp): 127–157.
Persson, Karl Gunnar, Marcus Lampe, and Paul Sharp. 2025. *An Economic History of Europe: Knowledge, Institutions and Growth, 600 to the Present*, 113–130. Cambridge: Cambridge University Press.
Piketty, Thomas P., and Emmanuel Saez. 2006. The Evolution of Top Incomes: A Historical and International Perspective. *American Economic Review* 96 (2): 200–205.
Ravallion, Martin. 2012. Fighting Poverty One Experiment at a Time. A Review of Abhijit Banerjee and Esther Duflo's Poor Economics. *Journal of Economic Literature* 50 (1): 103–114.
Ravallion, Martin. 2019. Comment. In *The State of Economics, The State of the World*, ed. Kaushik Basu, David Rosenblatt, and Claude Sepulveda, 494–498. Cambridge: MIT Press.
Sims, Christopher A. 2010. But Economics Is Not an Experimental Science. *The Journal of Economic Perspectives* 24 (2): 59–68.
Spolaore, Enrico, and Romain Wacziarg. 2013. How Deep are the Roots of Economic Development? *Journal of Economic Literature* 51 (2): 325–369.

Voth, Hans-Joachim. 2021. Persistence-Myth and Mystery. In *The Handbook of Historical Economics*, ed. Alberto Bisin and Giovanni Federico, x–243. Amsterdam: Elsevier.

Voigtländer, Nico, and Hans-Joachim Voth. 2013. How the West 'Invented' Fertility Restrictions. *American Economic Review* 103 (6): 2227–2264.

Webber, Sophie, and Carolyn Prouse. 2017. The New Gold Standard: The Rise of Randomized Control Trials and Experimental Development. *Economic Geography* 94 (2): 166–187.

Wooldridge, Jeffrey M. 2009. *Introductory Econometrics. A Modern Approach.* Southwestern: Cengage Learning.

New Perspectives of Economic History of South and Southeast Asia and the Middle East

Bishnupriya Gupta

Abstract The use of granular data and new statistical methods has led to new insights into the short-term and long-term effects of colonial connections. This chapter places South and Southeast Asia and the Middle East in the context of the Great Divergence debate. It explores the role of trade and the changes in factor markets arising from colonial interventions and its implications for economic development. It asks if modernization led to industrial development and structural change.

Introduction

Economic history of several regions in Asia is about the consequences of colonization. This is especially true for South and Southeast Asia. Undivided India, Ceylon, Malay and Singapore were part of the British Empire; the Indonesian islands were ruled by the Dutch Empire. Vietnam and Cambodia came under French colonization. Independence came at different points in time after 1945. The history of the Middle East is also one of colonization. Much of the Middle East was a part of the Ottoman Empire and included Egypt. However, this region too was touched by the quest for markets by the European Empires. The history of this region stands apart from that of South and Southeast Asia and will form parts of the discussion in this chapter. Egypt belongs to the Middle East rather than to the continent of Africa.

Early work on economic history aimed to understand the impact of colonization mainly by considering macro data on income, trade, structural change, capital flows and extraction of resources. Descriptive narratives dominated the literature: How much of wealth was drained from the colonies to the imperial countries? How did trading connections shift the structure of production? What were the broad patterns of development in fiscal capacity? The empirical methods involved quantification of drain of wealth from the colony to the mother country, trade in manufactured goods

B. Gupta (✉)
University of Warwick, Coventry, UK
e-mail: b.gupta@warwick.ac.uk

C. Diebolt, M. Haupert (eds.), *The State of Economic History*, Frontiers in Economic History, https://doi.org/10.1007/978-3-032-01624-9_5

for primary products and capital flows to the building of infrastructure and industries. The source for most of this data was the balance of payments and patchy employment data from surveys on sectoral shares.

Economic historians of South Asia and Southeast Asia adopted a conceptual approach to understand the role of colonial connections. The early history of colonization was documented by historians within a Marxian framework of imperialism and a quest for markets. The economic outcomes in the colonies were described in the context of unequal political and economic relationships between the imperial country and the colony. Trade was central to this framework. Colonies were the source of raw materials and markets for industrial goods produced in Europe. Colonization changed the economic structure of colonies from producers of traditional textiles and other industrial products to specializing in agriculture. Deindustrialization of the colonies has a significant space in this literature. The literature has compiled commodity-level details on the composition of trade and explored theoretically and with regional case studies the response of peasants to marketization of agriculture and their vulnerability to economic shocks. The role of commercialization of agriculture on living standards of cultivators and development of rural and urban labour markets for wage labour formed a part of this conceptual framework, but was not empirically established.

An alternative historiography, often seen as an imperialist perspective has focused on the modernizing impact of the integration of the colonies in a global network of European Empires. The access to the European capital markets given to the colonies funded the development of the railways and other infrastructure. Much of this discussion has been theoretical in parts and based on descriptive statistics based on macro level data.

Economic historians used archival evidence from national or regional archives to construct narratives on the state of agriculture, industry and living standard of the population. Given the time-consuming data collection from archives and libraries by hand, the histories written focused on small areas or sub-sectors rather than spatial variation within countries with subregional data. The narratives formed rich, but disconnected histories of a country or a region. Without systematic data it was difficult to have a picture of the economy of a country and its diversity within.

The new research on the economic history of the countries in South and Southeast Asia has been more data intensive. The European trading companies left detailed accounts of prices of goods bought and sold in the colonies and wages that were paid to skilled and unskilled employees and casual workers. Colonial governments produced reports and censuses from the late nineteenth century. Researchers in the last few decades have used the records maintained by the European trading companies and reports, maps, gazetteers and censuses of colonial governments. This has allowed systematic analysis of agricultural production, industrialization and the development of physical and social infrastructure recorded at a sub-region level, such as a county or district granular data on occupation, migration, agricultural output and infrastructural investment has opened the possibilities of rigorous statistical analysis and generated new insights into the economic history of Asia and in particular the role of colonial interventions. This literature has moved away from broad themes of development and underdevelopment to more specific questions that arise from economics: Who invested in industries in Asia? How did foreign and domestic firms interact under colonization? What occupational choices did women and men make and why? Did coercive labour systems prevail? Commodity-level trade data has allowed analysis of country-specific trading relationships. Were colonies locked into the production of agricultural goods due to free trade with the imperial country that produced industrial goods? How important was colonial trade?

Data digitization has provided access to new resources. Maps and text analysis tools have provided new methods of analysis. For example, maps of planned infrastructure and the maps of those constructed can be used in conjunction to study the impact of a railway line or a canal. This method can be used for causal analysis of railways and irrigation canals on economic outcomes. Maps of location of Christian Missions or temples also provide a rich source to create proxies for provision of education or state capacity. Text as data has not been used systematically in the study of economic history of these regions in Asia yet, but this opens up the door to new questions. Evidence from a folklore dataset created by Michalopoulos and Xue (2021) has been used by Dincecco et al. (2022) to understand gender bias.

In this chapter, I will discuss in what ways new data has led to evidence-based research in several broad themes. Some of these are big questions such as Asia's divergence with Europe, but also new insights based on granular data on a variety of questions relating to structural change, returns to factors of production, investment in physical and human capital, and impact of changes in law. I will focus on how the availability of new data and application of new statistical tools have been used by researchers to throw light on many of these questions. This chapter will be divided into topics that have used granular data to provide new insights into the following: Living standards, income, growth and divergence with Europe, land and its productivity, labour markets, capital and investment in industry, infrastructure, human capital, religion and finally the legacy of colonization over the longer term.

The Great Divergence Between Europe and Asia: Measuring Living Standards

Wages and National Incomes

The early literature was more qualitative in nature. Descriptions of travel writers, records of medieval courts and temples formed the basis of assessment of living standards. These documents were often biased towards the urban economy. They described the vibrant markets in India, Java and Malay and the dynamism of the trading networks. The new literature has systematically collected data on wages of workers, weavers and servants and prices of commodities in the average consumption basket. Though the data is urban biased, this has made it possible to construct estimates of silver and grain wages for a number of countries in Asia. The first is a measure of money wage and the second provides a measure of the real wage using the price of the locally consumed grain (Allen 2005; Broadberry and Gupta 2006; Pamuk 2007; De Zwart and Lucassen 2020; Bassino and Van der Eng 2021). These papers have also provided estimates of wages of unskilled and skilled workers and a measure of the skill premium and its implications for the Great Divergence (Van Zanden 2009). Relative measures of real wages have been constructed based on hypothetical barebones consumption baskets going back in time for cities in Asia (Allen et al. 2011). This has been used to study if Asian economies were above the barebones subsistence line using the concept of welfare ratio that equals one when wages cover the cost of one barebones basket of goods (Allen 2007). Welfare ratios above one show that the economy was above subsistence. We can think of this as the poverty line. Several Asia cities showed living standards to be above the poverty line and a decline over the nineteenth century.

For a long period of time, our understanding of income and growth across countries relied on the valuable work of Angus Maddison. His book on the World Economy, published in 2001, put together a series of estimates of per capita GDP for most countries of the world. The most reliable estimates came from countries in Europe and North America, where good data was available. Where good data was missing, as in most Asian countries, Maddison assumed several of these countries to be at subsistence and constructed the series based on what would be subsistence income until the end of the nineteenth century. The series covered a period from 1000 AD to the end of the twentieth century and were reported in 1990 Geary Khamis dollars. An exciting development in this literature has been new estimates of GDP based on new data and a more rigorous methodology. The new series are brought in one place in the Maddison Historical Statistics Project hosted at Groningen University. These historical national accounts diverge from the original estimates of 2001 and have provided a statistically sound basis to understand the rise and decline of nations from the nineteenth century to recent years. Figure 1 illustrates the regional comparisons. It is clear that reliable data cannot go back to 1000 AD for most countries. The world average only starts in the twentieth century. The divergence between Western Europe and the regions of Asia is visible. Asian incomes stagnated up to the middle of the twentieth century. Figure 2 shows a disaggregated picture by countries in Asia. Decolonization marks the structural break in growth. The divergence is post independence growth within Asia resulted from differences in historical conditions as well as differences in policies after independence. Table 1 shows India's divergence with Britain. India's GDP declined from 61% of British GDP in 1600 to 14% in 1871. Such comparisons have been made possible due to the application of new methods in historical national accounting.

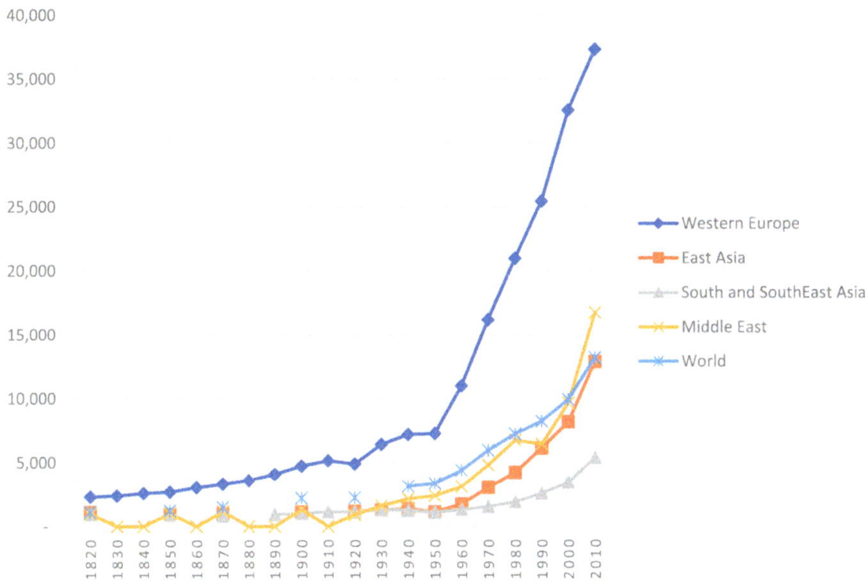

Fig. 1 GDP per capita by Regions in 2011 GK$. Source: Maddison database 2020

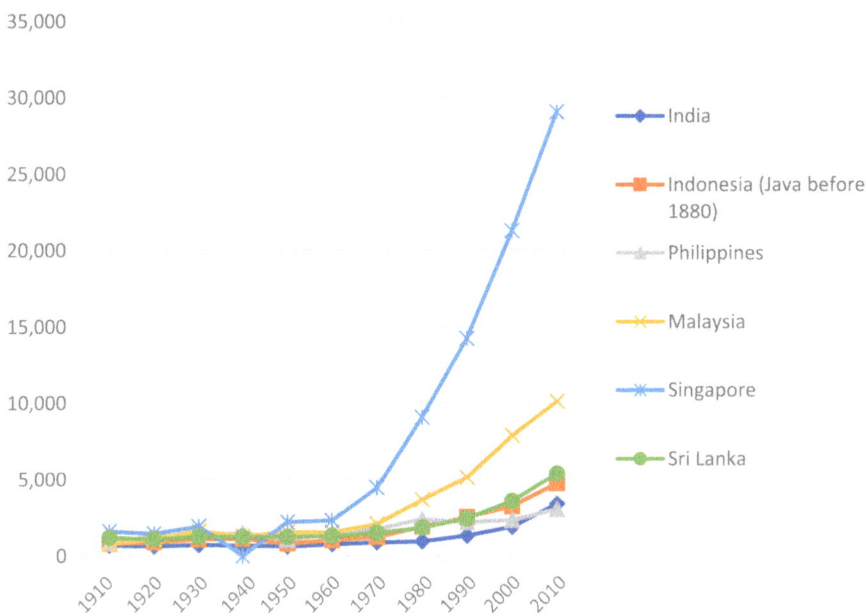

Fig. 2 GDP per capitain 2011 GK$ of selected countries in Asia. Source: Maddison database

Table 1 Indian and British GDP per capita, 1600–1871 (1990 Geary Khamis $)

Year	Indian GDP per capita	Indian GDP per capita/British GDP per capita (%)
1600	682	61
1650	638	58
1700	622	40
1750	576	36
1801	569	27
1811	519	25
1821	520	24
1831	510	22
1841	555	21
1851	556	19
1861	528	16
1871	526	14

Source: Broadberry et al. (2015) Table 14

Market Integration

Measuring market integration and market efficiency is another new development in the literature on economic development and the Great Divergence. A well-known paper by Shiue and Keller (2007) use systematically collected grain prices to measure the market integration in Europe and China. They suggests that the two regions were comparable in the functioning of markets in late eighteenth century although China did not industrialize at the same time as Europe. Availability of commodity prices over time and across sub-regions has made this possible for other parts of Asia. Similar methodology has been used by Studer (2008) to show that the grain market in India was less integrated compared to Europe in the eighteenth and nineteenth centuries and reflects India's relative underdevelopment. District-level price data on commodities have been used to measure market integration following the construction of the transportation network to understand the developmental effect of the railways in India (Andrabi and Kuehlwein 2010; Donaldson 2018). It marks a departure from the traditional view of economic historians of India that railways were a tool of colonization and exploitation. Recent work by Donaldson (2018) shows convergence in prices across districts connected to a railway network a positive effect on income. For Indonesia, Marks (2010) shows that rice markets were well integrated across different cities of the archipelago and functioned efficiently in the colonial period due to a well-developed infrastructure. World War II and the independence movement led to disintegration of the rice market.

Alternative Measures of Living Standards

Availability of data on heights from a variety of sources has led to using heights as indicators of living standards. Nutrition and disease environment are good indicators of well-being (Deaton 2007). Changes in heights indicates changes in living standard. Baten and co-authors have systematically collected data on heights across countries. They use data from military records and surveys. Several countries in South and Southeast Asia show no clear trend reflecting the stagnant real wages and incomes (Baten and Blum 2014). Guntupalli and Baten (2006) find little change in height inequality in India. The average height of a relatively tall population in the Middle East declined in the twentieth century (Stegl and Baten 2009). The paper argues that low population density and access to animal protein is likely to explain better health of this population. These conditions changed in the twentieth century.

Booth (2012) considers per capita rice availability as a measure of cross-country variation in living standards in Southeast Asia. This shows a decline over the first decades of the twentieth century. She argues that conclusions based on urban wages and incomes may be misleading.

Economic Inequality

Availability of income tax data for India and Indonesia has allowed estimation of income inequality over the twentieth century. Top income shares are estimated to be an indicator of income inequality. Income tax mainly applied to urban incomes and only to those working in the formal sector. In Indonesia, top income shares grew in the interwar years and declined after World War II (Leigh and Van der Eng 2009). Similar patterns are shown for India by Alvaredo et al. (2017) and Banerjee and Piketty (2005). Although limited in scope, this data provides some indication of changes in economic inequality during and after the colonial period.

Structural Change

Sector-level data over a long period of time has been compiled by researchers for several countries. This has made it possible to construct bilateral sector-level relative productivity estimates and a look at how relative productivity has changed over time. Broadberry and Gupta (2010) find that India reduced the difference in labour productivity with Britain in service sector, but there was no change in relative productivity in industry over the twentieth century. The paper explores the conditions that led to India's service sector advantage.

Decline in the share of traditional industries in various parts of the continent has been one of the big themes in the discussion of colonization. For India, this refers to the displacement of a vibrant cotton textiles industry that used traditional technology and sold cotton cloth in the world market before the Industrial Revolution in Britain. The early literature was based on limited data from regional surveys and selected province-level census on agricultural employment (Bagchi 1976) and trade data of the East India Company (Chaudhuri 2006). More recent literature has focused on the question of input costs, and competitive advantage and changes in terms of trade between agriculture and industry. Data on prices and wages form the basis of these empirical work. In the case of deindustrialization of India in the nineteenth century, Broadberry and Gupta (2009) construct estimates of relative input costs and changes in total factor productivity in the cotton textiles industry in India and Britain and show the changes in relative prices of the cotton textiles manufactured in the two countries The decline in the price of British textile goods reflect the changing competitive advantage in the textile market. Clingingsmith and Williamson (2008) show that changes in the terms of trade between agriculture and industry arising from domestic supply shocks in agriculture in India, led to the decline of industrial activity (Clingingsmith and Williamson 2008).

Price data has been used by Bassino and Williamson to explore deindustrialization in Southeast Asia in the nineteenth century. Competition from India and Britain saw a dramatic decline in the market share of domestic industry in Indonesia from 82% in 1822 to 11% in 1913. The Philippines, Burma and Thailand, similarly lost out to import of industrial goods. Bassino and Williamson (2017) construct agricultural terms of trade with respect to industry and attribute the decline in industry to the rise in agricultural prices. After World War II, when agricultural prices dampened down, some industrial activities re-emerged. But systematic industrialization did not begin until after 1960. Economic shocks and changes in terms of trade between agriculture and industry is shown to explain agricultural specialization in selected colonial economies.

The question of deindustrialization and industrialization in the Middle East was explored in the series of papers by Pamuk and Williamson (2011), Panza and Williamson (2015) adopt a similar method of analysis using data on terms of trade between agriculture and industry. Pamuk and Williamson (2011) point to the trade-led rise in agricultural terms of trade in the periphery in the nineteenth century, which affected the Ottoman Empire and Egypt more than South Asia and Latin America and led to deindustrialization (Fig. 3). Panza and Williamson (2015) emphasize the success of state-led industrialization under Muhammad Ali in Egypt in the first half of the nineteenth century by lowering the terms of trade in agriculture and the squeezing the peasantry Egypt. They show that its impact was short lived and did not survive after his reign.

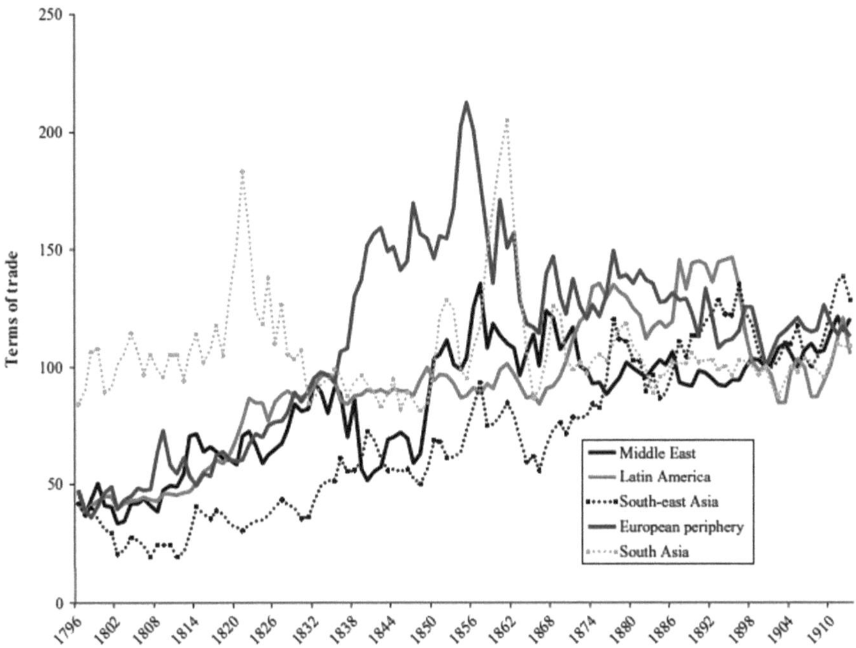

Fig. 3 Terms of trade changes: Agriculture relative to industry. Source: Pamuk and Williamson (2011), Fig. 3

Trade and Colonial Connections

The literature on the cost of imperialism through trade focussed on the trade surplus of a colony as a measure of extraction that was then syphoned off to the imperial country through the payment of interest of capital flows and profit on investment. Using disaggregated trade data, Van der Eng (1998) shows the declining importance of colonial trade. This can also be calculated for India using statistical Abstract of British India. The two colonies show quite different relationships with the imperial country. India was more dependent on Britain compared to Indonesia on the Netherlands in 1870. The dependence changed over time with the imperial countries becoming less important for trade for the colonies (see Table 2). Understanding what changes occurred over decades or if pattern of dependence had not been uniform across colonies was challenging without analyzing disaggregated trade statistics and broad generalizations characterized the literature on trade and colonization. Arthi et al. use commodity-level trade data for India to show that following the Ottawa Agreement of Imperial Preference in 1932 that created a favoured status for countries within the British Empire in tariffs, there was trade diversion from the rest of the world to Britain. This increased Britain's share in imports to India although the total imports declined. This analysis used data on 114 commodities that were trade across 42 countries.

Table 2 The share of the imperial country in trade of the colonies

	Share of Netherlands in Indonesian trade (%)		Share of UK in Indian trade (%)	
	Import	Export	Import	Export
1870–79	47	69	92	52
1900–09	34	32	61	26
1920–29	22	16	47	28

Source: Van der Eng (1998), Statistical Abstract of British India

Factor Endowments: Land and Labour

The Geography of South Asia is diverse. The sub-continent relies on the Monsoons for water. There are fertile and rain abundant regions that are densely populated. There are also dry regions in the rain-shadow areas that are sparsely populated, and the inhabitants were pastoral. Most of Southeast Asia is tropical and fertile. Geography of the region is diverse, and a variety of crops are grown from rice, coffee and rubber. Here land was abundant and labour scarce. Several countries in this region saw immigration.

Unlike in Europe, the property rights to land were not legally defined. Customary rights allowed cultivation rights to be passed on from generation to generation. Land in most cases belonged to the state and could not be bought and sold. Colonization introduced major changes. European colonizers introduced legal property rights to land to confer well-defined property rights to owners that would incentivize them to raise productivity and contribute more to state coffers. Most of the revenue came from land taxes. The European colonizers set out in search of the rightful owner and introduced a legal definition of ownership. The digitization of sub-region level data has made it possible to ask new questions and use new methods and statistical analysis. The two broad strands related to land and labour are discussed in the following section:

Land

The idea that geography determined the type of land ownership has been important in the context of the literature on land ownership and inequality. Land suitable for food grains, such as wheat or rice, saw cultivation by peasant proprietors. Regions suitable for plantation crops, such as sugar, had more concentrated ownership (Engerman and Sokoloff 2000). This literature mainly refers to the context of the Americas, where labour was in deficit relative to the abundance of land. Crop suitability determined what type of ownership emerged as European migration populated the continent. The land ownership system that emerged in Asia is difficult to be classified in a similar way. Population density in Asia was higher in comparison with the Americas, although there was a variation within the Asian continent. South Asia was more densely populated than Southeast Asia.

Precolonial agriculture was based on customary rights to cultivate land. The British introduced landlords in the regions of early conquest and assigned them property rights. The motivation was giving property rights to landlords would encourage them to invest in land and raise productivity on plots cultivated by tenants. This did not materialize. Land was scarce in labour abundant fertile regions. The landlords increased rents and lived a luxurious life often in the urban centres. British policy of land revenue settlement changed during the 1820s, and, in the new regions conquered, a different land tenure system was adopted. Ownership was given to cultivating peasants or village communities, depending on who held the customary rights. Banerjee and Iyer (2005) use the timing of conquest of regions in South Asia by the British to classify districts as landlord or non-landlord. They treat the assignment as exogeneous as it depended on the timing of conquest and look at long-term outcomes on agricultural productivity. The landlord-based districts have worse long-term outcomes as well as lower yields in the late nineteenth century.

A different context is studied in the work of de Zwart and Soekhradj (2022). In the Dutch colony of Java, customary ownership of land also differed from European norms as in South Asia. Where land was privately owned, compulsory labour services were provided to the State. On land under community ownership, the right of cultivation could be passed on from generation to generation. A third category of land tenure was on communal land that could be periodically redistributed among the village population, so that individual peasants did not cultivate the same plot of land year by year. Land suitable for sugar, used communal land as the crop was labour intensive and required processing. Sugar production by the state and private entrepreneurs was done on communal land in Java. The paper finds a decline in land inequality under sugar cultivation unlike the case of the Americas. Southeast Asia had a large indigenous population cultivating a wide variety of crops. Even in areas where labour was in short supply, the ownership rights in land were not given to immigrants in new settlements.

Rice cultivation was the main part of the agricultural economy in Southeast Asia and a major export. Van der Eng (2004) finds that high labour productivity in rice cultivations in Burma, Thailand and Southern Vietnam gave these countries a comparative advantage in the international market.

The data in South and Southeast Asia is at the district level and comes of decennial censuses or records compiled by district administrators. New research has used these data to ask new questions. Chankrajang and J Vechbanyongratana (2020) study the canal network in Thailand to understand the effect of canals and market access on labour productivity in orchards. The data comes from land deeds in orchard growing regions. The paper finds that properties located adjacent to canals had significantly higher productivity of labour than those located inland.

In Thailand, construction of the railways due to strategic reasons led to agricultural growth and urbanization (Paik and Vechbanyongratana 2024).

Labour

Did coercive institutions prevail across these regions? The land-labour ratio created conditions for labour coercion. In land abundant regions of Southeast Asia, corvee labour was used in agriculture (Marks 2010). Hup (2024) constructs a new panel dataset of sub-regions and finds a transition from compulsory corvee labour as a form of taxation to a head tax during 1874–1905.

In labour abundant regions, economic shocks led to loss of land for small cultivators. Many of whom became indentured workers to different parts of the European Empires. The system was widespread in South Asia. Thousands of workers entered into indentured contracts to travel to distant lands, such as Mauritius, Fiji, South Africa and the Caribbean to work on sugar plantations, railway construction and mines (Persaud 2019; Hui and Kambhampati 2022). Both studies use granular data to empirically test what the determinants of migration and return migration were. Migration data can be found aggregated at the district level at points of departure and at individual level at the point of entry. Information on migrants arriving at the destination was recorded. It included the name, age, marital status and caste of the migrant. Researchers can connect families and study who stayed and who returned. The return flows of migrants are discussed with reference to the social group of workers who returned (Hui and Kambhampati 2022). The paper finds that low caste workers were less likely to return. Persaud (2019) finds that volatility of agricultural prices in sending districts was a determinant of indentured migration in the late nineteenth century. Saleh (2023) studies labour coercion in the Middle East. During the cotton boom of the 1860s, the globalized economy of Egypt responded to the rising demand for raw cotton and increased the use of coercive labour. The peasantry began to rely on import of slaves.

Economic Development

Industrialization

There are two different theoretical approaches to understand the timing of industrialization in South and Southeast Asia. In the context of Southeast Asia, factor endowments offer an explanation of slow industrialization in the late nineteenth and early twentieth century. Except in Java and the western Philippines, labour scarcity in kept wages high and delayed industrialization in Southeast Asia (Bassino and Williamson 2015). Chinese and Indian migration did not lower wages significantly. However, using the Vent for surplus theory, Huff and Caggiano (2007) argue that surplus land was brought into cultivation as a result of migrant labour coming from labour surplus regions in South Asia and China and kept wages stagnant.

A different approach is used to understand the emergence and growth of a cotton textile industry in India following the years of boom in raw cotton exports in the 1860s. The India cotton textile industry was not protected by tariffs under colonial policies and faced competition from British imports. When the cotton boom ended, Indian traders, who had been involved in this trade used their social network to start investing in a local cotton textile industry. Business directories are a source of a rich data on entrepreneurs in Indian industry. This information has been used by Gupta et al. (2022) to construct a dataset of early entrepreneurs in the modern cotton textile. Using this panel dataset of social networks of entrepreneurs that belonged to various caste and religion-based communities, the paper documents the role of social networks in early industrialization when market institutions are weak and state does not play a supportive role.

Fiscal Capacity

Research on fiscal capacity continues to be mainly descriptive using data on taxation and revenues for government reports (Booth An exception is Dincecco et al. (2022)). The paper applies Tilly's idea of 'wars makes states' to India. They construct a measure of conflict exposure for districts using descriptions of battles fought in South Asia and show that higher conflict exposure increased fiscal capacity.

Human Capital

Colonial South Asia recorded literacy by district in the decadal censuses. Maps can be used to find location of Catholic and Protestant Missions that were education providers. Chaudhary (2009) uses district-level literacy and population by caste and religion data to show greater caste and religious diversity led to lower educational spending. Castelló-Climent et al. (2018) predict the district-level variation in higher education in recent times using location of Catholic Missions in 1911. Calvi et al. (2022) do a similar exercise with Protestant Missions.

When systematic data is missing, biased reporting of age can be used by researchers to predict numeracy. The method, known as age heaping, captures the heaping on age that end in 0 or 5. A higher value of the index indicates lower numeracy. Although age heaping has been declining in all regions, South Asia shows the highest values followed by the Middle East in the nineteenth century. Southeast Asia has lower values (Crayen and Baten 2010). All three regions have lower numeracy compared to Europe and East Asia. Panza (2020) used a dissimilarity index in cities in Mandate Palestine to measure ethnic segregation and its impact of the schooling outcome of the Arab Children.

Colonial Legacy

One of the new methodologies in understanding the role of colonization has been to study the long-term persistent effects of colonial institutions, Banerjee and Iyer (2005) show that districts in India under different systems of land ownership and revenue collection have differences in land productivity and provision of public goods after independence. Although the landlord system was abolished, historical landlord districts have worse economic outcomes today. Dell and Olken (2020) consider the regions where sugar was cultivated in colonial Indonesia. The production process combined cultivation of sugarcane and processing in Java. They show that areas where the sugar factories were located in the nineteenth century are more industrialized today and have better infrastructure. These regions also have a more educated population and are richer today.

Role of Religion

Religion has been brought into the discussion of economic history in different ways in the new literature. Differences in religious norms and practices have been shown to result in differences in economic outcomes. The systems of inheritance under Hinduism and Islam led to differences in business practices. In South Asia, Muslims made a slower transition to modern businesses. Hindu inheritance practices preserved wealth within the joint family system and created conditions for capital accumulation. The Islamic inheritance system fragmented family wealth (Kuran and Singh 2013). The Middle East's divergence with Europe also relates to the Islamic inheritance system that kept enterprises small and prevented organizational changes as in Europe (Kuran 2003).

Jha (2013) shows that the complementarity in occupations of Hindus and Muslims in medieval trading ports led to more harmonious relationship between the communities, and these towns experienced fewer Hindu Muslim conflicts in the following centuries.

A theoretical framework has offered a valuable tool to understand the taxation of minorities in the nineteenth century Egypt. Saleh and Tirole (2021) show that in a context of a society with religious minorities, rulers can use the trade-off between maintaining minority identity and compliance, by taxing minorities more, which creates incentives for minorities to convert to the religion of the majority. Using enterprise-level data from Turkey, Ağır and Artunç (2019) shows that a wealth tax imposed in 1842 differentially affected the non-Muslim minorities and led to the demise of minority-owned enterprises.

Use of Geography

Temperature, rainfall patterns, wind directions, terrain and access to rivers and oceans or more generally geography is increasingly being used in the economic history literature to measure economic shocks or trading connections between two countries or cities. Pascali (2017) considers that ease of shipping following the introduction of steam ships, which allowed ships to shorten time of transit as they no longer relied on routes permitted by wind directions. Estimating bilateral trade by country pairs, the paper finds that not all countries benefitted from the first phase of globalization, and this may have contributed to the Great Divergence. Coastlines that have the contours of natural harbours similarly can increase trade between two cities (Bakker et al. 2021).

In the context ofAsia, historical climate data has made it possible to statistically measure economic shocks and study its impact on crime (Papaioannou 2017) or spread of epidemics (Fenske et al. 2022). Rainfall variation is used to predict increasing conflict between the rural population of Arab farmers and the urban Jewish population with implications for economic inequality in Mandate Palestine (Panza and Swee 2023).

Conclusion

In this chapter, I have argued that the availability of granular data has changed the questions for new research. In the last decades, new data and new statistical methods have changed the way economic historians think of the history of colonization in South and Southeast Asia and the Middle East. Many of the questions are rooted in economics, and empirical tests are rigorous to provide causal connections between colonial interventions, the response of economic agents and their impact on economic outcomes in the short and medium term, but also those that persist over the long run.

References

Ağır, S., and C. Artunç. 2019. The wealth Tax of 1942 and the disappearance of non-Muslim enterprises in Turkey. *The Journal of Economic History* 79 (1): 201–243.

Allen, R. C. 2005. Real wages in Europe and Asia: A first look at the long-term patterns. *Living Standards in the Past: New Perspectives on Well-Being in Asia and Europe* 1:111–131.

Allen, R. C. 2007. *India in the Great Divergence. The New Comparative Economic History: Essays in Honor of Jeffrey G. Williamson*, 9.

Allen, R.C., Bassino, J.P., Ma, D., Moll-Murata, C. and Van Zanden, J.L., 2011. Wages, prices, and living standards in China, 1738–1925: in comparison with Europe, Japan, and India. The economic history review, 64: 8–38

Alvaredo, F., A. Bergeron, and G. Cassan. 2017. Income concentration in British India, 1885–1946. *Journal of Development Economics* 127:459–469.

Andrabi, T., and M. Kuehlwein. 2010. Railways and price convergence in British India. *The Journal of Economic History* 70 (2): 351–377.

Bagchi, A. K. 1976. De-industrialization in India in the nineteenth century: Some theoretical implications. *The Journal of Development Studies* 12 (2): 135–164.

Bakker, J. D., S. Maurer, J. S. Pischke, and F. Rauch. 2021. Of mice and merchants: Connectedness and the location of economic activity in the Iron Age. *Review of Economics and Statistics* 103 (4): 652–665.

Banerjee, A., and L. Iyer. 2005. History, institutions, and economic performance: The legacy of colonial land tenure systems in India. *American economic review* 95 (4): 1190–1213.

Banerjee, A., and T. Piketty. 2005. Top Indian incomes, 1922–2000. *The World Bank Economic Review* 19 (1): 1–20.

Bassino, J. P., and Williamson, J.G. 2015. From commodity booms to economic miracles: why Southeast Asian industry lagged behind (No. 2015-07). UPSE Discussion Paper.

Bassino, J. P., and P. van der Eng 2021. *The First East Asian Economic Miracle: Wages, Living Standards and Foundations of Modern Economic Growth in Southeast Asia, 1880-1938* (No. 05). Centre for Economic History, Research School of Economics, Australian National University.

Bassino, J. P., and Williamson, J. G. 2017. From commodity booms to economic miracle. *The Spread of Manufacturing to the Global Periphery* 256–286.

Baten, J., and M. Blum. 2014. Why are you tall while others are short? Agricultural production and other proximate determinants of global heights. *European Review of Economic History* 18 (2): 144–165.

Booth, A. 2012. Measuring living standards in different colonial systems: Some evidence from South East Asia, 1900–1942. *Modern Asian Studies* 46 (5): 1145–1181.

Broadberry, S., and B. Gupta. 2006. The early modern great divergence: Wages, prices and economic development in Europe and Asia, 1500–1800 1. *The Economic History Review* 59 (1): 2–31.

Broadberry, S., and B. Gupta. 2009. Lancashire, India, and shifting competitive advantage in cotton textiles, 1700–1850: The neglected role of factor prices 1. *The Economic History Review* 62 (2): 279–305.

Broadberry, S., and B. Gupta. 2010. The historical roots of India's service-led development: A sectoral analysis of Anglo-Indian productivity differences, 1870–2000. *Explorations in Economic History* 47 (3): 264–278.

Broadberry, S., J. Custodis, and B. Gupta. 2015. India and the great divergence: An Anglo-Indian comparison of GDP per capita, 1600–1871. *Explorations in Economic History* 55:58–75.

Calvi, R., L. Hoehn-Velasco, and F. G. Mantovanelli. 2022. The Protestant legacy: Missions, gender, and human capital in India. *Journal of Human Resources* 57 (6): 1946–1980.

Castelló-Climent, A., L. Chaudhary, and A. Mukhopadhyay. 2018. Higher education and prosperity: From Catholic missionaries to luminosity in India. *The Economic Journal* 128 (616): 3039–3075.

Chankrajang, T., and Vechbanyongratana, J. 2020. Canals and orchards: the impact of transport network access on agricultural productivity in nineteenth-century Bangkok. The Journal of Economic History, 80(4), pp.996-1030

Chaudhary, L. 2009. Determinants of primary schooling in British India. *The Journal of Economic History* 69 (1): 269–302.

Chaudhuri, K. N. 2006. *The Trading World of Asia and the English East India Company: 1660-1760*. Cambridge University Press.

Clingingsmith, D., and J. G. Williamson. 2008. Deindustrialization in 18th and 19th century India: Mughal decline, climate shocks and British industrial ascent. *Explorations in Economic History* 45 (3): 209–234.

Crayen, D., and J. Baten. 2010. Global trends in numeracy 1820–1949 and its implications for long-term growth. *Explorations in Economic History* 47 (1): 82–99.
De Zwart, P., and J. Lucassen. 2020. Poverty or prosperity in northern India? New evidence on real wages, 1590s–1870s. *The Economic History Review* 73 (3): 644–667.
Deaton, A. 2007. Height, health, and development. *Proceedings of the national academy of sciences* 104 (33): 13232–13237.
Dell, M., and B. A. Olken. 2020. The development effects of the extractive colonial economy: The Dutch cultivation system in java. *The Review of Economic Studies* 87 (1): 164–203.
Dincecco, M., J. Fenske, A. Menon, and S. Mukherjee. 2022. Pre-colonial warfare and long-run development in India. *The Economic Journal* 132 (643): 981–1010.
Donaldson, D. 2018. Railroads of the Raj: Estimating the impact of transportation infrastructure. *American Economic Review* 108 (4-5): 899–934.
Fenske, J., B. Gupta, and S. Yuan. 2022. Demographic shocks and women's labour market participation: Evidence from the 1918 influenza pandemic in India. *The Journal of Economic History* 82 (3): 875–912.
Guntupalli, A. M., and J. Baten. 2006. The development and inequality of heights in North, West, and East India 1915–1944. *Explorations in Economic History* 43 (4): 578–608.
Gupta, B., D. Mookherjee, K. Munshi, and M. Sanclemente. 2022. Community origins of industrial entrepreneurship in colonial India. *Journal of Development Economics* 159:102973.
Huff, G., and G. Caggiano. 2007. Globalization, immigration, and Lewisian Elastic Labour in Pre–World War II Southeast Asia. *The Journal of Economic History* 67 (1): 33–68.
Hui, N., and U. S. Kambhampati. 2022. Between unfreedoms: The role of caste in decisions to repatriate among indentured workers. *The Economic History Review* 75 (2): 421–446.
Hup, M. 2024. Labour coercion, fiscal modernization, and state capacity: Evidence from colonial Indonesia. *Explorations in Economic History* 94:101632.
Jha, S. 2013. Trade, institutions, and ethnic tolerance: Evidence from South Asia. *American political Science review* 107 (4): 806–832.
Kuran, T. 2003. The Islamic commercial crisis: Institutional roots of economic underdevelopment in the Middle East. *The Journal of Economic History* 63 (2): 414–446.
Kuran, T., and A. Singh. 2013. Economic modernization in Late British India: Hindu-Muslim differences. *Economic Development and Cultural Change* 61 (3): 503–538.
Leigh, A., and P. Van der Eng. 2009. Inequality in Indonesia: What can we learn from top incomes? *Journal of public economics* 93 (1-2): 209–212.
Marks, D. 2010. Unity or diversity? On the integration and efficiency of rice markets in Indonesia, c. 1920–2006. *Explorations in Economic History* 47 (3): 310–324.
Paik, C., and J. Vechbanyongratana. 2024. Reform, rails, and rice: Political railroads and local development in Thailand. *The Journal of Economic History* 84 (3): 807–837.
Pamuk, Ş. 2007. The Black Death and the origins of the 'Great Divergence' across Europe, 1300–1600. *European Review of Economic History* 11 (3): 289–317.
Pamuk, Ş., and J. G. Williamson. 2011. Ottoman de-industrialization, 1800–1913: Assessing the magnitude, impact, and response. *The Economic History Review* 64:159–184.
Panza, L. 2020. The impact of ethnic segregation on schooling outcomes in Mandate Palestine. *Journal of Development Economics* 146:102514.
Panza, L., and E. L. Swee. 2023. Fanning the flames: Rainfall shocks, inter-ethnic income inequality, and conflict intensification in Mandate Palestine. *Journal of Economic Behaviour & Organization* 206:71–94.
Panza, L., and J. G. Williamson. 2015. Did M Muhammad A li foster industrialization in early nineteenth-century Egypt? *The Economic History Review* 68 (1): 79–100.
Papaioannou, K. J. 2017. Hunger makes a thief of any man: Poverty and crime in British colonial Asia. *European Review of Economic History*, pp.1–28.
Persaud, A. 2019. Escaping local risk by entering indentureship: Evidence from nineteenth-century Indian migration. *The Journal of Economic History* 79 (2): 447–476.

Pascali, L. 2017. The wind of change: Maritime technology, trade, and economic development. American Economic Review, 107(9), pp.2821–2854.
Saleh, M. 2023. Trade, slavery, and state coercion of labour: Egypt during the first globalization era. *Journal of Economic History*.
Saleh, M., and J. Tirole. 2021. Taxing identity: Theory and evidence from early Islam. *Econometrica* 89 (4): 1881–1919.
Shiue, C. H., and W. Keller. 2007. Markets in China and Europe on the Eve of the Industrial Revolution. *American Economic Review* 97 (4): 1189–1216.
Sokoloff, K. L., and S. L. Engerman. 2000. History lessons: Institutions, factor endowments, and paths of development in the new world. *Journal of Economic perspectives* 14 (3): 217–232.
Stegl, M., and J. Baten. 2009. Tall and shrinking Muslims, short and growing Europeans: The long-run welfare development of the Middle East, 1850–1980. *Explorations in Economic History* 46 (1): 132–148.
Studer, R. 2008. India and the great divergence: Assessing the efficiency of grain markets in eighteenth-and nineteenth-century India. *The Journal of Economic History* 68 (2): 393–437.
Van der Eng, P. 1998. Exploring exploitation: The Netherlands and colonial Indonesia 1870–1940. *Revista de Historia Economica-Journal of Iberian and Latin American Economic History* 16 (1): 291–321.
Van der Eng, P. 2004. Productivity and comparative advantage in rice agriculture in South-East Asia since 1870. *Asian Economic Journal* 18 (4): 345–370.
Van Zanden, J. L. 2009. The skill premium and the 'Great Divergence'. *European Review of Economic History* 13 (1): 121–153.
de Zwart, P. and Soekhradj, P. 2023. Sweet equality: Sugar, property rights, and land distribution in colonial Java. *Explorations in Economic History, 88*, p.101513.

The State of Economic History in Japan

Yutaka Arimoto, Tomoko Hashino, Masaki Nakabayashi, Tetsuji Okazaki, Osamu Saito, Kaoru Sugihara, and Yoshihiro Sakane

Abstract This paper surveys the changes in economic history research in Japan. In recent decades, the internationalization of research has progressed, and the influence of economics and econometrics has increased, and related to these changes, more economic historians are working on new topics using new approaches. Japan's economic history research was internationalized prior to World War II, but only in the sense that economic historians in Japan "imported" theoretical frameworks, concepts, and perspectives from the Western literature. In recent decades, the situation has changed. Economic historians in Japan, equipped with analytical tools from economics and econometrics, have generated new insights and "exported" them to the international academic community.

Y. Arimoto
Metrics Work Consultants Inc. and Hitotsubashi University, Tokyo, Japan

T. Hashino
Kobe University, Kobe, Japan

M. Nakabayashi
The University of Tokyo, Tokyo, Japan

T. Okazaki (✉)
Meiji Gakuin University, Tokyo, Japan

O. Saito
Hitotsubashi University, Tokyo, Japan

K. Sugihara
Research Institute for Humanity and Nature, Kyoto, Japan

Y. Sakane
Hiroshima Shudo University, Hiroshima, Japan

C. Diebolt, M. Haupert (eds.), *The State of Economic History*, Frontiers in Economic History, https://doi.org/10.1007/978-3-032-01624-9_6

Introduction

Economic history research in Japan has a long history. The Socio-Economic History Society (*Shakai Keizaishi Gakkai*), Japan's largest academic society for economic history with around 1300 members, was founded in 1930. This is four years later than the foundation of the Economic History Society in the United Kingdom, and 10 years earlier than the foundation of the Economic History Association in the United States (https://sehsjp.org/). Since its foundation, the Socio-Economic History Society of Japan has produced numerous insights through many studies by economic historians. Because it is impossible to survey all of these studies, we focus on the new trends in economic history research in Japan in recent decades. Specifically, the internationalization of research has progressed and the influence of economics and econometrics has increased, and related to these changes, more economic historians are working on new topics using new approaches. In section "Progress of Internationalization", we highlight the progress of internationalization by reviewing the publishing records in major economic history journals. Section "Increasing Influence of Economics and Econometrics" describes the increasing influence of economics and econometrics. Section "New Topics and New Approaches" surveys studies on new topics using new approaches. Section "Conclusion" concludes.

Progress of Internationalization

One of the major changes in economic history research in Japan in recent decades has been the emergence of internationally focused economic historians. In the 1980s, the major outlets for studies by economic historians in Japan were Japanese economic history journals and books, whereas submitting and publishing papers to international journals in English was quite exceptional. However, the situation has changed after that. This section reviews the process of the internationalization of economic history research in Japan.

To visualize the progress of internationalization, we survey the publications of Japanese economic historians in international journals from the 1980s to the 2010s. More specifically, we surveyed all papers published in the three major economic history journals, *Economic History Review* (EHR), *Explorations in Economic History* (EEH), and *Journal of Economic History* (JEH), and listed the Japanese authors (the authors who were affiliated with institutions in foreign countries at the time of publication are excluded from the list).[1]

Figure 1 shows the trend in the number of papers published by Japanese scholars working in Japan (simply called "Japanese scholars" hereafter). There is a clear increasing trend, which accelerated in the 2000s. In the 1980s, only five papers were

[1] The list of papers appears in the appendix.

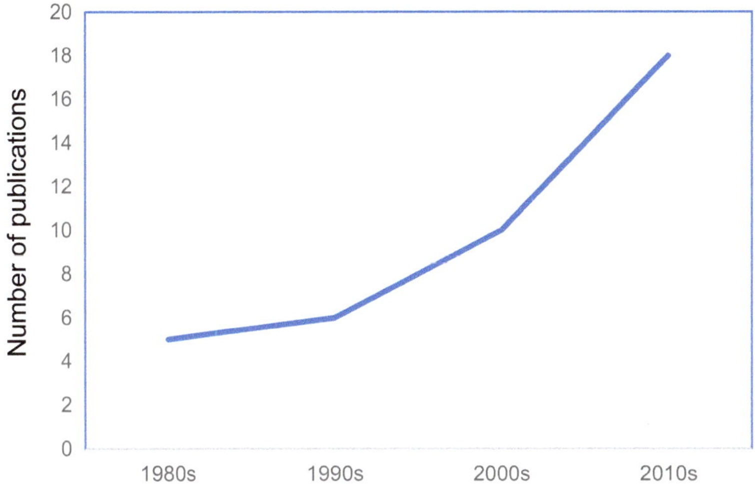

Fig. 1 Number of publications of scholars in Japan in the three major economic history journals

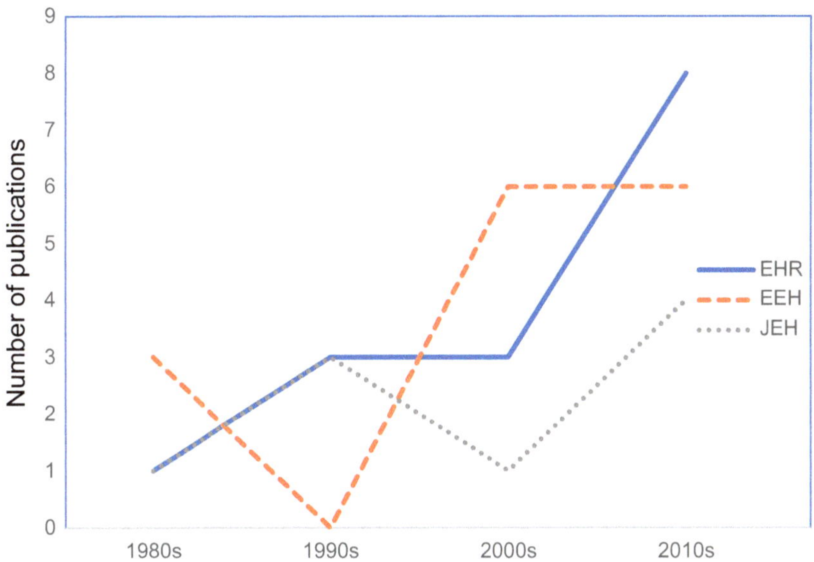

Fig. 2 Number of publications by journal

published over the 10 years, that is, 0.5 papers per year. In the 1990s, the number of publications increased marginally to six. Then, in the 2000s, the number increased to 10, and finally to 18 in the 2010s. Given the number of economic historians in Japan the number of publications in the 2010s is small, but the progress of internationalization in the past two decades is noteworthy. Figure 2 breaks down the data

Table 1 Number of publications by institution

	Total	1980s	1990s	2000s	2010s
Total	46	5	6	11	24
University of Tokyo	12	0	0	5	7
Hitotsubashi University	6	1	0	1	4
Osaka University	4	2	1	0	1
Kobe University	4	0	2	0	2
Bank of Japan	3	0	0	0	3
Keio University	2	0	0	1	1
Nomura Research Institute	1	1	0	0	0
Toyo Yuniversity	1	1	0	0	0
Hosei University	1	0	1	0	0
Kansai University	1	0	1	0	0
Osaka Gakuin University	1	0	1	0	0
Ministry of Finance	1	0	0	1	0
Nagoya City University	1	0	0	1	0
Nagoya Gakuin University	1	0	0	1	0
Soka University	1	0	0	1	0
National Graduate Institute for Policy Studies	1	0	0	0	1
Nihon University	1	0	0	0	1
Osaka Sangyo University	1	0	0	0	1
Saitama University	1	0	0	0	1
Tokyo Institute of Technology	1	0	0	0	1
Tokyo University of Science	1	0	0	0	1
Yokohama National University	1	0	0	0	1

Note: In case of a joint work written by multiple authors at different institutions in Japan, the number is double counted

of Fig. 1 into the three journals. We find that publications in EHR and EEH drive the increasing trend.

Table 1 shows the number of publications by institution. If the author of an article was affiliated with institution A, this counts as one publication for institution A. If an article was by two Japanese authors who were affiliated with institutions A and B, this counts as one publication for both institutions (hence, the total number in the table is larger than the total in Fig. 1). Looking at the first column indicating the total number of publications from the 1980s to the 2010s, we find that major universities in Japan and the Bank of Japan, which has a section for historical research at the Institute for Money and Economic Studies, all have at least two publications. At the same time, it is notable that scholars of the other 16 institutions also published papers in major journals. This implies that the internationalization of economic history research involves numerous institutions. This trend arguably reflects the internationalization of the work environment of economic historians in Japan. That is, most economic historians are affiliated to economics departments of universities, and the community of economists has undergone internationalization, where publishing papers in top international journals is highly valued, and hence is essential to the academic career of a scholar. The culture of the economist community has penetrated the economic historian community, who often work in the same department.

Over time, changes in the number of publications by institution are also of interest. Prior to the 2000s, when the number of publications surged, Osaka and Kobe were the leading institutions, whereas the University of Tokyo had no recorded publications. However, in the 2000s and the 2010s, the University of Tokyo drove the increase in publications. As noted, until the 1990s, most economic historians in Japan did not have an interest in publishing their papers in international journals, and this mode of thinking was typical of the scholars at the University of Tokyo, who were prestigious in the academic community in Japan.

Table 2 classifies the papers by subject area. In total, papers on Japan account for 56.4% (22/39) of all papers, and they drove the increasing trend in the number of publications. This is not surprising because many Japanese scholars are not only interested in Japan's history, but have various advantages in conducting research on Japan, including language and access to materials. Looking closely at the topics of the papers on Japanese economic history, while most papers until the 1990s were on macro issues in a broad sense, such as economic growth and standard of living, those in the 2000s and 2010s addressed a broader range of issues, such as industrial organization, industrial relations, regional economies, war economy, and natural disasters. Notably, most of these papers exploit data at the micro level, which is consistent with the global trend in economic history research.

Papers on European and North American economic history soon followed those on Japanese economic history. Economic historians in Japan have long been interested in the economic history of the West, especially Europe, which preceded Japan in terms of economic and social development. In this area of Western studies, most of the papers had been published in Japanese-language journals. Many, if not all, of those scholars who published their papers in international journals seem to have motivations that differ from those in the academic community in Japan. They address issues such as the labor market for Japanese immigrants in the USA and the Great Depression in the USA.

Papers on Asia, excluding Japan, followed those on the West. It is notable that three of the five papers focus on Korea in the period of colonization by Japan, and were all published in the period before 2000 by one scholar. He was one of the few internationally minded economic historians in pre-2000 Japan. However, since the turn of the century, the number of papers on global and comparative economic history has increased; most of these are motivated, not surprisingly, by the Great Divergence debate.

Table 2 Number of publications by object area

	Total	Japan	Asia	Europe and North America	Global, comparative
Total	39	22	5	8	4
1980s	5	3	1	1	0
1990s	6	1	3	2	0
2000s	10	7	0	2	1
2010s	18	11	1	3	3

Increasing Influence of Economics and Econometrics

In this section, we review the history of economic history research in Japan, which is characterized by the increasing influence of economics and econometrics.[2] Arimoto (2022) stresses the difference in economic history research between Japan and Western countries. He contends that economic history research in Japan is more history oriented in that it emphasizes the description of "what happened and how it happened." In contrast, economic history research in Western countries seeks to explain "why it happened," emphasizing a strict identification of causality (Arimoto 2022, p. 24). In other words, he claims that Japanese economic history research is mostly descriptive and differs from research in Western countries that attempts to identify causality. This characteristic of early economic history research in Japan reflects that it had not yet been influenced by the methods of economics and econometrics, unlike economic history research in Western countries.

Indeed, most papers published in international economic history journals in recent years are economics and/or econometrics oriented. For example, most of the papers published in the three major journals in the field of economic history (*EEH*, *EHR*, and *JEH*)use the methods of economics and econometrics, and could be published in journals in applied economics. The same is true for *Cliometrica* and *European Review of Economic History*, which approach these three major journals in terms of reputation and quality, as well as *Australian Economic History Review* (now *Asia-Pacific Economic History Review*) and *Scandinavian Economic History Review*.

While many international journals in economic history are economics and/or econometrics oriented, the influence of economics and econometrics started only recently among Japanese economic historians. Yamamoto (2018) argues that the degree of "quantification" or influence of economics and econometrics among Japanese economic historians is much lower than among international historians. He demonstrates this by comparing the papers published in *EHR* and *Shakai Keizai Shigaku* (*Socioeconomic History*), one of Japan's economic history journals. Quantification in *Socioeconomic History is* much lower than in *EHR*, which is less "quantified" than *JEH* or *EEH* (Yamamoto 2018). Whereas the proportion of papers using quantitative analysis in *EHR* was 46.9% in 2013–17, it was only 4.4% in *Socioeconomic History* in 2013–18 (Yamamoto 2018, pp. 72–73). More recent issues of *Socioeconomic History* show that the diversification of analytical methods has somewhat progressed, but compared with the trends in European countries and the USA, the influence of economics and econometrics has been substantially smaller in Japan.

The origins of this characteristic of economic history research in Japan were examined by Saito (2016, 2017), Yamamoto (2018), and Nakamura et al. (2021), who provide detailed accounts of the emergence and development of economic history and socioeconomic history research in Japan. Economic history research in

[2] In this section, we depend on Hashino (2024, forthcoming) unless noted otherwise.

Japan was traditionally located at the boundary between history and economics, and each economic historian started her/his research in either of the two disciplines and learned the other discipline later in their career (Nakamura et al. 2021, p. 27). In addition, the economic theories they relied on were primarily those of the German historical school and Marxian economics. Since the fall of the Berlin Wall in 1989, the influence of Marxian economics has rapidly faded, and Japanese economic history research has become detached from economic theories and more history oriented. Meanwhile, some economic historians introduced comparative institutional analysis and the economics of organizations into their economic history research, which contributed to a revival of the interaction between economics/econometrics and economic history (Nakamura et al. 2021, p. 34). As a result, a stark change in economic history research has emerged, as described in sections "Increasing Influence of Economics and Econometrics" and "New Topics and New Approaches", although its influence is not substantial at present.

It should be noted that this recent change has an important prehistory. Saito (2016) points out that a "quiet revolution of quantification" took place in economic history research in Japan in the late 1960s. One noteworthy example of this quiet revolution was the demographic research by Akira Hayami, who utilized village population registers compiled under the Tokugawa shogunate. He applied demographic concepts, measures, and methods to those micro data (Saito 2016, p. 202). Economic historians and economists, including Hayami, founded the Quantitative Economic History Group (QEH Group) as a cross-university research organization. Economists working with historical national accounts at the Institute of Economic Research (IER) at Hitotsubashi University joined the group's historians. Based on the recognition that economic development should be conceived as a long-term historical phenomenon, the group members, both economists and historians, conducted quantitative economic history research, while the IER finalized the work for the Long-Term Economic Statistics (LTES) series in 1988. Since then, numerous economic historians, both in Japan and abroad, have benefited from the 14-volume LTES and its one-volume English-language publication (Ohkawa et al. 1965–88; Ohkawa and Shinohara 1979).

The activities of the QEH Group came to fruition with eight volumes of *Japanese Economic History* (Umemura et al. 1988–1990; Saito 2016, p. 202). The recently published *Iwanami Series on the History of the Japanese Economy* (six volumes), edited by Fukao et al., inclusing Fukao (2017a, b, c, and d), is a new series that incorporates updates since the publication of *Japanese Economic History* and emphasizes the application of economics and econometrics (Nakamura et al. 2021, pp. 40–41). Indeed, the authors of the *Iwanami Series on the History of the Japanese Economy* include not only historians and economic historians, but also economists, and it is an attempt to engage economic historians in dialogue with economists/econometricians, while valuing the tradition of careful empirical research based on historical sources and materials.

As noted, the methods of economics and econometrics have been gradually diffusing within Japanese economic history research. In such a situation, it is somewhat ironic that foreign researchers of Japanese economic history let us know that they are actively introducing such methodologies and beginning a new image, arguably something like a new illusion of economic history of Japan. Japan has been accumulating resources and data since the early stages of its economic development, and much of the quantitative data provided by government agencies are now accessible online. In other words, the "entry barrier is low" (Kumon 2020) for foreign researchers to undertake research on the economic history of Japan. As a result, there has been an increase in the number of foreign researchers publishing papers on Japanese economic history in international journals. Of course, it is beneficial that foreign researchers have become interested in the economic history of Japan. However, in some cases, those papers have shortcomings, partly because they do not incorporate knowledge of the extant literature on Japanese economic history, which is mainly written in Japanese. This means that there is a critical need for interaction between economic historians in Japan and researchers abroad who are interested in Japanese economic history.

New Topics and New Approaches

Estimates of Gross Domestic Product and Population

Although the Great Divergence debate on the eighteenth century has attracted considerable attention (Pomeranz 2000), "little divergences" in Europe and Asia are also the subject of interest. These refer to divergences in terms of per capita GDP between northwestern European economies in Europe and between Japan and China in Asia in the eighteenth century (Broadberry et al. 2018). Takashima (2017) and Bassino et al. (2019) demonstrate that Japan's productivity improvement accelerated, whereas China's stagnated in the eighteenth century so that Japan's per capita GDP surpassed China's for the first time in its history in the eighteenth century and caught up with those of peripheral European economies such as Portugal and Poland in the mid-nineteenth century. Estimates of the per capita GDP of premodern Japan and premodern China appear in the 2023 version of the Maddison Project database (https://www.rug.nl/ggdc/historicaldevelopment/maddison/) and are based on Broadberry et al. (2018) and Bassino et al. (2019). Estimates by Bassino et al. (2019) were revised and extended by Nakabayashi et al. (2020), who revised GDP estimates, using the estimates of agricultural output by Midorikawa (2019) for the year 1150, and revised per capita GDP for that year accordingly.

Nakabayashi et al. (2020) also extend GDP estimates using four estimate point years, 1600, 1721, 1804, and 1846 for early modern times from Bassino et al. (2019) to annual series from 1651 to 1841. They use descriptive and anecdotal evidence to estimate nonfarm output in medieval times. Estimates of GDP in modern times were updated by Fukao et al. (2015), on which the Maddison Project's database is reliant. Fukao et al. (2020) and Fukao and Paul (2021) further elaborate on the sources of productivity improvement in modern times.

One factor that improved productivity in medieval Japan was the transformation from extensive farming to intensive farming that continuously pursued land and labor productivity improvement from the fourteenth to the sixteenth century (Nishitani 2017). This transformation also implied a profound change in Japanese society. The very dense "Japanese" local communities, based on villages where the same farming households cultivated the same plots of farmland, were first formed in the transition to intensive farming from the fourteenth century in economically developed regions and from the sixteenth century in less developed regions (Oyama and Mieda 2018).

Saito (2018) reestimated population for the year 1600 substantially upward from Hayami's estimate of 12 million (Hayami 2010) to 17 million. For 1150, Nakabayashi et al. (2020) revised the estimate by Farris (2006, 2009) substantially downward based on the estimates of agricultural output by Midorikawa (2019). In total, population growth in medieval times is thought to have been more rapid after the disastrous ancient period than previously estimated. Such updates require us to fully reexamine Japanese economic history, a process started by Fukao et al. (2017a, b, c, 2018a, b), along with other developments in studies on economic history of Japan.

Comparative Historical Institutional Analyses on Traditional Japanese Society

The early modern Japanese state provided farming households with property rights over the plots of farmland that the household cultivated by means of detailed cadastral surveys (Nakabayashi 2020, 2021). The protection of the property rights of farmers inevitably encourages farmers to take greater risks because properties protected by the state would serve as safe collaterals when they were pledged to borrow, and hence farmers could borrow more cheaply than otherwise. To prevent owner-farmers from taking too many risks, the shogunate regulated the trade of farmland and financing by pledging farmland (Mandai and Nakabayashi 2018). The shogunate also encouraged single inheritance, and when consanguineous sons were considered incapable of running family businesses, adoption of more talented persons. This regulation achieved a balance between growth and stability. The shogunate collapsed in 1868, and as of 1873, when the deregulation of farmland sales and farmland-collateral loans was implemented, the tenanted land ratio was estimated to be just 27% of farmland (Furushima 1958, p. 332). Nakabayashi et al. (2020) note that, on balance, early modern Japan experienced modest growth in productivity and social stability.

Protection of smallholders' property rights in early modern Japan enabled its civilians to accept a high taxation rate, which is referred to as "state capacity" (Nakabayashi 2012, 2021; Sng and Moriguchi 2014; Koyama et al. 2018) compared with other merging powers such as China, Turkey, and Spain. The higher state capacity, or higher taxation rate, delivered room for spending on modernization, including of the military after the Meiji Restoration of 1868.

The stability of owner-farming households enabled owner-farmers to carry on farming while expanding nonfarm production using the family workforce in slack seasons. Thus, the division of labor deepened within, not between, farming households in early modern Japan (Saito 2009). After all, Tokugawa Japan maintained a relatively equal society (Saito 2015b). Stable governance under the Tokugawa shogunate regime also reduced the frequency of famines and pandemics, which raised and smoothed productivity growth over the long term (Saito 2015a).

However, the preserved equity incurred costs. While the shogunate's regulations on farmland trades and inheritance succeeded in protecting the smallholder class, they hindered improvement in resource allocations (Kumon 2025, forthcoming). After the Meiji Restoration, farmland sales and farmland-collateral loans were fully deregulated.

The reforms resulted in an increase in the ratio of tenanted land to 45% around 1900 (Furushima 1958, p. 332). Even with consolidation of landownership, farming methods barely changed. Former smallholders continued to cultivate their former properties as tenant farmers. Thus, the goal of tenancy contracts was something other than technological gain from a consolidation of acreage. Indeed, Arimoto (2005) and Arimoto et al. (2010) demonstrate that risk-taking by landlords after the Meiji Restoration was an equilibrium between landlords and tenant farmers. While the shogunate and lords before the Meiji Restoration shared weather risk with farmers through a temporary reduction of land tax, the Meiji Government defied such risk-bearing. Landlordism took over the role of risk-bearing.

The greater responsibility of households for risk-bearing in early modern times cast a long shadow. Nakabayashi (2019) argues that greater reliance on family security made a larger welfare state less able to maintain economic growth. The experiences of patriarchal societies such as Japan and continental European nations thus reasonably explain their heavy welfare states.

Conclusion

In this chapter, we briefly surveyed the changes in economic history research in Japan. Japan's economic history research was internationalized prior to World War II, but only in the sense that economic historians in Japan "imported" theoretical frameworks, concepts, and perspectives from the Western literature. In recent decades, the situation has changed. Economic historians in Japan, equipped with analytical tools from economics and econometrics, have generated new insights and "exported" them to the international academic community.

The material covered in this chapter is limited in that it basically focuses on economic history research on Japan. One distinctive characteristic of this research field in Japan is the contribution of scholars on Western and Asian economic history; however, a review of such work is beyond the scope of the present chapter.

Appendix: Publication of Scholars in Japan in the Major Three Economic History Journals in the 1980s, 1990s, 2000s, and 2010s

1980–1989

Akimoto, H. (1981) "Capital formation and economic growth in Mid-19th century Japan," *Explorations in Economic History* 18(1): 40–59.

Kimura, M. (1989), "Public finance in Korea under Japanese rule: Deficit in the colonial account and colonial taxation," *Explorations in Economic History* 26(3): 285–310.

Murayama, Y. (1984) "Contractors, collusion, and competition: Japanese immigrant railroad laborers in the Pacific Northwest, 1898-1911," *Explorations in Economic History* 21(3): 290–305.

Yasuba, Y (1986) "Standard of living in Japan before industrialization: From what level did Japan begin? A comment," *Journal of Economic History*, March 1986, 46(1): 217–24.

Yonekawa, S. (1985) "Recent writing on Japanese economic and social history," *Economic History Review* 38(1): 107–23.

1990–1999

Kimura, M. (1993) "Standards of living in colonial Korea: Did the masses become worse off or better of under Japanese rule?" *Journal of Economic History* 53(3): 629–52.

Kimura, M. (1995) "The economics of Japanese imperialism in Korea, 1910-1939," *Economic History Review* 48(3): 555–74.

Murayama.Y. (1991) "Information and emigrants: Interprefectural differences of Japanese emigration to the Pacific Northwest, 1880-1915," *Journal of Economic History*, March 1991, 51(1): 125–47.

Nishimura, S. (1995) "The French provincial banks, the Banque de France, and Bill Finance, 1890-1913," *Economic History Review* 48(3): 536–54.

Yasuba, Y. (1996) "Did Japan ever suffer from a shortage of natural resources before World War II? " *Journal of Economic History* 56(3): 543–60.

2000–2009

Fukao, K, D. Ma, and Y. Tangjun (2006) "International comparison in historical perspective: Reconstructing the 1934-1936 benchmark purchasing power parity for Japan, Korea, and Taiwan," *Explorations in Economic History* 43(2): 280–308.

Kanzaka, J. (2002) "Villein rents in thirteenth-century England: An analysis of the hundred rolls of 1279-1280," *Economic History Review* 55(4): 593–618.

Miwa, Y. and M. Ramseyer (2006) "Japanese industrial finance at the close of the 19th century: Trade credit and financial intermediation," *Explorations in Economic History* 43(1): 94–118.

Okazaki, T. (2005) "The role of the merchant coalition in pre-modern Japanese economic development: An Historical institutional analysis," *Explorations in Economic History* 42(2): 184–201.

Okazaki, T. (2006) "'Voice' and 'exit' in Japanese firms during the Second World War: Sanpo revisited," *Economic History Review* 59(2): 374–95.

Okazaki, T. (2007) "Micro-aspects of monetary policy: Lender of last resort and selection of banks in pre-war Japan," *Explorations in Economic History* 44(4): 657–79.

Okazaki, T., M. Sawada, and K. Yokoyama (2005) "Measuring the extent and implications of director interlocking in the prewar Japanese banking industry," *Journal of Economic History* 65(4):1082–1115.

Solomou, S. and M. Shimazaki (2007) "Japanese episodic long swings in economic growth," *Explorations in Economic History* 44(2): 224–41.

Suzuki, A. (2009) "Measles and the spatio-temporal structure of Modern Japan," *Economic History Review* 62(4): 828–56.

Suzuki, M. (2002) "Selective immigration and ethnic economic achievement: Japanese Americans before World War II," *Explorations in Economic History* 39(3): 254–81.

2010–2019

Bassino, J., S. Broadberry, K. Fukao, B. Gupta, and M. Takashima, (2019) "Japan and the Great Divergence, 730-1874," *Explorations in Economic History* 72: 1–22.

Hashino, T. and K. Otsuka, "Hand looms, power looms, and changing production organizations: The case of the Kiryu weaving district in early twentieth-century Japan," *Economic History Review* 66(3): 785–804.

Hunter, J. and K. Ogasawara (2019) "Price shocks in regional markets: Japan's Great Kanto Earthquake of 1923," *Economic History Review*. 72(4): 1335–62.

Imaizumi, A., K. Ito, and T. Okazaki (2016), "Impact of natural disasters on industrial agglomeration: The case of the Great Kanto Earthquake in 1923," *Explorations in Economic History* 60: 52–68.

Kobayashi, A. (2019) "International bimetallism and silver absorption in Singapore, 1840-73," *Economic History Review* 72(2): 595–617.

Nakabayashi, M. (2018) "From the substance to the shadow: The role of the court in Japanese labour markets," *Economic History Review* 71(1): 267–89.

Nakajima, K. and T. Okazaki (2018) "The expanding empire and spatial distribution of economic activity: The case of Japan's colonization of Korea during the prewar period," *Economic History Review* 71(2): 593–616.

Nakamura, Y. (2017), "The relationship between the real and financial economies in the Soviet Union: An analysis of government debts using newly available data," *Explorations in Economic History*. 66: 65–84.

Okazaki, T. (2011) "The Supplier network and aircraft production in wartime Japan," *Economic History Review*. 64(3): 973–94.

Okazaki, T., T. Okubo, and E. Strobl (2019) "Creative destruction of industries: Yokohama City in the Great Kanto Earthquake, 1923," *Journal of Economic History* 79(1):1–31.

Okazaki, T. and M. Sawada (2017) "Measuring the extent and implications of corporate political connections in prewar Japan," *Explorations in Economic History* 65: 17–35.

Onji, K. and J. Tang (2017) "Taxes and the choice of organizational form in late nineteenth century Japan," *Journal of Economic History* 77(2): 440–72.

Saito, O. (2015) "Growth and inequality in the Great and Little Divergence debate: A Japanese perspective," *Economic History Review* 68(2): 399–419.

Sasaki, Y.(2014) "Publishing nations: Technology acquisition and language standardization for European ethnic groups," *Journal of Economic History*, December 2017, v. 77, iss. 4, pp. 1007–47.

Shibamoto, M. and M. Shizume (2014) "Exchange rate adjustment, monetary policy and fiscal stimulus in Japan's escape from the Great Depression, *Explorations in Economic History* 53: 1–18.

Shizume, M. (2011) "Sustainability of public debt: Evidence from Japan before the Second World War," *Economic History Review* 64(4): 1113–43.

Tangjun, Y., K. Fukao, and H. Wu (2010) "Comparative output and labor productivity in manufacturing between China, Japan, Korea and the United States for ca. 1935: A production-side PPP approach, *Explorations in Economic History* 47(3): 325–46.

Watanabe, S. (2016) "Technology shocks and the Great Depression," *Journal of Economic History* 76(3): 909–33.

References

Arimoto, Y. 2005. State-Contingent Rent Reduction and Tenancy Contract Choice. *Journal of Development Economics* 76 (2): 355–375.

Arimoto, Y. 2022. Economic History and 'Economic History. *Keizai (Economics) Seminar*, February-March: 23–38.

Arimoto, Y., T. Okazaki, and M. Nakabayashi. 2010. Agrarian Land Tenancy in Prewar Japan: Contract Choice and Implications on Productivity. *The Developing Economies* 48 (3): 1746–1049.

Bassino, J., S. Broadberry, K. Fukao, B. Gupta, and M. Takashima. 2019. Japan and the Great Divergence, 730–1874. *Explorations in Economic History* 72:1–22.

Broadberry, S., H. Guan, and D. D. Li. 2018. China, Europe, and the Great Divergence: A Study in Historical National Accounting, 980–1850. *The Journal of Economic History* 78 (4): 955–1000.

Farris, W. W. 2006. *Japan's Medieval Population: Famine, Fertility, and Warfare in a Transformative Age*. Honolulu: University of Hawai'i Press.

Farris, W. W. 2009. *Daily Life and Demographics in Ancient Japan*. Ann Arbor: Center for Japanese Studies, University of Michigan.

Fukao, K., J. Bassino, T. Makino, R. Paprzycki, T. Settsu, M. Takashima, and J. Tokui. 2015. *Regional Inequality and Industrial Structure in Japan: 1874–2008*. Tokyo: Maruzen Publishing.

Fukao, K., T. Makino, and T. Settsu. 2020. Structural Change, Capital Deepening, and TFP Growth in Japan: 1885–1970. *Social Science Japan Journal* 23 (2): 185–204.

Fukao, K., N. Nakamura, and M. Nakabayashi eds. 2017a. *Iwanami Kouza Nihon Keizai no Rekishi Dai 1 Kan Chusei: 11 Seiki kara 16 Seiki kohan (Iwanami Lecture Series, History of the Japanese Economy*, Volume 1, The Medieval Period: From the Eleventh Century to the Second Half of the Sixteenth Century). Tokyo: Iwanami Shoten (in Japanese).

Fukao, K., N. Nakamura, and M. Nakabayashi eds. 2017b. *Iwanami Lecture Series, History of the Japanese Economy*, Volume 2 (The Early Modern Period: From the End of the Sixteenth Century to the First Half of the Nineteenth Century). Tokyo: Iwanami Shoten (in Japanese).

Fukao, K., N. Nakamura, and M. Nakabayashi eds. 2017c. *Iwanami Kouza Nihon Keizai no Rekishi Dai 3 Kan Kindai 1: 19 Seiki Kouhan kara Dai Ichiji Sekai Taisen Mae (1914–1936) (Iwanami Lecture Series, History of the Japanese Economy*, Volume 3, The Modern Period 1: From the Late Nineteenth Century to 1913). Tokyo: Iwanami Shoten (in Japanese).

Fukao, K., N. Nakamura, and M. Nakabayashi eds. 2017d. *Iwanami Kouza Nihon Keizai no Rekishi Dai 3 Kan Kindai 2: Dai Ichiji Sekai Taisen-ki kara Nicchu Senso Mae (1914–1936) (Iwanami Lecture Series, History of the Japanese Economy*, Volume 3, The Modern Period 2: From the First World War to the Eve of the Second Sino-Japanese War (1914–1936)). Tokyo: Iwanami Shoten (in Japanese).

Fukao, K., N. Nakamura, and M. Nakabayashi eds. 2018a. *Iwanami Kouza Nihon Keizai no Rekishi Dai 5 Kan Gendai 1: Nicchu Sensou Ki kara Koudo Seichou Ki (1937–1972) (Iwanami Lecture Series, History of the Japanese Economy*, Volume 5, The Contemporary Period 1: From the Sino-Japanese War to the Rapid Growth (1937–1972)). Tokyo: Iwanami Shoten.(in Japanese).

Fukao, K., N. Nakamura, and M. Nakabayashi eds. 2018b. *Iwanami Kouza Nihon Keizai no Rekishi Dai 6 Kan Gendai 2: Antei Seichou Ki kara Kouzou Kaikaku Ki (1973–2010) (Iwanami Lecture Series, History of the Japanese Economy*, Volume 6, The Contemporary Period 2: From the Stable Growth to the Structural Reforms (1973–2010)). Tokyo: Iwanami Shoten (in Japanese).

Fukao, K., and S. Paul. 2021. Baumol, Engel, and Beyond: Accounting for a Century of Structural Transformation in Japan, 1885–1985. *Economic History Review* 74 (1): 164–180. https://doi.org/10.1111/ehr.13021.

Furushima, T. 1958. "Chiso Kaisei go no jinushiteki tochi shoyu no kakudai to nogyo rippo" (Expansion of landlordism and the land policy after the Land Tax Reform of 1873). In *Nihon Jinushisei Shi Kenkyu (Study on the history of the Japanese Landlord System)*, ed. T. Furushima, 315–357. Tokyo: Iwanami Shoten (in Japanese).

Hashino, T. 2024. "Swallowed" Economic History: The Significance of Economic History Research in Economics. In *Next Generation of Empirical Research in Economics*, ed. K. Otsuka et al. Springer. (forthcoming).
Hayami, A. 2010. Population trends in Tokugawa Japan: 1600–1868. In *Population, Family and Society in Pre-Modern Japan*, ed. Hayami, Akira, 99–112. Leiden: Brill (first published in 1987).
Koyama, M., C. Moriguchi, and T. Sng. 2018. Geopolitics and Asia's Little Divergence: State Building in China and Japan After 1850. *Journal of Economic Behavior & Organization* 155:178–204.
Kumon, Y. 2020. "Kono Hito wo Tazune te" (Visiting This Person). *Keizai Seminar,* 18:5–6. (in Japanese).
Kumon, Y. 2025. Adoption, Inheritance and Wealth Inequality in Pre-industrial Japan and Western Europe. *Journal of Economic History* (forthcoming).
Mandai, Y., and M. Nakabayashi. 2018. Stabilize the Peasant Economy: Governance of Foreclosure by the Shogunate. *Journal of Policy Modeling* 40 (2): 305–327.
Midorikawa, K. 2019. Nihon kodai-chusei no suiden seisanryoku (Estimating the Productivity of Paddy Fields in Ancient and Medieval Japan)," *Shakai-Keizai Shigaku (Socio-Economic History)* 85 (2): 3–24 (in Japanese).
Nakabayashi, M. 2012. The Rise of a Japanese Fiscal State. In *The Rise of Fiscal States: A Global History, 1500–1914*, ed. B. Yun-Casalilla, P. K. O'Brien, and F. C. Comín, 327–409. Cambridge: Cambridge University Press.
Nakabayashi, M. 2019. From Family Security to the Welfare State: Path Dependency of Social Security on the Difference in Legal Origins. *Economic Modelling* 82:280–293.
Nakabayashi, M. 2020. The Thin Line Between Economic Dynamism and Social Stability: Regulation and Deregulation in Japan (12th to the 19th C.). In *Capitalisms: Towards A Global History*, ed. K. Yazdani and D. Menon, 277–305. New Delhi: Oxford University Press.
Nakabayashi, M. 2021. Tokugawa Japan and the Foundations of Modern Economic Growth in Asia. In *The Cambridge Economic History of Modern World*, ed. S. Broadberry and K. Fukao, vol. 1, 67–96. Cambridge: Cambridge University Press.
Nakabayashi, M., K. Fukao, M. Takashima, and N. Nakamura. 2020. Property Systems and Economic Growth in Japan, 730 – 1874. *Social Science Japan Journal* 23 (2): 147–184.
Nakamura, N., M. Takashima, and M. Nakabayashi. 2021. Current Empirical Economic History Research. *Social Science Research* 72 (2): 27–53.
Nishitani, M. 2017. Chusei no nogyo kozo (Structure of the medieval agriculture). In *Iwanami Koza Nihon Keizai no Rekishi Dai 1 Kan: 11 seiki kara 16 seiki kohan (Iwanami Lecture Series, History of the Japanese Economy, Volume 1: From the Eleventh Century to the Late Sixteenth Century)*, ed. K. Fukao, N. Nakamura, and M. Nakabayashi, 148–177. Tokyo: Iwanami Shoten (in Japanese).
Ohkawa, K., and M. Shinohara, eds. 1979. *Patterns of Japanese Economic Development: A Quantitative Appraisal.* New Haven: Yale University Press.
Ohkawa, K., M. Shinohara, and M. Umemura, eds. 1965–88. *Chōki Keizai Tōkei* (Estimates of Long-Term Economic Statistics of Japan). Tokyo: Tōyō Keizai Shimpōsha.
Oyama, K., and A. Mieda, eds. 2018. *Kodai Chūsei no Chiiki Shakai: Mura no "Kosekibo" no Kanousei (Regional Communities in Ancient and Medieval Times: Possibilities of "Registration Records" of Villages).* Shibunkaku Shuppan (in Japanese): Kyoto.
Pomeranz, K. 2000. *The Great Divergence: China, Europe, and Making the Modern World Economy*. Princeton: Princeton University Press.
Saito, O. 2009. "Land, Labour and Market Forces in Tokugawa Japan," *Continuity and Change* 24 (1): 169–196.
Saito, O. 2015a. Climate, Famine, and Population in Japanese History: A Long-Term Perspective. In *Environment and Society in the Japanese Islands: From Prehistory to the Present*, ed. Bruce L. Batten and Philip C. Brown, 213–329. Corvallis: Oregon State University Press.

Saito, O. 2015b. Growth and Inequality in the Great and Little Divergence Debate: A Japanese Perspective. *Economic History Review* 68 (2): 399–419.
Saito, O. 2016. A Very Brief History of Japan's Economic and Social History Research. *Jahrbuch für Europäische Überseegeschichte* 15:193–204.
Saito, O. 2017. Quantitative Economic History: Reflections on the Modern Japanese Historiography. In *Toward a Reinterpretation of Japanese Economic History: Quantitative and Comparative Approaches*, ed. M. Matao and M. Sawai (International Advanced Research Report 1103).
Saito, O. 2018. 1600 nen no zenkoku jinko: 17 seiki jinko keizaishi saikouchiku no kokoromi (Japan's Population in 1600: An Attempt to Reconstruct the History of the Population and Economy in the Seventeenth Century). *Shakai Keizai Shigaku (Socio-Economic History)* 84 (1): 3–23. (in Japanese).
Sng, Tuan-Hwee, and Chiaki Moriguchi. 2014. Asia's Little Divergence: State Capacity in China and Japan Before 1850. *Journal of Economic Growth* 19:439–470.
Takashima, M. 2017. *Keizai Seicho no Nihonshi (Economic Growth in the Japanese Past)*. Nagoya: Nagoya University Press. (in Japanese).
Umemura, M. et al. eds., 1988. *Nihon Keizai-shi (Japanese Economic History)*, Vol.1-8, Tokyo: Iwanami Shoten (in Japanese).
Yamamoto, C. 2018. The Role of Economic History. *Japanese Educational History* 61:69–75.

The Rise and Fall and Rise (?) of Economic History in Australia

Andrew Seltzer, Martin Shanahan, and Claire Wright

Abstract In this chapter, we examine the history of economic history in Australia. We trace its evolution from its English-influenced roots through its concern with colonial development, business history, cliometrics, comparative studies and, more recently, Asian topics. The field emerged in the early-1900s, with rapid expansion after the Second World War through free-standing economic history departments at several leading Australian universities. From the 1990s, a more corporatist approach to university management contributed to a decline in Australian economic history and, in particular, cliometric work. In the 1990s and early-2000s, the free-standing departments were all closed, and the hiring of economic historians virtually ceased. In the past decade and a half, there has been something of a revival, with economic history increasingly again reemerging in both history and economics departments. Over this period, the discipline has developed supportive institutional infrastructure, including scholarly societies, an annual conference, and an academic journal. This infrastructure proved robust and adaptive during the period of department closures and has again expanded over the past decade. In addition to examining the history of the discipline, we also look at some challenges for the future, focussing on the

We wish to thank Claude Diebolt and Michael Haupert for inviting us to participate in the WEHC session "The future of economic history", which led to this paper. The paper title is a nod to Meredith and Oxley (2015)—"The Rise and Fall of Australian Economic History".

A. Seltzer
Royal Holloway, University of London, London, UK

London School of Economics, London, UK

M. Shanahan
University of South Australia, Adelaide, SA, Australia

University of Gothenburg, Göteborg, Sweden

C. Wright (✉)
University of Technology Sydney, Ultimo, NSW, Australia
e-mail: Claire.Wright@uts.edu.au

C. Diebolt, M. Haupert (eds.), *The State of Economic History*, Frontiers in Economic History, https://doi.org/10.1007/978-3-032-01624-9_7

collection of still unextracted historical data and its usefulness in addressing various topics.

Introduction

Economic history in Australia has undergone dramatic changes over the century since its inception as an academic discipline. The source materials for the field were produced in the context of invasion, colonisation, and European settlement of the continent, as planning for the economic development of the colonies required a comprehensive system of colonial record keeping. After several influential, but ultimately sporadic contributions throughout the first half of the twentieth century, the field experienced substantial post-WWII expansion. During the next four decades, the field became more professionalised with the expansion of universities and the establishment of free-standing economic history departments. Collaborative research programmes developed, particularly at Australian National University (ANU) under Noel Butlin, and professional structures drew on the semi-captive market for economic historians. The influence of Butlin's orthodox school, particularly its focus on high-quality statistics and integration with mainstream economic theory, provided a foundation for early cliometrics research. However, beginning in the late-1980s, government policies forced Australian universities to adopt a corporate approach to management and resourcing. Funding pressures and competitive markets for students and research contributed to the closure of economic history departments and a virtual cessation of new hiring for almost two decades. This led to a "missing generation" of scholars, a dwindling supply of new contributions, and neglect of the "big data" revolution reshaping cliometrics work overseas. In the new millennium, economic history in Australia has experienced something of a revival. Hiring has resumed in small numbers, courses are once again being offered, and the research programme appears secure. While these latest developments mean that the field is more stable today than in the 1990s and early-2000s, it remains far smaller and in a much more precarious position than during the era of free-standing departments.

With each of these changes to the environment, there have been changes in how scholars have perceived the state of the field and the security of its future. Disciplinary introspection is a common pursuit among academics, satisfying intellectual curiosity, allowing practitioners to take stock, and providing an opportunity to think about how external factors—such as technology and university funding—impact upon our research and teaching. Arguably, more introspection is needed in the case of economic history, as its status as an interdisciplinary field—caught between disciplinary juggernauts of economics and history—has contributed to different expressions of the field based on the time, place, and context (Boldizzoni 2011; Boldizzoni and Hudson 2015; Lyons et al. 2008; Lamoreaux 2015). In Australia, scholars have published numerous articles on the state of economic history, with many of these featuring in the main journal of the field the *Australian Economic History Review* (henceforth *AEHR*) (see Table 1 for a full list).

Articles offering predictions addressing either the shape of research or commenting on the current health and future prospects for the field have generally aligned with the then-current state of affairs. Commentaries in the 1950s and 1960s were frequent and optimistic, focussing on how best to exploit the advantages created by

Table 1 Papers on the practice and future of business or economic history: *AEHR*, 1956–2022

Year	Author/s	Title
1958	Hartwell, R.M.	The Use of Business History
1959	Blainey, G.	The Future of Australian Business History: A Writer's View
1959	Anon	A Summing up of the First Australian Conference on Business History
1961	Tauman, M.	A Critical Comment of Australian Business Histories
1962	Birch, A.	The Study of Business History in Australia
1963	Hughes, H.	Business History Or The History of Business?
1967	Dowie, J.A.	As If Or Not As If: The Economic Historian as Hamlet
1967	Schedvin, C.B.	Economic History In Australian Universities, 1961–1966
1969	Pritchard, M.F.L	Economic History in New Zealand Universities.
1988	Pincus, J.J. & Snooks, G.D.	The Past And Future Role of the *Australian Economic History Review*
1989	Clarkson, L.A.	The Transformation of Australian Economic And Social History
1997	Boot, H.M.	Special Report: Teaching Economic History at Australian Universities
1997	Boot, H.M.	Some Developments in Teaching Practice in the Department of Economic History at the Australian National University
1997	Lloyd, C.	Can Economic History Be the Core Of Social Science? Why the Discipline Must Open And Integrate to Ensure the Survival of Long-Run Economic Analysis
1997	Nicholas, S.	The Future Of Economic History in Australia
1997	Whitwell, G.	Future Directions for the *Australian Economic History Review*
2004	van der Eng, P. & Shanahan, M.	The Current And Future Role of *AEHR*: Editorial Reflections
2007	Dick, H.	Big Questions in Australian Economic History: from the Outside Looking in
2007	McLean, I.W. & Shanahan, M.	Australian Economic History: Research Challenges and Big Questions
2010	Morgan, S. & Shanahan, M.	The Supply Of Economic History in Australasia: The *Australian Economic History Review* at 50
2017	Wright, C. & Ville, S.	The Evolution of an Intellectual Community Through the Words of Its Founders: Recollections of Australia's Economic History Field
2018	Seltzer, A.J.	Publication Trends And Future Challenges for the *Australian Economic History Review*: A Bibliometric Analysis
2020	Keneley, M.	Reflections on the Business History Tradition: Where Has It Come from and Where Is It Going To?
2021	Lloyd, P.J.	Big Economic History
2022	De Jong, A.	Research in Business History: From Theorising to *Bizhismetrics*

the post-war environment (Hartwell 1958; Blainey 1959; Tauman 1961; Birch 1962; Hughes 1963; Dowie 1967; Schedvin 1967; Pritchard 1969). Boris Schedvin, in particular, commented on the field's "secure future" within economics and commerce faculties, noting that "there is no reason why it should not maintain its place as it has done in [recent] years" (Schedvin 1967, p. 18). These commentaries vanished from the pages of the *AEHR* through the 1970s and remained absent well into the 1980s. The field's settled state and (apparently) secure place within economics were reflected in the lack of discussion about the future of the discipline for well over a decade, with the exception of papers by J.A. Dowie (1972) and H.F. Cruise (1975) on the role of economic historians for contemporary economics.

The first signs that the mood in Australian economic history had changed appeared in 1988, with the *Review*'s editors Jonathan Pincus and Graeme Snooks, arguing that "the future of economic history [...] may well depend upon whether we can present a united front to those who covet the resources we now control" (Pincus and Snooks 1988, p. 5). The caution of the late-1980s turned into outright pessimism by the late-1990s, as economic historians began to worry about their collective academic future. Coinciding with austerity in the tertiary sector and the loss of economic history departments around Australia, many questioned the scope, methodology, and place of economic and business history within the university. In a special issue in 1997, Stephen Nicholas, Greg Whitwell, and Chris Lloyd discussed the decline of the field, arguing that it had become the "poor cousins" of business faculties, and that their professional lives were now characterised by a "vain quest for students and recognition" (Whitwell 1997, p. 276). Nicholas argued that the future of teaching economic history was "bleak" and that it was "impossible" for the field to convince other disciplines of the subject's relevance (Nicholas 1997, p. 270–1). In two articles on teaching the subject in Australian universities, Mac Boot (1997a, b) noted "...economic historians are possibly less confident about their place in universities than at any time in the history of the discipline" (1997a, p. 158). In outlining solutions to the largely "institutional" issues they faced, scholars examined various adaptations designed to protect jobs that had become vulnerable, including changing the names of departments, aligning with disciplines like business and management, and adjusting the curriculum. Lloyd and Whitwell both advocated the field's disciplinary broadening: Lloyd as part of the broader social sciences, and Whitwell into business disciplines like marketing (Lloyd 1997; Whitwell 1997).

A cautious optimism has returned in the early twenty-first century, although most acknowledge considerable challenges still facing the field. In 2004, the then *AEHR* editors Pierre van der Eng and Martin Shanahan reported on the Society's annual conference and a panel session on "The Future of Economic History" held the previous year (van der Eng and Shanahan 2004). While the field's status in universities was still tenuous, the number of institutional subscribers to the journal (over 750) and the appointment of economic historians to university departments outside economic history were cited as reasons for optimism. The now familiar pattern of a conference panel on "future directions" complemented with papers appearing in the

AEHR was repeated in 2007. Once again, scholars proposed several suggestions about how to broaden the scope and perceived relevance of economic history research. By 2010, the journal's then editors, Stephan Morgan and Martin Shanahan were feeling sufficiently buoyed to celebrate the 50th year of the journal (Morgan and Shanahan 2010). In 2018, the then editor Andrew Seltzer again raised questions about the challenges still facing the profession in Australia. Nonetheless he was determined to "conclude on a note of cautious optimism", citing the frequency of Australian-based scholars publishing in leading international journals, high-quality submissions to the *AEHR*, and the first crop of new Australian-based PhD students in two decades (Seltzer 2018, p. 132).

We contribute to these efforts by documenting the history of economic history down under. We examine institutional changes in the field's funding and organisation, and corresponding changes to the teaching and research programme. We focus on the development of cliometric research in Australia, and the consequences of the "missing generation" for the collection of new data and undertaking of new quantitative projects. Finally, we reflect on the challenges and opportunities for Australian economic history, particularly the implications of data quality and accessibility, retirements and new hires, an internationalised research programme, and corporatized universities, for the nature of research in the field. We finish by offering some of our own speculations as to the likely future of the research programme going forward.

Early Economic History

The intellectual predecessors of Australian economic history were a variety of nineteenth-century colonial writings by administrators, policymakers, and journalists. These works were typically intended for the broader public and covered various aspects of the nature, history, and future of economic matters. Quantitative, data-driven economic history was largely the domain of government work at this time, with the British Government using quantitative information as a technique of surveillance and control throughout their Empire (Huf 2018; Cook 2017). The output of these public agencies included data-rich *Census Reports*, *Blue Books*, *Government Gazettes*, and others. By the mid- to late-nineteenth century, as Australia's first universities were established, government statisticians collected extensive data on the nature and progress of the economy. One of the first and best-known chroniclers of Australian economic development was the New South Wales government statistician, Sir Timothy Coghlan (1855–1926), whose *Labour and Industry in Australia* (1918) is still regarded as the foundation volume for Australian economic history prior to Federation. In an overwhelming 2449 pages, Coghlan provided a "pullulating Victorian panorama in words and numbers that seemingly capture every person, law, and landmark" (Coleman 2015). Although *Labour and Industry* was not the first to capture Australia's economic advance, it focussed on describing and explaining rather than promoting the benefits of the country (Coleman 2015; see also Coghlan 1890, 1891).

While economic history in the United Kingdom and United States experienced a professional consolidation in the first half of the twentieth century with the founding of academic societies and journals, in Australia the field remained in relative infancy until the late-1940s (Lamoreaux 2015; Hudson 2015). In the interwar period, institutional co-operation between government statisticians, universities, and the Workers' Educational Association (WEA) encouraged a small community of economic-historical scholars with an eclectic mix of interdisciplinary pursuits (Wright 2022). Interwar scholars moved between paradigms and institutions, with few identifying as an "economic historian". Over time, an identifiable discipline emerged, defined by interest in Australia's "progress"—analysis of international trade, capital imports, land settlement, and the role of government—and the lens of overlapping disciplines including economics, history, politics, and sociology. E.O.G. Shann and Brian Fitzpatrick, the most prominent scholars in this tradition, combined a reliance on quantitative data, skilled command of the written word, and underlying theoretical frameworks to broaden the appeal of Coghlan's dry account of Australia's economic past (Fitzpatrick 1939, 1941; Shann 1929). The more widely known post-war growth of economic history, therefore, did not spring out of barren ground, but had been growing, slowly and haphazardly, for decades.

The Second World War was a watershed for Australian economic history. During the war, campus grounds and facilities were used for training, university students enlisted in the services, research was directed towards work perceived to be relevant to the nation, and academics were seconded to public service planning roles. The total war developed a partnership between public and academic work, with the reconstruction effort centred on universities and the development of "useful" knowledge as the source of equality and prosperity (Forsyth 2014; Macintyre 2010). Many Western nations, including Australia, invested heavily in higher education after WWII, expanding the state-based "sandstone" universities and the establishing new tertiary institutions to mass-educate the population. University enrolment in Australia skyrocketed, approximately doubling in the immediate aftermath of the War (from 14,236 in 1939 to 30,477 in 1947) and continuing to experience high growth through the 1980s (Booth and Kee 2011). There was a concurrent emphasis on research, with new opportunities for funding, and the establishment of the Australian National University (ANU) in 1946 allowing professors to dedicate themselves to new research programmes and the training of graduate students (Wright 2022).

The Departmental Era

The expansion of universities led to enormous growth in the discipline, with separate economic history departments established at the University of Melbourne (1947), Australian National University (1957), University of New England (1965),

University of Sydney (1970), Flinders University (1970), University of New South Wales (1970), Monash University (1972), and Latrobe University (1990). For three decades, the ANU even had two separate departments, one in the teaching faculty and the other in the research school. Each of these departments was kitted out with a small group of scholars led by their "God Professor" (Anderson and Eaton 1982; Forsyth 2014; Macintyre 2010).

Alongside the field's expansion came the professionalisation of research methods, led by Noel Butlin, who arrived at the ANU in the late-1940s. Borrowing methodological advances from overseas and working with numerous colleagues, graduate students, and research assistants, Butlin set about collecting a wealth of national income accounting statistics. In his two path-setting volumes published in the early 1960s—colloquially termed "the numbers" and "the words"—Butlin argued that domestic factors (namely, urbanisation, manufacturing, and construction) had a far greater influence on Australia's economic fortunes in the second half of the nineteenth century than integration with the international economy through commodity exports and capital inflows (Butlin 1962, 1964). The "numbers" compiled Australian historical statistics within a national income accounting framework. The "words" described the sectoral mechanism of growth in the latter half of the nineteenth century, applying neoclassical and Keynesian economic concepts to the evidence. Although some criticised his method and conclusions, Butlin's "orthodox school" was largely supported within both economics and history, and inspired generations of economic historians that followed (see, for example, Forster 1964, 1970; Barnard 1958; Sinclair 1955, 1956; Snooks 1974; McLean 1973). The orthodox focus on high-quality data and integration with mainstream economics would prepare the conditions for the cliometric revolution to later come to Australia.

The main institutional structures of the discipline came into existence around this time as well. The field's journal—the *Australian Economic History Review*—was first published in 1956 as the *Bulletin of the Business Archives Council of Australia*. The early mission of the journal was to "form a bridge between businesspeople and academic researchers interested in the development of Australian business and the economy" rather than to publish high-quality research in economic history (Morgan and Shanahan 2010, p. 217). Conferences and curricula on the subject were reported on its pages. Scholars reflected on the value of historical research to the business community, and the need to tread a path between censorship and freedom of expression in the writing of company histories (Blainey 1959; Birch 1962). Early contributions also reflected enduring tensions around the appropriate focus, method, style, and audience for the field. Common debates included the field's identity in the social sciences and humanities, and difficulties in finding congruence amongst the field's "multiplicity of independent studies" (Tauman 1961, p. 64; Hughes 1963, p. 14).

The journal was slowly colonised by the growing number of academic economic historians. The name was changed first to *Business Archives and History* in 1962 and then to *Australian Economic History Review* in 1966, at which time the journal was transferred to the University of Sydney under the editorial leadership of Schedvin and John McCarty. The Economic History Society of Australia and New

Zealand (EHSANZ) was established in the early 1970s, and ownership of the *AEHR* was transferred to the Society shortly thereafter.

The 1970s and the 1980s were periods of stability for Australian's economic historians. The growth and legitimacy of the "orthodox school" coincided with the "golden age" of higher education, with economic history one of the beneficiaries of post-WWII expansion of Australian universities. Economics and commerce degrees increasingly required undergraduate courses in economic history, guaranteeing a student base and helping to ensure the generational renewal of scholars. The number of dedicated economic history staff grew from 12 in 1960, 30 in 1970, to a peak of about 50 in the 1980s (Wright 2022).

From the 1960s, the research frontier increasingly moved away from business history and towards the quantitative macroeconomic work that epitomised the "orthodox school" and the cliometric revolution. In a 1967 reflective symposium, Dowie assessed the applicability of the US-based cliometric revolution to Australian "economist-historians" and Schedvin discussed the connection (or lack thereof) between economics and economic history (Dowie 1967; Schedvin 1967). The first use of econometrics in the *AEHR* occurred in 1971 (Pope 1971; Schedvin 1971). A few years later cliometric work comprised a larger share of articles in the *AEHR* than any other economic history journal published outside of North America.[1] A reflective article by Deirdre McCloskey published in 1978 cited Butlin's work on national income accounts as an example of how the cliometric methodology had spread beyond its North American origins (McCloskey 1978). The publication of Antipodean articles in leading international economic history journals peaked towards the end of the departmental era. Figure 1 shows that about 1% of articles published between 1980 and 2000 in "Top 5" journals in economic history were on Australian topics (*Journal of Economic History*, *Explorations in Economic History*, *Economic History Review*, *European Review of Economic History*, and *Cliometrica*).[2]

Decline and Adaptation

The first storm clouds appeared in the late-1980s. John Dawkins, Federal Minister for Education, Employment and Training from 1987 through 1991, introduced a suite of higher education reforms designed to upgrade the skills of the workforce and improve the performance of university graduates (Forsyth 2014; Woelert and Yates 2015; Marginson and Considine 2000). As the Dawkins reforms were rolled out through the sector, universities began to look and act more like corporations.

---

[1] The 1973 share of papers with a regression was 27.8% for the *Journal of Economic History*, 12.5% for *Explorations in Economic History*, 11.1 in the *AEHR*, and 0.0% in the *Economic History Review*, *Scandinavian Economic History Review*, and *Revista de Historia Economica*. A decade later, these figures were 20.8, 45.8, 12.5, 13.6, 0.0, and 0.0%, for these same journals, respectively.

[2] The Top 5 listed above have been widely used in the bibliometric literature. See, for example, Fourie (2019).

Reform was based on principles of deregulation and competition, with institutions competing for student income through the new Higher Education Contribution Scheme (HECS), and research funding allocated competitively through the Australian Research Council (ARC). Smaller institutions were amalgamated, technical colleges were converted to universities, and student numbers almost doubled in the decade to 1996 (Forsyth 2014; Connell 2019; Woelert and Yates 2015). Tertiary study became the gateway to work, and for an increasing number of overseas students, the passport to migration. Students seeking degrees in business, commerce, finance, and management increased rapidly in number while programmes in economics and economic history and other less "occupation-focused" electives struggled for numbers (Forsyth 2014; Marginson and Considine 2000).

This new environment placed pressure on small economic history departments to earn their keep, while also making it difficult to seek the protection of larger disciplines. Economics was under its own pressure from declining student numbers and began removing compulsory economic history units (Millmow 2006). The trend towards mathematical theory and statistics within economics globally in the latter decades of the twentieth century helped to construct an identity for economists as "scientists", meaning they sought continual, linear improvements in practice and theory, and rarely looked to the past for insights (Docherty 2014; Thornton 2013; Blaug 2001). Economic historians were thus seen as a separate, but less scientific version of economics—and an easy group to jettison under pressure. Historians, who had once engaged in genuine dialogue with economic history, became preoccupied with their 'cultural turn', which left little room for an interest in the large, faceless structures of economic, social, and labour history (Forsyth and Loy-Wilson 2017; Curthoys 1994).

This combination of disciplinary and institutional isolation made economic history vulnerable, with each of the ten economic history departments transforming or closing between 1992 and 2003. Most academics from these departments were absorbed into economics or business/management groups. There was an almost complete removal of economic history from the taught curriculum, and economic historians had to adapt their teaching to core economics or management subjects. Although many economic historians were able to continue with their research areas and found external funding success through the ARC (Wright 2022), there was a steady decline of papers in leading economic history journals on Antipodean topics (Fig. 1).

In addition to the closure of departments, there was also a virtual cessation of progress on data collection and cliometric work. Many of the scholars involved in the first wave of Australian cliometrics either moved to greener pastures or were no longer active by the late-1990s or early-2000s.[3] By the end of the decade, these departures coupled with virtually no new hiring meant that there was much less

[3] Departures among the relatively small group of scholars who had published in the Top 5 international economic history journals in the 1980s and 1990s included the following. David Pope retired early from ANU due to ill health and died in 2003. Deborah Oxley, Andrew Seltzer, and John Singleton emigrated to the UK. Boris Schedvin, Stephen Nicholas, and Gary Magee became uni-

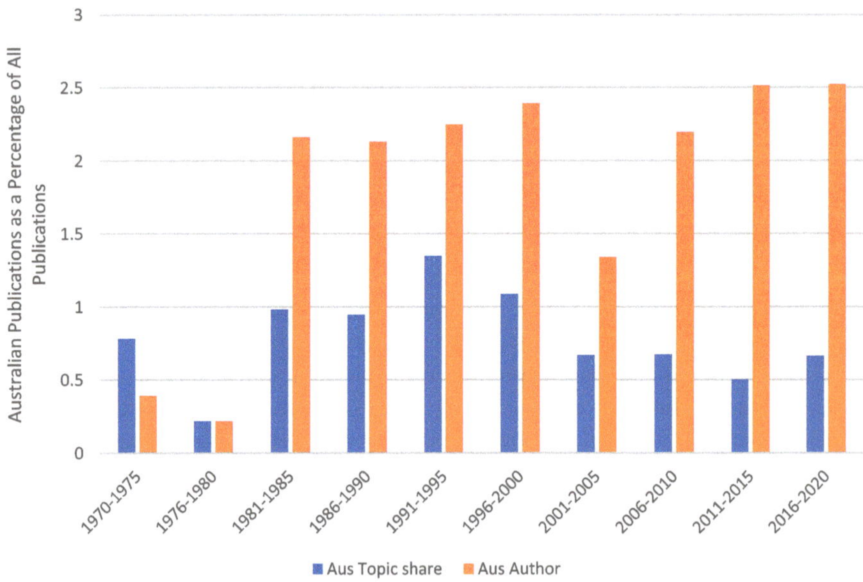

Fig. 1 Antipodean Share of Total Publications in Top 5 Economic History Journals. Sources: Fourie (2019); Authors' calculations

Antipodean cliometric work being produced than a decade or so earlier, as evidenced by a steep decline in publications in the Top 5 economic history journals (Fig. 1) and in the use of econometrics in the *AEHR* from the mid-1980s (Seltzer 2018). At the same time, there were significant advances in cliometric methodology overseas. Data collection became more efficient through automated extraction of primary sources. New computer technology, software, and statistical techniques made working with large datasets much easier and increased the sort of analyses that can be done with these datasets. A growing norm of requiring scholars to share data from published articles made it easier to replicate and extend others' research. In short, there has been a "big data" revolution in cliometrics, which has made it possible to address many important research questions far more rigorously than was previously possible. This big data revolution largely bypassed Australia until very recently.

Cliometric work in Australia has experienced a modest resurgence in the early twenty-first century. Economics departments at ANU, Melbourne, Monash, and Adelaide have hired a small number of quantitatively trained economic historians. The first meeting of the Australian Cliometrics Workshop was held in Adelaide in 2014, with the OzClio group growing in size and prominence over the past decade. However, the group of cliometricians in Australia is still relatively small. Moreover, most of the quantitative economic historians hired from overseas over the past two

versity administrators. Jonathan Pincus, Glen Withers, Peter Shergold, Rod Maddock left academia to take jobs in the public sector. Grant Fleming left academia for the private sector.

decades have mostly maintained their existing research agendas. Today most cliometric work being done *in* Australia is not being done *on* Australia. In the most recent Australian Cliometrics Workshop in 2021, only one of six papers had any Australian content. Similarly, the growth in quantitative research in the *AEHR* since 2005 has been more a result of increased numbers of Asian scholars publishing in the journal, rather than a resurgence of qualitative work on Australia (Seltzer 2018).

The changes in professional and institutional conditions since the 1990s described above have had several substantial influences on the field's research practices. Reflecting the field's integration with the history discipline and the mid-century character of the economics discipline, major monographs were once a mainstay of the profession. Most "god professors" from the era of free-standing departments built their reputations on the back of a small number of "big books". Scholars such as Noel and Syd Butlin, Coghlan, Ian McLean, Nicholas, Pincus, Shann, Schedvin, Sinclair, and Whitwell have written books that have amassed over 200 citations in Google Scholar.[4] However, since the closure of economic history departments and the absorption of academics into economics and business groups, these scholars have been incentivised to publish journal articles rather than monographs. Most of the small number of major monographs published since the 1990s were authored by scholars based in history departments or those who no longer faced institutional publication pressure after retirement.[5]

Since the end of the free-standing departments, economic historians have been increasingly required to publish in well-ranked, international journals such as the Top 5 and others ranked highly by the Australian Business Deans' Council (ABDC). Figure 1 shows that even as the number of papers published on Antipodean topics in the Top 5 declined from the mid-1990s, the number of papers with at least one Antipodean-based author increased slightly, albeit with a downwards blip in 2001–05. This seeming contradiction can be explained by the fact scholars coming to Australia are increasingly able to maintain their existing research agendas on other countries because it has become easier to work virtually with co-authors overseas and because of increased availability of machine-readable datasets and digital archival sources.[6]

---

[4]This list may be incomplete. Individuals who were on the periphery of the discipline are particularly likely to be missing.

[5]The case of Ian Mclean is perhaps particularly illustrative. Mclean was based in the Economics Department at Adelaide for most of his professional career (1974–2007). His prolific set of publications during this time largely reflects the values of economics departments, with the economic history Top 5 and other leading economics journals being frequent outlets for his work. Despite working under Noel Butlin at ANU, he did not write a research monograph and only co-edited one book during the time in which he was formally employed at Adelaide. After his retirement in 2007, his sole publication is his magisterial book *Why Australia Prospered* (2012).

[6]Maintaining an existing research agenda is an optimal strategy for junior academics facing publication pressures inasmuch as it eliminates fixed costs associated with "tooling up" in a new research area. It has also been suggested that European and North American research is seen more favourably by leading international journals (Wright 2022; Collyer et al. 2019; Connell 2007).

A final change to research strategy over the period has been an increasingly regional focus, exploiting geographic and increasingly social and economic links with colleagues in the Asia-Pacific region. In 2005, the annual conference was renamed the Asia-Pacific Economic and Business History Conference (APEBH). Two scholars of the Asian economies, Pierre van der Eng and Stephen Morgan, served as editors of the *AEHR* in the early 2000s. More recently, Yan Se, Li Dan, John Tang, and Chicheng Ma have served as co-editors. The editorial board has been expanded to include scholars with expertise on China, India, Japan, Korea, and Singapore. The journal's research internationalised greatly from the 1990s onwards. Special issues on international economic history and comparative research have increased fourfold. Pages on Asian topics have increased from 1% in the 1980s, to almost 20% in the 2000s (Morgan and Shanahan 2010; Wright 2022). In 2020 and 2021, a majority of papers (16 of 27) covered Asian topics. Asian articles have won the Coghlan Prize for best article in the *AEHR* 11 times since the prize was founded in 2006. In 2005, the journal's subtitle was changed to "an Asia-Pacific Journal", reflecting the reorientation towards regional connections. In 2023, the journal was renamed *Asia-Pacific Economic History Review*.

Challenges and Opportunities

Although economic history in Australia is much smaller and its position is more precarious now than it was 40 years ago, there is cause for guarded optimism with regard to institutional structure and research programme. The Economic History Society of Australia and Zealand and the *AEHR* have survived the closure of departments and adopted to the new environment. The *AEHR* has been published digitally, as well as in print, since 2007. In 2018, issues dating back to the 1950s were digitised and made available online. The journal's impact factor in 2022 was 0.66, the highest in its long history. There have been an increased number of viable submissions in recent years—largely on Asian topics—leading to an increase in the number of published articles and page count. Following the recent name change, the journal has had an unprecedented number of submissions, buoyed by an increase in Asian articles. The Society's conference has had stable attendance in recent years. After being dormant for more than a decade, the Butlin Prize for best PhD dissertation on an Australia/New Zealand topic has been revived and received a record number of applicants in 2020. The Society added two important new awards, the Asia-Pacific Prize for best PhD dissertation on an Asia-Pacific topic in 2017 and the E.O.G. Shann Award for lifetime contribution to the economic history of Australia and New Zealand in 2018.

The publication of the long-awaited, collaborative *Cambridge Economic History of Australia* (2015) coincided with a new edition of Barry Dyster and David Meredith's *Australia in the Global Economy* (2012), McLean's *Why Australia Prospered* (2013), and the establishment of the ANU Centre for Economic History (2012). The CEH now has over 60 research affiliates, publishes several newsletters each year, operates a working paper series, and provides a platform for old ANU Source Papers in Economic History from the free-standing departments' era. Interest in economic history—from economists seeking to understand the long-run trajectory of financial crises, global development, inequality, and wellbeing; and from historians interested in the contingency of global capitalism—has increased the legitimacy of the field in Australia and abroad.

Economics, history, and business/management departments at several major Australian universities have again begun hiring economic historians, and the number of appointments over the past 10 years has far outpaced the two previous decades. The group appointed to economics departments includes Laura Panza and John Tang at Melbourne (in 2013 and 2019), Martine Mariotti and Tim Hatton at ANU (in 2004 and 2008), Florian Ploeckl at Adelaide (in 2013), Sascha Becker at Monash (in 2019), and Jordi Vidal Robert at Sydney (in 2015). In 2023, Professor James Kai-Sing Kung was appointed to the University of Melbourne as the inaugural Griffin Chair in Economic History. New hiring in economics departments, in particular, means the number of quantitative economic historians in Australia is probably higher than it has ever been.

A final cause for optimism is that research on Australian (and New Zealand) has continued to have broad intellectual influence, measured in the now-standard manner of citations. We use Johan Fourie's bibliometric data on all articles published in "Top 5" economic history journals between 1997 and 2021 to examine this impact (Fourie 2019). We have extended Fourie's data backwards to 1970, to examine journal publications during the period of free-standing departments and also collected similar data for the *AEHR* between 1970 and 2021. The data contain a list of all original articles published in these journals, a breakdown of coverage by continent for each article, and the number of Google Scholar citations for each article.[7] Almost all articles on Antipodean topics published in Top 5 journals (40 of 43) and in the *AEHR* (5542 of 5562) have been cited at least once.[8] A large share of these, 69.8% and 37.2%, respectively, have been cited at least 10 times. Eight articles on Antipodean topics have been cited over 100 times. Figure 2 shows the median number of citations for articles published in each 5-year period since 1970. The median citations for Antipodean papers in Top 5 journals have exceeded 10 for all 5-year periods, except for the most recent period (which has had little time to accumulate citations). Although Fig. 2 also shows Antipodean research has been somewhat less cited than research on other geographic areas, but the gap between non-Antipodean papers (28) and Antipodean papers (19) in the Top 5 is relatively small. There is

[7] Fourie collected citation data in early 2022. Our extension to his dataset took place towards the end of 2022, implying that articles published prior to 1997 will have had a few additional months to be cited. However, we expect that the number of additional citations per article will typically be quite low because these articles had been published 26–52 years earlier.

[8] We are somewhat agnostic as to the classification of top economic history journals and also consider the "Top 3" following Seltzer and Hamermesh (2018), which excludes the two newer journals in the Top 5, *European Review* and *Cliometrica* and the *JEH* separately. We report statistics for the Top 5 in this chapter, but the results are broadly similar for the Top 3 and the *JEH*.

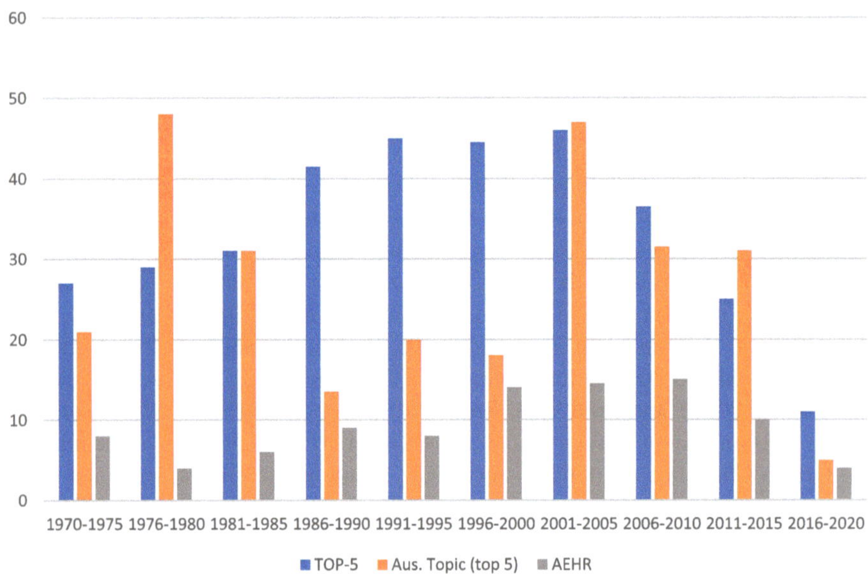

Fig. 2 Median Citations of Antipodean Economic History Papers. Sources: Fourie (2019); Authors' calculations

considerable overlap between the distribution of citations, with 37.2% of Antipodean papers in the Top 5 in the top half of the citation distribution for all papers published in these journals.

Although the Society and Journal are generally strong, they continue to face challenges. The reduction in personnel since the closure of departments has reduced the volume of economic history research on Australian and New Zealand topics. Leadership of the Society and the journal will also likely be a major challenge over the next decade. In the past, the main leadership roles have normally been filled by senior economic historians in Associate Professor or Professorial positions. During the era of free-standing departments, there was a steady stream of hiring and thus there were always suitable people available for these important leadership positions. With the cessation of hiring and the closure of departments, the number of suitable scholars has shrunk and there has effectively been a "missing generation" of economic historians. Since 1997, the Society and Journal have thrived only because a small number of people have been willing to take long turns in these roles.[9] Finding new people from the generation who were first hired after the closure of the free-standing departments to take on these roles will be essential for the continued survival and success of these institutions.

[9] Simon Ville, Pierre van der Eng, Martin Shanahan, Stephen Morgan, and Andrew Seltzer have all spent at least 5 years as editor of the *AEHR* since 1997. Ville, Shanahan, and Lionel Frost have all had lengthy tenures as President of the Society.

The incentives created by the institutional structures of modern Australian universities also present challenges for the Society and the Journal. Hiring, tenure, and promotion in all three parent disciplines are governed by a strong, well-defined hierarchy of journals and book publishers. Journal rankings are based on relative citation rates, which are lower for regional and interdisciplinary journals (Rafols et al. 2012). Although top international economic and business history journals are generally well-recognised in ABDC rankings, the *AEHR* is ranked below metropole outlets due to lower circulation and citations (Collyer et al. 2019).[10] Figure 2 shows that papers in the *AEHR* (median citations of 7) are considerably less influential than those in the Top 5. While the *AEHR* is ranked well for the history discipline and has a higher impact factor than key national history journals, the discipline values books over journal articles. Consequently, departments in all three parent disciplines give relatively little credit for publishing in the *AEHR* and, thus, attracting papers from junior scholars has been difficult. Encouragingly, in recent years, the journal has begun to overcome these barriers. Several younger scholars have engaged with the *AEHR* as associate editors, members of the editorial board, or referees. For the first time in three decades, there has been a discernible increase in the number of submissions from young, Australian-based scholars.

Although hiring of economic historians has resumed in the parent disciplines, institutional separation has resulted in fragmentation between the field's various "streams". The over the past decade or so, there is little collaboration or collective action between the different groups, with each negotiating space and legitimacy with their respective parent disciplines to the detriment of economic history professional structures. The OzClio group and the ANU Centre for Economic History have created institutional links to the economics discipline. The "new histories of capitalism" has provided a focus for Australian historians working on Australian economic history topics, adding an Antipodean voice and a global and comparative frame to the US movement of the same name (Forsyth and Loy-Wilson 2017; Huf et al. 2020; Huf and Sluga 2019). In business schools, many former labour historians and management scholars have engaged with AAHANZBS as well as EHSANZ in their work on firm and industry structure, and the history of work, technology, and education (Patmore and Balnave 2018; Wright 2019; Bishop 2015; Bailey 2020).

Although the citations of Antipodean research are generally a cause for optimism, there remain challenges. Perhaps the biggest challenge pertains to the well-documented pattern of "blockbusters" in academic citations, e.g. that the distribution is highly right-skewed, with average and particularly maximum citations dominated by a handful of rare articles that are seen as pathbreaking (Brouthers et al. 2012; Hamermesh 2018). As can be seen in Fig. 2, the median number of citations for Antipodean papers in the Top 5 is only slightly lower than for all articles in these journals. However, the relatively small market for Antipodean research means that

[10] In the initial ABDC rankings in 2007, the *AEHR* received an "A" ranking. This was downgraded to a "B" in 2013. Economics departments, particularly top ranked departments such as those in the sandstone universities, make a clear distinction between these rankings, valuing publications in B-rated journals much less than those in A-rated journals.

there is a much larger gap at the mean and particularly the maximum number of citations. The most-cited Antipodean article (Schedvin 1990) ranks in the top 3% of articles published in the Top 5 journals with 248 citations, but only has 3.6% of the number of citations as the most cited article (North and Weingast 1989). There are seven papers published in the Top 5 with over 1000 citations, plus an additional 140 papers with more citations than Schedvin (1990). To the extent that journal editors consider the impact of related work when making decisions about whether to accept papers, the absence of Antipodean "blockbusters" will make it harder for work on Antipodean topics to be accepted into top journals.

The Future of Cliometric Research

Despite the continued low number of scholars undertaking quantitative research on Australia, there is cause for guarded optimism about the future of cliometric work. The recent wave of hiring by economics departments has resulted in a larger cliometrics group based in Australia than ever before, although most of these scholars do not work on Australian topics. "Big data" is slowly starting to appear in Australian research.

The original source material for Australia is, in general, excellent. The planned nature of Australian settlement meant that from the very beginning, colonial administrators compiled comprehensive and high-quality data. These records are easy to access at the National and State libraries and archives and are largely comparable to, and in some ways better than, similar original source materials for the USA and UK. Many of these sources are now freely available online, albeit as pdf images rather than extracted machine-readable files.

Official records which have been used by economic historians include convict ships' musters, the *Colonial Blue Books*; the *Colonial Year Books* (and later *State Year Books*); the *Commonwealth Year Books*; the *Report of the Chief Inspector of Factories, Work-Rooms, and Shops* (Victoria); the *Australasian Insurance and Banking Record*; service records of World War I veterans in the Australian Imperial Forces; and many others. In recent years, these records have been used to examine topics such as the nature of convict labour in Australia (Nicholas 1988), the health consequences of Australian industrialisation (Cranfield and Inwood 2015), the impact of minimum wages on Australian labour markets (Seltzer and Borland 2018), living standards (Panza and Williamson 2020), levels of inequality prior to Federation (Panza and Williamson 2021), and the evolution of tariff policy (Lloyd 2008, 2017).

In addition to government records, Australia possesses many corporate records with excellent quantitative data. Banking records are high quality and have been widely utilised, with the enduring dominance of large banks contributing to arguably the most complete set of banking statistics in the world. Banking records have been used by Syd Butlin and collaborators to compile monetary and banking statistics (Butlin et al. 1971; Butlin 1986) and by Andrew Seltzer and collaborators to examine personnel practices (Seltzer and Merrett 2000; Seltzer and Simons 2001). Some other examples of corporate data from Australian archives that have been used by economic historians include the mining industry (Pottenger and Leigh 2016) and manufacturing (Fahey and Sammartino 2013). The availability of high-quality corporate archival data has also led to a strong research group in business history which has examined, amongst other industries, banking (Butlin 1961; Merrett 1985) and the pastoral sector (Ville 2000). Fleming et al. (2004) provide a broad overview of the evolution of Australian corporate leadership, and Terwiel et al. (1998) provide a comprehensive description of corporate archival sources in Australia.

Although Australia has a wealth of original source materials, it lags behind other countries in the collection and dissemination of "big data". In many countries, research grants require data be made publicly available, and many leading publications now make it easy for researchers to upload and access data collected by other researchers. In contrast, much Australian data is not easily accessible, with historical statistics either undigitised or only digitised as pdf photos, requiring researchers to collect or extract data before undertaking analysis. This presents a particularly serious barrier for PhD students and junior academics, who often lack the funding to prepare data infrastructure, and need to publish quickly to establish themselves in the profession. It also presents a barrier to research replication and extension, with this only being possible for a limited number of topics. This places Australian researchers at a substantial disadvantage relative to their peers overseas and in other fields of study who can easily download existing datasets. Unleashing the potential of the excellent Australian source materials described above will require increased data collection and dissemination.

"Big data" poses particular challenges. From the 1980s, research overseas has undergone a big data "revolution", boosted by improvements in collection and analysis of data. The result has been the collection of ever-larger datasets, enabling increasingly advanced analyses. Australia has been slow to this revolution, but recently Australian economic historians have started to produce large datasets. In the late-1990s, Andrew Seltzer led the collection of data covering employment records and branch deposits, advances, staff numbers, and profits at the Union Bank of Australia from the mid-nineteenth through mid-twentieth centuries (Seltzer and Merrett 2000; Seltzer and Simons 2001). Andre Sammartino collected data covering a large near-random sample of employment records of the Victorian Railways (Sammartino 2002; Sammartino and Seltzer 2011). Kris Inwood and co-authors have used height dataset of over 20,000 recruits into the First Australian Imperial Force, 1914–1920 and a smaller sample of British born recruits serving in the Australian forces during the Anglo-Boer War (Cranfield and Inwood 2015; Fourie et al. 2020). The most ambitious Australian big data project so far is the *Tasmanian Historical Dataset*, a longitudinal dataset which, when completed, will link information from convict records; Colonial courts; censuses and musters; migration records; births, deaths and marriages; property and financial records; hospital and pauper records; military records; and weather records for a large (though non-random) share of the Tasmanian population between 1803 and 1928 (Cowley et al.

2023). The *THD* includes 1,666,157 observations across all record groups and is (by far) the largest Australian historical dataset produced to date.

Finally, the almost complete absence of Australian *Census* microdata presents a challenge to cliometricians. With the exception of early colonial Tasmania, the original returns of the *Australian Census* containing individual microdata have been destroyed in order to ensure permanent confidentiality. Since 1981, there have been official releases of anonymised samples of *Census* microdata, comparable to samples released by the USA and UK. While these samples useful for some research questions, they are limited in scope and content and, of course, do not date back to before 1981. The anonymisation of these records also limits the ways in which they can be used. One of the most important methodological developments in economic history overseas since the 1990s has been the linkage of records across censuses and from the censuses to external data sources in order to create panel datasets. Linked records have been used to examine important topics in economic history such as migration, development of labour markets, and long-term health outcomes in a manner than was not previously possible (Long and Ferrie 2013; Abramitzky et al. 2012). Because of the absence of original *Census* records, there been very few historical panel datasets constructed for Australia.

New Directions

Many of the most important issues being addressed by scholars today were also of concern to previous generations. In some sense, history does not change, rather it is scholarly interests and the available set of materials and analytical tools used to explain history that have evolved. Economic historians frequently revisit old topics as new archival sources, datasets, theoretical approaches, and statistical techniques become available. In some cases, this means directly revisiting old questions. In other cases, it means new approaches to address previously unanswerable questions. Looking overseas to the USA and UK, the broad topics of interest today are not dissimilar to those of 20 or 40 years ago. For example, the first generation of cliometricians were aware of the importance of migration and migration policy to American economic growth (Neal and Uselding 1972). A generation later, the topic of immigration remained central to US economic history but both data and methodology had advanced (see, e.g., Hatton and Williamson 1998). More recent examinations of American migration have been able to take advantage of big data and the associated techniques, for example, linking records of migrants entering the USA at Ellis Island to subsequent *US Census* records to examine longer-term outcomes (see Abramitzky and Boustan 2017 for a summary).

Australian scholarship has to an extent been characterised by the same pattern. Peter Lloyd's work developing a database of Australian tariffs (Lloyd 2008, 2017) and Seltzer's work building a database of Victorian minimum wages (Seltzer 2018) follow much earlier work by scholars who examined the same topics, but without the benefit of computer technology or statistical methodology capable of handling large amounts of data (Clark 1908 and Reeves 1899 on tariffs; Hammond 1913, 1915; Rankin 1916; Webb 1912 on minimum wages). The difference between Australia and North America is the pace at which this is occurring. Scholars "stand on the shoulders of giants"—in other words, work being done today routinely builds on the work of earlier generations. Even during the era of free-standing departments, Australia had fewer economic historians than the USA or UK and far fewer quantitative economic historians. Since the 1990s, this gap has grown ever larger. Australia simply has fewer giant shoulders to stand on and thus there is a bigger gap between the research that is possible given available data and methodology and the research that has already been done. This suggests that virtually any important topic in Australian economic history will have several important unresolved questions and renders our list of potential research directions outlined below as necessarily incomplete.

Comparative and Regional Economic History

The geographic broadening of Australian economic history in the 2000s was specifically focussed on developing comparative research. Comparative research with the USA and UK (Panza and Williamson 2019; McLean 2013; Gregory and Butlin 1988; Frost 1991, 2020) and Argentina (Duncan and Fogarty 1984; Dingle and Merrett 1985; McLean 2006) has been followed by a broader settler economy framing, such as Lloyd et al. (2013), which includes chapters examining Uruguay, the UK, Sweden, Switzerland, Finland, Spain, France, the USA, Canada, South Africa, and Israel. There is still much to say about Australia as a settler economy, with comparisons based on political institutions, trade and industry structures, and climate, natural resources, and geography important themes for the future.

Connections with Asian and regional research are important to the field's future. The field's Asian connections expanded in the 2000s, and the editorial team at the journal has included a growing number of Asian scholars over time. Special issues on comparative or Asia-Pacific economic history have established the *AEHR* as a key regional (rather than national) outlet. The history of capitalism movement also presents opportunities for regional and comparative research. The movement originated and is still largely based in the USA, so much of the Australian research has been framed with this particular comparison in mind. As with other work in the field, we see regional research (similar to Lionel Frost's "Pacific Rim" frame, see Jones et al. 1993) and comparative research with Asia as a key future research direction.

Inequality

Since Atkinson and Piketty (2007) and Piketty (2014) revived interest in income and wealth inequality, several scholars have returned to this topic, often with new datasets and techniques (Atkinson and Leigh 2007). High-quality aggregated government data has existed in Australia for most of its European history. Unfortunately access to historical individual census data or personal tax returns is not possible in Australia, as these records were consciously destroyed for privacy reasons. This means that studies such as Atkinson and Jenkins (2020) which use tax data are not replicable for Australia and scholars need alternative data to examine these research questions. Clark et al. (2020) have used electoral roles and lists of the eighteenth-century Tasmanian convicts linked to graduation lists from the University of Sydney and the University of Melbourne to examine the extent of social mobility of individuals with rare surnames in Australia and the UK. Other records await transcription, digitisation, and analysis. For example, state-based probate records are slowly being digitised, as are individual wills. Future research that replicates, for example, the recent UK probate-based study by Cummins (2021) awaits.

Labour

There is a long tradition of non-cliometric research on the history of labour in Australia, much of which is related to the broad interests of economic historians. This research has a dedicated outlet, the journal *Labour History*, which is almost as old as the *AEHR*. There is also a limited amount of cliometric work on labour markets, for example, David Pope and Glen Withers' work on migration (Pope 1976; Withers and Pope 1985, 1993) and Seltzer's work on internal labour markets and minimum wages (Seltzer and Merrett 2000; Seltzer and Simons 2001; Seltzer and Borland 2018). What is largely missing from the academic landscape is quantitative work exploiting untapped employment records in business archives, union membership records, and even public records such as the *Colonial Blue Books*. Another important, and as far as we are aware under-addressed, question is the relative importance of basic supply/demand factors and Australia's unique system of protective labour legislation in achieving the comparatively favourable living and working conditions of the working and semi-skilled classes.

Trade and International Finance

Australia's trade with the rest of the world has long been a subject of study by Australian (and other) economic historians (Clark 1908; Reeves 1899). From first European settlement, Australia's position as a frontier economy heavily dependent on overseas linkages saw the production of detailed records of the flow of goods, services, and capital. Confounding later interpretation of these records, however, was the unrecorded trade between colonies and then states; a problem that continues to complicate historical analysis. Trade and tariffs have been cited as important drivers of growth, particularly in the context of the "infant industry" theory (Corden 1997). Recent work has only just begun to exploit the rich colonial records, for example, Peter Lloyd's work on tariffs (Lloyd 2008, 2017) and Kilian Rieder and Leonhard Sauerhammer's work looking at tariffs and growth, using town-level data from "free trade" New South Wales and "protectionist" Victoria (Rieder and Sauerhammer 2021). Future work based on tracing the detailed flow of goods, services, capital, and people awaits the digitisation and matching of individual colonies' detailed blue books, government records, and official files sent to the UK pre-Federation. The brake on this work is the transfer of the extensive official records from their dispersed, paper-based media to electronic systems.

Environment

Australian environmental history is another area awaiting significant contributions by economic historians, While this field of research has been expanding significantly since the 1980s, the recent input of economic historians has been modest relative to the contributions by geographers, biologists, historians, and other scientists both social and physical (Isenberg 2014; Griffiths 2015). This is despite early work on the interaction between humans, economics, and the environment (Hancock 1972; Blainey 1975, 1980; and Bolton 1981 among others). The past quarter century has seen a considerable increase in the scientific and social data necessary to unpick some of the complex interactions between the environment, markets, and humans. These data, integrated with an economic historian's perspective, remain to be explored.

Conclusion

If the growth of Australian economic history could be represented by the life-cycle of a classic, but relatively rare native species—the snow gum (*Eucalyptus pauciflora*)—then this species reached its zenith in Australia in the mid-twentieth century. Thereafter, corporatisation and restructuring of Australian Universities acted much like the nation's endemic bushfires, virtually burning out the majority of the discipline. After the bushfires passed through the previously flourishing gum trees remain as skeletons—their leaves gone and their trunks blackened. With time and some rain, however, shoots emerge from the lower parts of the tree, beginning anew the cycle of regrowth and new life.

Australian economic history and Australian economic historians, while not completely burned by past events, experienced severe decline from the late-1980s through the early-2000s. All free-standing departments were closed, hiring virtually ceased, and many of the leading scholars either passed away or headed for new challenges outside the discipline. The analogy of the blackened tree grove with a few survivors seems appropriate to the landscape of the discipline two decades ago. In recent years, new academic shoots are slowly emerging in a sparse landscape. The shape of a new tree will differ from the old; scholars have dispersed into the disciplines of history, economics, and business/management. However, its shoots build on well-established and deep roots, as the core institutional structures of the discipline (the Society and Journal) remain strong and new institutions have developed (OZClio and the CEH).

Bibliography

Abramitzky, R., and L. Boustan. 2017. Immigration in American economic history. *Journal of Economic Literature* 55 (4): 1311–1345.

Abramitzky, R., L. Boustan, and K. Eriksson. 2012. Europe's tired, poor, huddled masses: Self-selection and economic outcomes in the age of mass migration. *American Economic Review* 102 (5): 1832–1856.

Anderson, D., and E. Eaton. 1982. Part 1: Post-war reconstruction and expansion 1940 - 1965. *Higher Education Research and Development* 1 (1): 8–93.

Anon. 1959. A summing up of the first Australian conference on business history. *Business History and Archives* 1 (5): 21–23.

Anon [McCarty, J. W.] 1962. Editorial. *Bulletin of the Archives of Australia* 2:8.

Anon [McCarty, J. W. and C. B. Schedvin] 1966. Australian Economic History Review. *Business History and Archives* 6:203–204.

Atkinson, A. B., and S. P. Jenkins. 2020. A different perspective on UK income inequality. *Review of Income and Wealth* 66 (2): 253–266.

Atkinson, A. B., and A. Leigh. 2007. The distribution of top incomes in Australia. In *Top Incomes over the Twentieth Century: A Contrast Between Continental European and English-Speaking Countries*, eds. A. B. Atkinson and T. Piketty, 309–332. Oxford: Oxford University Press.

Atkinson, A. B., and T. Piketty, eds. 2007. *Top Incomes over the Twentieth Century. A Contrast Between Continental Europe and English-Speaking Countries*. Oxford: Oxford University Press.

Bailey, M. 2020. *Managing the Marketplace: Reinventing Shopping Centres in Post-war Australia*. Oxford and New York: Routledge.

Bambrick, S. 1968. Indexes of Australian import prices, 1900 to 1927-28. *Australian Economic History Review* 8 (1): 62–70.

Barnard, A. 1958. *The Australian Wool Market, 1840-1900*. Melbourne: Melbourne University Press.

Birch, A. 1962. The study of business history in Australia. *Bulletin of the Business Archives Council of Australia* 2 (1): 86–87.

Bishop, C. 2015. *Minding Her Own Business: Colonial Businesswomen in Sydney*. Sydney: NewSouth Publishing.

Blainey, G. 1954. *The Peaks of Lyell*. Melbourne: Melbourne University Press.

Blainey, G. 1959. The future of Australian business history: A writer's view. *Bulletin of the Business Archives Council of Australia* 1 (5): 12–15.

Blainey, G. 1975. *Triumph of the Nomads: A History of Ancient Australia*. Melbourne: Macmillan.

Blainey, G. 1980. *A Land Half Won*. Melbourne: Macmillan.

Blaug, M. 2001. No history of ideas, please, we're economists. *Journal of Economic Perspectives* 15 (1): 145–164.

Boadle, D. 1995. Origins and development of the NSW Regional Depositories System. *Archives and Manuscripts* 23 (2): 244–274.

Boldizzoni, F. 2011. *The Poverty of Clio: Resurrecting Economic History*. Princeton: Princeton University Press.

Boldizzoni F and Hudson P. 2015. *Routledge handbook of global economic history*. London: Routledge

Bolton, G. 1981. *Spoils and Spoilers*. Sydney: George Allen & Unwin.

Boot, H. M. 1997a. Special report: Teaching economic history at Australian universities. *Australian Economic History Review* 37 (2): 158–164.

Boot, H. M. 1997b. Some developments in teaching practice in the Department of Economic History at the Australian National University. *Australian Economic History Review* 37 (3): 282–297.

Booth, A. L., and H. J. Kee. 2011. A long-run view of the university gender gap in Australia. *Australian Economic History Review* 51 (3): 254–276.

Brouthers, K., R. Mudambi, and D. Reeb. 2012. The blockbuster hypothesis: Influencing the boundaries of knowledge. *Scientometrics* 90:959–982.

Butlin, S. J. 1953. *Foundations of the Australian Monetary System 1788-1851*. Melbourne: Melbourne University Press.

Butlin, S. J. 1961. *Australia and New Zealand Bank*. Croydon: Longmans.

Butlin, N. G. 1962. *Australian Domestic Product, Investment and Foreign Borrowing 1861 - 1938/9*. London: Cambridge University Press.

Butlin, N. G. 1964. *Investment in Australian Economic Development, 1861 - 1900*. London: Cambridge University Press.

Butlin, S. J. 1986. *The Australian Monetary System 1851-1914*. Sydney: Ambassador Press.

Butlin, N. G. 1994. *Economics and the Dreamtime: A Hypothetical History*. Sydney: Cambridge University Press.

Butlin, S. J., A. R. Hall, and R. C. White. 1971. *Australian Banking and Monetary Statistics, 1817-1945*. Sydney: Reserve Bank of Australia.

Cappie, F., and A. Weber. 1985. *A Monetary History of the United Kingdom, 1870–1982*. London: George Allen & Unwin.

Clark, V. S. 1908. Australian economic problems: II. the tariff. *Quarterly Journal of Economics* 22 (4): 576–601.

Clark, G., A. Leigh, and M. Pottenger. 2020. Frontiers of mobility: Was Australia 1870–2017 a more socially mobile society than England? *Explorations in Economic History* 76.

Clarkson, L. A. 1989. The transformation of Australian economic and social history. *Australian Economic History Review* 29 (2): 79–82.

Coghlan, T. A. 1890. *A Statistical Account of the Seven Colonies of Australasia 1895-6*, sixth issue. Sydney: Government Printer.

Coghlan, T. A. 1891. *The Wealth of Australasia*. Sydney: Government Printer.

Coghlan, T. A. 1918. *Labour and Industry in Australia*. London: Oxford University Press.

Coleman, W. 2015. The historiography of Australian economic history. In *The Cambridge Economic History of Australia*, ed. S. Ville and G. Withers, 11–28. Melbourne: Cambridge University Press.

Collyer, F., R. Connell, J. Maia, et al. 2019. *Knowledge and Global Power: Making New Sciences in the South*. Johannesburg, SA: Wits University Press.

Connell R. 2007. *Southern theory: The global dynamics of knowledge in social science*. Allen & Unwin

Connell, R. 2019. *The Good University: What Universities Actually do and why its Time for Radical Change*. London: Zed Books Ltd.

Conrad, A., and J. Meyer. 1958. The economics of slavery in the Ante Bellum South. *Journal of Political Economy* 66 (2): 95–130.

Cook, E. 2017. *The Pricing of Progress: Economic Indicators and the Capitalization of American Life*. Cambridge, MA: Harvard University Press.
Corden, W. M. 1997. *Trade Policy and Economic Welfare*. 2nd ed. Oxford: Clarendon Press.
Cowley, T., L. Frost, K. Inwood, R. Kippen, H. Maxwell-Stewart, M. Schwarz, J. Shepherd, R. Tuffin, M. Williams, J. Wilson, and P. Wilson. 2023. Reconstructing a Longitudinal Dataset for Tasmania. In *Sowing: The Construction of Historical Longitudinal Population Databases*, eds. Kees Mandemakers George Alter Hélène Vézina Paul Puschmann. Nijmegen: Radboud University Press.
Cranfield, J., and K. Inwood. 2015. A tale of two armies: Comparative growth in the mirror of the First World War. *Australian Economic History Review* 55 (2): 212–233.
Cruise, H. 1975. The economic historian and the growth debate. *Australian Economic History Review* 15 (2): 83–106.
Cummins, N. 2021. Where is the middle class? Evidence from 60 million English death and probate records, 1892-1992. *Journal of Economic History* 81 (2): 359–404.
Curthoys, A. 1994. Labour history and cultural studies. *Labour History* 67:12–22.
Dick, H. 2007. Big questions in Australian economic history: From the outside looking in. *Australian Economic History Review* 47 (3): 316–322.
Dingle, A. E., and D. T. Merrett. 1985. *Argentina and Australia: Essays in Comparative Economic Development*. Clayton: Economic History Society of Australia and New Zealand.
Docherty, P. 2014. The role of economic history and the history of economic thought in macroeconomics and finance courses after the Global Financial Crisis. *Australasian Journal of Economics Education* 11 (2): 1–24.
Dowie, J. A. 1967. As if or not as if: The economic historian as Hamlet. *Australian Economic History Review* 7 (1): 69–85.
Dowie, J. 1972. Economic history: Time for some anti–growth. *Australian Economic History Review* 12 (2): 161–173.
Duncan, T., and J. Fogarty. 1984. *Australia and Argentina: On Parallel Paths*. Melbourne: Melbourne University Press.
Dyster, B., and D. Meredith. 2012. *Australia in the Global Economy: Continuity and Change*. Cambridge: Cambridge University Press.
Fahey, C., and A. Sammartino. 2013. Work and wages at a Melbourne factory, the Guest Biscuit works 1870–1921. *Australian Economic History Review* 53 (1): 22–46.
Fitzpatrick, B. C. 1939. *British Imperialism and Australia, 1783- 1823*. London: Allen & Unwin.
Fitzpatrick, B. C. 1941. *The British Empire in Australia*. Melbourne: Melbourne University Press, Macmillan.
Fleming, G., D. Merrett, and S. Ville. 2004. *The Big End of Town: Business and Corporate Leadership in the Twentieth Century*. Port Melbourne, VIC: Cambridge University Press.
Forster, C. 1964. *Industrial Development in Australia 1920-1930*. Canberra: ANU Press.
Forster, C., ed. 1970. *Australian Economic Development in the Twentieth Century*. Sydney: Australasian Publishing Company.
Forsyth, H. 2014. *A History of the Modern Australian University*. Sydney: University of New South Wales Press.
Forsyth, H., and S. Loy-Wilson. 2017. Seeking a new materialism in Australian history. *Australian Historical Studies* 48 (1): 169–188.
Fourie, J. 2019. Who writes African economic history? *Economic History of Developing Regions* 34 (2): 111–131.
Fourie, J., K. Inwood, and M. Mariotti. 2020. Military technology and sample selection bias. *Social Science History* 44 (3): 485–500.
Frost, L. 1991. *The New Urban Frontier: Urbanisation and City-Building in Australasia and the American West*. Sydney: UNSW Press.
Frost, L. 2020. Water technology and the urban environment: Water, sewerage, and disease in San Francisco and Melbourne before 1920. *Journal of Urban History* 46 (1): 15–32.

Gregory, R. G., and N. G. Butlin. 1988. *Recovery from the Depression: Australia and the World Economy in the 1930s*. Cambridge: Cambridge University Press.
Grief, A. 1989. Reputation and coalitions in medieval trade: Evidence on the Maghribi traders. *Journal of Economic History* 49 (4): 857–882.
Griffiths, T. 2015. Environmental history Australian style. *Australian Historical Studies* 46 (2): 157–173.
Hamermesh, D. S. 2018. Citations in economics: Measurement, uses, and impacts. *Journal of Economic Literature* 56 (1): 115–156.
Hammond, M. B. 1913. Judicial interpretation of the minimum wage in Australia. *American Economic Review* 3 (2): 259–286.
Hammond, M. B. 1915. Wages boards in Australia: IV. Social and economic results of wages boards. *Quarterly Journal of Economics* 29 (3): 563–630.
Hancock, W. K. 1930. *Australia*. London: Jacaranda Brisbane.
Hancock, W. K. 1972. *Discovering Monaro*. Cambridge: Cambridge University Press.
Hartwell, R. M. 1958. The use of business history. *Business Archives and History* 1 (4): 20–22.
Hatton, T. J., and J. G. Williamson. 1998. *The Age of Mass Migration: Causes and Economic Impact*. New York: Oxford University Press.
Hudson P. 2015. Economic history in Britain: The 'first industrial nation'. In *Routledge handbook of global economic history*, eds. Boldizzoni F. and Hudson P, 17-34. London: Routledge
Huf, B. 2018. *Making Things Economic: Theory and Government in New South Wales, 1788-1863*. Canberra: Australian National University.
Huf, B., and G. Sluga. 2019. 'New' histories of (Australian) capitalism. *Australian Historical Studies* 50 (4): 405–417.
Huf, B., Y. Rees, M. Beggs, et al. 2020. Capitalism in Australia: New histories for a reimagined future. *Thesis Eleven* 160 (1):
Hughes, H. 1963. Business history or the history of business? *Business Archives and History* 3 (1): 1–19.
Inwood, K., R. Kippen, H. Maxwell-Stewart, and R. Steckel. 2020. The short and the tall: Comparing stature and socioeconomic status for male prison and military populations. *Social Science History* 44 (3): 463–483.
Isenberg, A. C. 2014. Introduction: A new environmental history. In *The Oxford Handbook of Environmental History*, ed. A. C. Isenberg, 1–22. Oxford: Oxford University Press.
Jackson, R. V. 1977. *Australian Economic Development in the Nineteenth Century*. Canberra: ANU Press.
Jones, E., L. Frost, and C. White. 1993. *Coming Full Circle: An Economic History of the Pacific Rim*. New York: Taylor & Francis Inc.
Keating, M. 1967. The Australian workforce and employment 1910-1960. *Australian Economic History Review* 7 (2): 150–173.
Lamoreaux N. 2015. The future of economic history must be interdisciplinary. *The Journal of Economic History* 75 (4): 1251–1257
Lloyd, C. 1997. Can economic history be the core of social science? Why the discipline must open and integrate to ensure the survival of long-run economic analysis. *Australian Economic History Review* 37 (3): 256–266.
Lloyd, P. J. 2008. 100 years of tariff protection in Australia. *Australian Economic History Review* 48 (2): 99–145.
Lloyd, C. 2015. Analytical frameworks of Australia's economic history. In *Cambridge Economic History of Australia*, ed. S. Ville and G. Withers, 52–69. Melbourne: Cambridge University Press.
Lloyd, P. J. 2017. The first 100 years of tariffs in Australia: The colonies. *Australian Economic History Review* 57 (3): 316–344.
Lloyd, C., J. Metzer, and R. Sutch. 2013. *Settler Economies in World History*. Leiden: Brill.
Long, J., and J. Ferrie. 2013. Intergenerational occupational mobility in Great Britain and the United States since 1850. *American Economic Review* 103 (4): 1109–1137.

Lyons J, Cain L and Williamson S. 2008. *Reflections on the cliometrics revolution: Conversations with economic historians*. New York: Routledge.

Macintyre, S. 2010. *The Poor Relation*. Melbourne: Melbourne University Press.

Macintyre, S., A. Brett, and G. Croucher. 2017. *No End of a Lesson: Australia's Unified National System of Higher Education*. Melbourne: Melbourne University Press.

Maddock, R., and I. W. McLean. 1987. *The Australian Economy in the Long Run*. Cambridge: Cambridge University Press.

Madsen, J. B., J. B. Ang, and R. Banerjee. 2010. Four centuries of British economic growth: The roles of technology and population. *Journal of Economic Growth* 15 (4): 263–290.

Marginson, S., and M. Considine. 2000. *The Enterprise University: Power, Governance and Reinvention in Australia*. Cambridge: Cambridge University Press.

Mariotti, M. 2012. Estimating the substitutability of African and white workers in South African manufacturing, 1950–1985. *Economic History of Developing Regions* 27 (2): 47–60.

McCloskey, D. N. 1978. The achievements of the cliometric school. *The Journal of Economic History* 38 (1): 13–28.

McLean, I. W. 1973. Growth and technological change in agriculture: Victoria 1870-1910. *Economic Record* 49 (128): 560–574.

McLean, I. W. 2006. Recovery from depression: Australia in an Argentine mirror 1895-1913. *Australian Economic History Review* 46 (3): 215–241.

McLean, I. W. 2013. *Why Australia Prospered: The Shifting Sources of Economic Growth*. Princeton, NJ: Princeton University Press.

McLean, I. W., and J. J. Pincus. 1983. Did Australian living standards stagnate between 1890 and 1940? *The Journal of Economic History* 43 (1): 193–202.

McLean, I. W., and M. P. Shanahan. 2007. Australasian economic history: Research challenges and big questions. *Australian Economic History Review* 47 (3): 300–315.

Meredith, D., and D. Oxley. 2015. The rise and fall of Australian economic history. In *Routledge Handbook of Global Economic History*, ed. Francesco Boldizzoni and Pat Hudson, 73–94. London: Routledge.

Merrett, D. 1985. *ANZ Bank: A History of the Australia New Zealand Banking Group and its Constituents*. Sydney: Allen & Unwin.

Millmow, A. 2006. Trends in economic degree enrolments within Australia 1990–2004. *Australasian Journal of Economics Education* 3 (1): 111–124.

Mitchell, B. R. 1988. *British Historical Statistics*. Cambridge: Cambridge University Press.

Morgan, S., and M. Shanahan. 2010. The supply of economic history in Australasia: The *Australian Economic History Review* at 50. *Australian Economic History Review* 50 (3): 217–239.

Neal, L., and P. Uselding. 1972. Immigration, a neglected source of American economic growth: 1790 to 1912. *Oxford Economic Papers* 24 (1): 68–88.

Nicholas, S., ed. 1988. *Convict Workers: Reinterpreting Australia's Past*. Melbourne: Cambridge University Press.

Nicholas, S. 1997. The future of economic history in Australia. *Australian Economic History Review* 37 (3): 267–274.

North, D., and B. Weingast. 1989. Constitutions and commitment: The evolution of institutions governing public choice in seventeenth-century England. *Journal of Economic History* 49 (4): 803–832.

Panza, L. 2014. De-industrialization and re-industrialization in the Middle East: Reflections on the cotton industry in Egypt and in the Izmir region. *The Economic History Review* 67 (1): 146–169.

Panza L and Williamson JG. 2019. Australian squatters, convicts, and capitalists: dividing up a fast-growing frontier pie, 1821–71. *The Economic History Review* 72 (2): 568–594.

Panza, L., and J. Williamson. 2020. Living costs and living standards: Australian development 1820-1870. *European Review of Economic History* 24 (1): 80–97.

Panza, L., and J. Williamson. 2021. Always egalitarian? Australian earnings inequality 1870-1910. *The Australian Economic History Review* 61 (2): 228–246.

Patmore, G., and N. Balnave. 2018. *A Global History of Co-operative Business*. London: Taylor and Francis.

Piketty, T. 2014. *Capital in the Twenty-first Century*. Cambridge: Belknap Press.

Pincus, J., and G. D. Snooks. 1988. The past and future role of the *Australian Economic History Review*: editorial reflections and aspirations. *Australian Economic History Review* 28 (2): 3–7.

Pope, D. 1971. Viticulture and phylloxera in north-east Victoria. *Australian Economic History Review* 10 (1): 21–37.

Pope, D. 1976. The push-pull model of Australian migration. *Australian Economic History Review* 16 (2): 144–152.

Pottenger, M., and A. Leigh. 2016. Long-run trends in Australian executive remuneration: BHP, 1887-2012. *Australian Economic History Review* 56 (1): 2–20.

Pritchard, M. F. L. 1969. Economic history in New Zealand universities. *Australian Economic History Review* 9:3–8.

Rafols, I. L., L. Leydesdorff, A. O'Hare, et al. 2012. How journal rankings can suppress interdisciplinary research: A comparison between innovation studies and business and management. *Research Policy* 41 (7): 1262–1282.

Rankin, M. T. 1916. *Arbitration and Conciliation in Australasia: The Legal Wage in Victoria and New Zealand*. London: Allen and Unwin.

Reeves, W. P. 1899. Protective tariffs in Australia and New Zealand. *Economic Journal* 9 (33): 36–44.

Rieder, K., and Sauerhammer, L. 2021. *The impact of tariff protection: Evidence from British colonies in Australia*. Unpublished manuscript.

Sammartino, A. 2002. *Human Resource Management Practices and Labour Market Structures in the Victorian Railways 1864–1921*. PhD thesis, University of Melbourne.

Sammartino, A., and A. J. Seltzer. 2011. Nominal wage rigidity prior to compulsory arbitration: Evidence from the Victorian Railways, 1902-21. *Cliometrica* 5 (1): 53–78.

Schedvin, C. B. 1967. Economic history in Australian universities, 1961-1966. *Australian Economic History Review* 7 (1): 1–18.

Schedvin, C. B. 1971. Monetary stability and the demand for money in Australia between the Wars. *Australian Economic History Review* 11 (2): 167–178.

Schedvin, C. B. 1990. Staples and regions of Pax Britannica. *Economic History Review* 43 (4): 533–559.

Seltzer, A. J. 2018. Publication trends and future challenges for the *AEHR*: A bibliometric analysis. Editorial comment. *Australian Economic History Review* 58 (2): 112–133.

Seltzer, A. J., and J. Borland. 2018. The impact of the 1896 Factory and Shops Act on the labor market in Victoria, Australia. *Journal of Economic History* 78 (3): 785–821.

Seltzer, A. J., and D. T. Merrett. 2000. Personnel practices at the Union Bank of Australia: Panel evidence from the 1887-1900 entry cohorts. *Journal of Labor Economics* 18 (4): 573–613.

Seltzer, A. J., and K. Simons. 2001. Salaries and career opportunities in the banking industry: Evidence from the personnel records of the Union Bank of Australia. *Explorations in Economic History* 38 (2): 195–224.

Shann, E. O. G. 1929. *An Economic History of Australia*. Cambridge: Cambridge University Press; Melbourne: Georgian House.

Sinclair, W. A. 1955. Public capital formation in Australia: 1919-20 to 1929-30. *Economic Record* 31 (61): 299–310.

Sinclair, W. A. 1956. *Economic Recovery in Victoria 1894-1899*. Canberra: ANU Press.

Sinclair, W. A. 1976. *The Process of Economic Development in Australia*. Melbourne: Cheshire.

Snooks, G. D. 1974. *Depression and Recovery in Western Australia 1928/29 – 1938/39*. Nedlands: University of Western Australia Press.

Tang, J. P. 2017. The engine and the reaper: Industrialization and mortality in late nineteenth century Japan. *Journal of Health Economics* 56:145–162.

Tauman, M. 1961. A critical comment of Australian business histories. *Bulletin of the Business Archives Council of Australia* 1 (9): 57–65.

Terwiel, D., S. P. Ville, and G. A. Fleming. 1998. *Australian Business Records: An Archival Guide*. Canberra: Australian National University. working paper.

Thornton, T. 2013. The narrowing of the Australian university economics curriculum: An analysis of the problem and a proposed solution. *The Economic Record* 89 (Suppl. S1): 106–114.

United States. Bureau of the Census. 1975. *Historical Statistics of the United States, Colonial Times to 1970*. Washington DC: US GPO.

Vamplew, W., ed. 1987. *Australians: Historical Statistics*. Broadway, N.S.W: Fairfax, Syme & Weldon Associates.

van der Eng, P., and M. P. Shanahan. 2004. The current and future role of *AEHR*: Editorial reflections. *Australian Economic History Review* 44 (2): 113–117.

Ville, S. 2000. *The Rural Entrepreneurs: A History of the Stock and Station Agent Industry in Australia and New Zealand*. Oakleigh, VIC: Cambridge University Press.

Ville, S., and G. Withers. 2014. *The Cambridge Economic History of Australia*. Cambridge: Cambridge University Press.

Webb, S. 1912. The economic theory of a legal minimum wage. *Journal of Political Economy* 20 (10): 973–998.

Whaples, R. 1991. A quantitative history of the *Journal of Economic History* and the cliometric revolution. *The Journal of Economic History* 51 (2): 289–301.

Whitwell, G. 1997. Future directions for the *Australian Economic History Review*. *Australian Economic History Review* 37 (3): 275–281.

Withers, G., and D. Pope. 1985. Immigration and unemployment. *Economic Record* 61 (2): 554–564.

Withers, Glen, and David Pope. 1993. Do migrants rob jobs? Lessons of Australian history, 1861-1991. *Journal of Economic History* 53 (4): 719–742.

Woelert, P., and L. Yates. 2015. Too little and too much trust: Performance measurement in Australian higher education. *Critical Studies in Education* 56 (2): 175–189.

Wright, C. E. F. 2019. The boarding pass: pathways to corporate networks in early twentieth-century Australia. *Australian Historical Studies* 50 (4): 441–462.

Wright, C. E. F. 2022. *Australian Economic History: Transformations of an Interdisciplinary Field*. Canberra: ANU Press.

Wright, C. E. F., and S. Ville. 2017. The evolution of an intellectual community through the words of its founders: recollections of Australia's economic history field. *Australian Economic History Review* 57 (3): 345–367.

Opportunities and Challenges in African Economic History

Johan Fourie

Abstract This chapter examines the renaissance that has characterised the field of African economic history since 2010. I trace this renewed interest, predominantly by economists, to influential theoretical and practical developments such as the emergence of New Historical Economics and the establishment of the African Economic History Network in 2011. Despite these promising advancements, this chapter raises two critical issues: the divergence of two schools within African economic history and the underrepresentation of African scholars in this discourse. I analyse recent publication trends in economic history journals, addressing questions such as: (1) To what extent has this renewed interest in African economic history been reflected in academic journals devoted to economic history? (2) Who are the predominant contributors to this specialised field? (3) What strategies can be implemented to foster increased participation from African academics? This chapter proposes actionable recommendations to enhance interdisciplinarity and inclusivity within the field.

Introduction

Africa is not at the margins of economic history any longer. In the last 5 years, research on Africa's economic past—on topics ranging from intergenerational mobility to missionaries, from violence to healthcare—has appeared in leading economics journals (Alesina et al. 2021; Jedwab et al. 2022; Heldring 2021; Lowes and Montero 2021b). Notably, even prestigious scientific publications such as *Nature*

This paper benefited from discussions at the World Economic History Congress in Paris (2022) and the Oxford-Cambridge-LSE meetings in London (2023). I acknowledge the excellent research assistance of Kudzai Chidamwoyo and Lauren Stevens.

J. Fourie (✉)
Stellenbosch University, Matieland, South Africa
e-mail: johanf@sun.ac.za

C. Diebolt, M. Haupert (eds.), *The State of Economic History*, Frontiers in Economic History, https://doi.org/10.1007/978-3-032-01624-9_8

and *Science* have begun to include articles on the subject (Nunn 2020; Alesina et al. 2023).

This interest in African economic history is relatively recent. A little more than two decades ago, Africa was largely absent in economic history publications and, as a consequence, from economic history debates. At least four factors explain the renewed interest: First, the emergence of New Historical Economics has offered a methodological and conceptual framework for integrating historical narratives into economic analysis. Second, the increased availability of rich datasets, including archival records and geospatial data, has enabled more robust and nuanced analyses, attracting wider scholarly attention to the field. Third, the establishment of academic forums specifically devoted to African economic history has provided a platform for focused research and dialogue. And, finally, the rising global interest in Africa's economic potential—a consequence, perhaps, of Africa's rapid economic progress in the 2000s—has led to a greater focus on understanding the continent's complex historical influences on its current economic landscape.

But the renaissance in African economic history has also caused two less-desired outcomes: First, a divergence of what Fourie and Obikili call the 'history matters' school from the 'historical reconstruction' school. And, second, the failure to encourage more scholars from Africa to participate in either of these schools. Both these outcomes require active efforts to prevent the field from becoming fragmented and disconnected from the African context. The divergence between the 'history matters' and 'historical reconstruction' schools could lead to a siloed research environment, undermining the richness that a unified approach could offer. The underrepresentation of African scholars in these discussions is a missed opportunity for incorporating local perspectives, building research capacity within Africa, and influencing policy decisions relevant to the continent.

In this chapter, I briefly describe the renaissance, highlighting only the main developments in the last two decades and referring, where necessary, to other, more detailed overviews. I then report, using an updated list of published papers in the top six economic history journals, the two trends: that of the divergence between the two schools and the underrepresentation of scholars based in Africa. I conclude with five suggestions on the way forward.

The Renaissance

A renaissance implies initial strength. As Antony Hopkins (2019) so eloquently summarised, African economic history attracted much interest from scholars, activists, and policymakers, both outside and within Africa, during the second half of the previous century. He divides its intellectual history into five eras. By the 1950s and the 1960s, as independence swept across Africa, modernisation theory, with its universalist prescriptions for 'traditional' societies to adopt Western values for development, held sway but eventually gave ground to dependency theory. The latter posited that global capitalism, particularly as orchestrated by the West, was the main culprit behind underdevelopment in Africa and other parts of the world. Dependency theory, while centring history in its analysis, led to a focus on external trade and somewhat limited the scope for understanding the agency of African societies in shaping their own destinies.

As dependency theory faced its own critiques, Marxist perspectives emerged, shifting the lens from external trade relations to internal modes of production and class relations. However, the rigidities and inherent Eurocentrism in classical Marxist theories found themselves at odds with the complexities and heterogeneities of African societies. By the early 1980s, as Marxism's political and academic influence waned, the Annales School gained traction by offering a nuanced approach that considered long-term social and economic structures, while also incorporating the roles of women, children, and environmental factors. However, unlike Marxism, the Annales School was more focused on understanding the world than changing it through ideological advocacy.

Postmodernism then took the spotlight, emphasising cultural history and deconstructing traditional narratives, but its focus on cultural representations and textual analyses left little room for considering economic realities. This shortcoming became apparent as global economic trends in the 1990s, such as the meteoric rise of China and India as global economic powerhouses, the ICT revolution, and increased global integration, seemed to suggest a narrative of universal progress and, as some argued, 'the end of history'. Africa, by contrast, appeared to be an exception to this trend, frequently mired in violence, social strife, and economic underperformance. The inability to explain Africa's economic woes forced a re-evaluation of intellectual trends that avoided materialist issues, giving space for more nuanced approaches, including those that recognised the multiplicity of forces—economic, social, and political—that shaped African histories and contemporary states.

While historians hoped to understand economic realities, economists yearned for historical depth. The resurgence of interest in history among economists can be partially attributed to the pioneering work of Douglass North (1990) and the emergence of New Institutional Economics (NIE). North emphasised the critical role that institutions—rules, norms, and practices—play in shaping economic outcomes. This was a vital corrective to conventional economic models that often oversimplified or altogether neglected the complexity of historical and institutional contexts.

By the 1990s, in particular, traditional economic theories fell short in explaining why African nations lagged behind even when factors like capital, labour, and technology were accounted for. Economists studying Africa struggled to explain the 'African dummy' in their cross-country growth regressions—a variable that stood in for being African countries that were consistently associated with poor economic performance (Englebert 2000; Burger and Du Plessis 2011). The inability to understand Africa's underperformance through conventional methods led to a search for more nuanced models and theories, further fuelling interest in economic history. With the aid of New Institutional Economics, researchers could delve into the historical and institutional variables that contributed to the present economic conditions in Africa. In this context, the rise of New Historical Economics (NHE) in the early 2000s can be seen as part of a long arc, offering empirical rigour and a deeper understanding of institutional structures while incorporating both external and internal factors.

The publication of two seminal papers marked a pivotal moment in the NHE within African economic history.[1] 'The Colonial Origins of Comparative Development' by Acemoglu et al. (2001) was first to incorporate historical change in a rigorous empirical analysis of the present. Using settler mortality rates as an instrumental variable, they were able to establish a causal relationship between colonial institutions and modern-day economic performance, thereby moving the field beyond mere correlations.

A few years later, Nathan Nunn (2008) used similar methods to the negative long-term impacts of the slave trades on economic development in Africa. Prior to Nunn's work, discussions around the long-term impact of the African slave trades on African societies were largely qualitative and seldom incorporated into economic models. By using detailed historical data on slave exports across African regions and employing advanced econometric techniques, Nunn offered a compelling causal argument that linked historical slave trading to contemporary underdevelopment in affected regions. Extensions to this studied the mechanisms responsible for the persistent impact (Nunn and Wantchekon 2011; Nunn and Puga 2012).

Many followed suit. By the 2010s, economists from some of the leading universities were publishing an increasing number of papers that connected historical events to present-day outcomes in Africa.[2] This burgeoning field, the 'History Matters' school [also known as the 'Persistence Studies' school (Cioni et al. 2021)], primarily employed sophisticated empirical methods, including causal analysis and econometric modelling, to integrate historical contexts into economic theory (Alesina et al. 2016; Alsan 2015; Lowes and Montero 2021a; Michalopoulos and Papaioannou 2013; Michalopoulos and Papaioannou 2016). In an article in the *Journal of Economic Literature*, Michalopoulos and Papaioannou (2020) summarise the key contributions of this school, such as the long-term impact of colonial infrastructure and extractive systems, the divisive outcomes of the 'Scramble for Africa', the enduring effects of slave trades, and the modern relevance of precolonial traits like political centralisation. The authors attribute the emergence of this literature primarily to the implementation of robust identification methods that focus on within-country variation, compared to older literature based on cross-country correlations.

In a *Nature* article, Nunn (2020) also emphasises the use of rigorous empirical methods as the defining feature of this new literature, using historical data to establish causal relationships with contemporary variables. But for Nunn, the value of NHE is not in its improved, causal understanding of the past, but in its ability to shape the future. Contrary to the perceived notion that these historical links left little scope for contemporary policy intervention, Nunn (2020: 6) emphasises its usefulness as natural

[1] Note that the New Historical Economics also include work on other (developing) regions, notably Latin America and Asia.

[2] For a comprehensive overview of these contributions, see Fourie and Obikili (2019) and Michalopoulos and Papaioannou (2020).

policy experiments, noting that '[n]ot only does a historical process of development not preclude the need for policy, it also can be leveraged to gain insights into policies and their effects. This, I feel, is where this line of research can have its greatest impact'.

The NHE also inspired a second group of researchers—the 'Historical Reconstruction' school. Spearheaded by Gareth Austin, this group was primarily concerned with filling the gaps in our understanding of Africa's economic history, rather than simply explaining contemporary issues. What mattered was understanding long-term trends in various areas such as GDP, population dynamics, taxation, wages, inequality, standards of living, education, and social mobility (Jerven 2010; Moradi 2010; Frankema and Van Waijenburg 2012; Fourie 2013; Frankema and Jerven 2014; Fourie and Green 2015; Bolt and Hillbom 2016; De Haas 2017; Van Waijenburg 2018; Bolt and Gardner 2020; Frankema and van Waijenburg 2023a). To do that, required new sources of evidence. The use of quantitative sources, often newly transcribed from archival records, characterised this group, rather than attempts at causal claims using sophisticated identification strategies. Fourie (2016) coined this the 'data revolution in African economic history'.

Though Austin was critical of the NHE approach to African history, he and other African economic historians welcomed the renewed interest in the field (Austin 2008; Hopkins 2009). At least during these early years, economists and economic historians engaged in frequent debates (Fenske 2010; Hopkins 2011; Jerven 2011; Fenske 2011). A revived journal dedicated to publishing the economic histories of African countries and other developing regions contributed (Schirmer et al. 2010), as did the establishment of a new African Economic History Network, with an annual conference. Figure 1 shows the number of papers presented at these conferences. The rapid growth in participation during the 2010s is quite evident.

The rising interest in African economic history is reflected in research output too. Figure 2 shows the annual output of the four leading economic history journals—*Journal of Economic History, The Economic History Review, Explorations in Economic History, and the European Review of Economic History*—from 1998 to 2022. Papers are classified by region.[3] As Fig. 2 demonstrates, papers on Africa increased substantially in the 2010s, an increase, to be precise, of 612%. In contrast, papers on Asia and Oceania increased to 63%, papers on Europe by 45%, and papers on the Americas declined by 13%.

Fragmentation

Despite the resurgence of interest in Africa's economic past, two main issues warrant attention. First, the increasing divergence between the 'History Matters' and 'Historical Reconstruction' schools of thought threatens to create a fragmented

[3] Papers with no regional focus (such as theory papers), as well as editorials, commentaries, and responses, are removed.

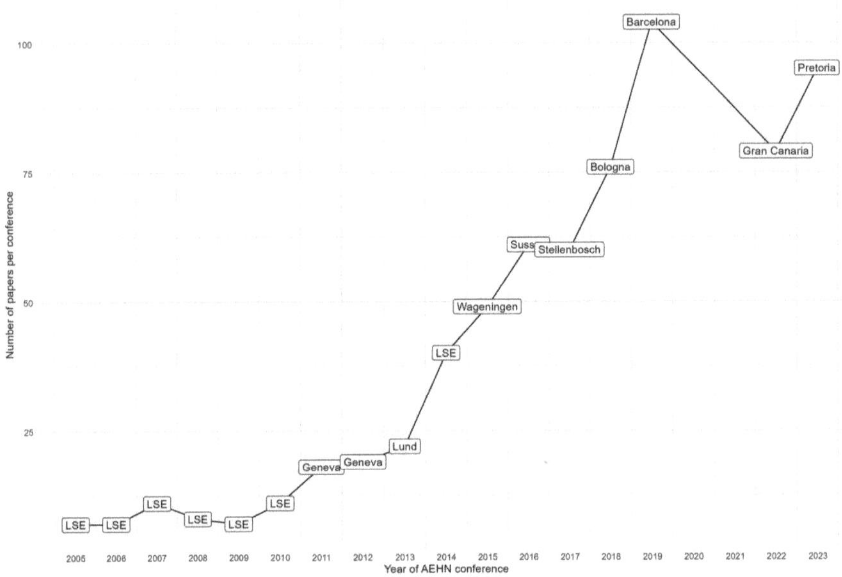

Fig. 1 Number of papers presented at AEHN conferences

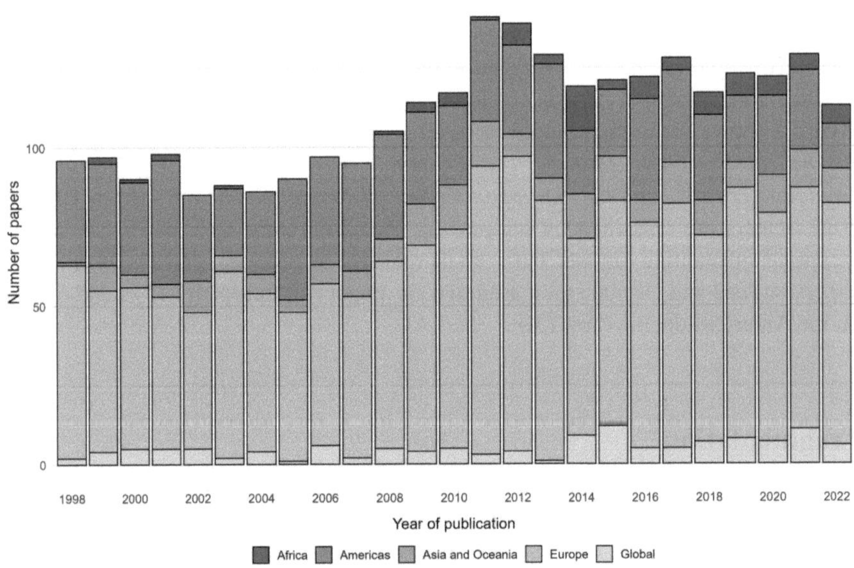

Fig. 2 Number of papers in the top four economic history journals, 1998–2022

research landscape.[4] This division could dilute the potential richness a more unified approach could bring to the field. Second, the notable underrepresentation of African scholars in these academic discussions poses a significant drawback. This lack of local participation not only misses the opportunity to incorporate invaluable local perspectives but also hinders the development of research capacity within Africa itself. It, furthermore, limits the influence of home-grown expertise in policy decisions that are directly relevant to the continent.

The first of these disconcerting trends is visible from a simple citation analysis. Consider, for example, the two review articles discussed above, by Michalopoulos and Papaioannou (2020) and Nunn (2020). Of the 434 papers cited by Michalopoulos and Papaioannou in the *Journal of Economic Literature*, only 15—less than 4%—were published in the top four economic history journals.[5] An additional one is published in EHDR, and four more are published in the *Journal of African History*.[6] Of the 83 papers cited by Nunn (2020), not a single one is published in an economic history journal.

Others have used more rigorous methods to come to the same conclusion. Cioni, Federico, and Vasta (2021) compare the Cliometric Revolution that transformed economic history in the 1960s with the transformation of economic history in the last two decades. To do so, they use all articles published in the top five economic history journals between 2001 and 2019 and compare those to papers with an economic history focus published in thirteen top economics journals.[7] They conclude:

> There is very little overlap between authors of articles in economic history journals and in economics journals. Out of the 2251 authors included in the database, 1630 have published only in economic history journals, 467 only in economics journals and a mere 154 (6.8% of the total) in both economic history and economics journals.

The trend towards fragmentation is not unique to African economic history. One reason for this bifurcation is the method of analysis. Papers published in economic history journals are more likely to be descriptive in nature, focusing on the historical context and the data-generating process (and related source critique). Papers published in economics journals are more likely to focus on rigorous study designs. To publish in top economics journals, Cioni, Federico, and Vasta (2023) also

[4] There is the additional concern of fragmentation between African economic historians using quantitative methods, on the one hand, and African social and cultural historians on the other. See Frankema and Van Waijenburg (2023b) for an excellent review article on the potential for crosspollination between these two subfields.

[5] Five in the *Journal of Economic History*, one in *Explorations in Economic History*, six in *The Economic History Review*, and three in the *European Review of Economic History*.

[6] Not a single paper in *Cliometrica*, a journal that 'encourages the methodological debate, use of economic theory, model building, and reliance upon quantification to support models with historical data', was cited.

[7] These are the *American Economic Review, Econometrica, Journal of Political Economy, the Quarterly Journal of Economics, the Review of Economic Studies, the Economic Journal, the Journal of Economic Theory, the Journal of Monetary Economics, the Journal of Public Economics, the Review of Economics and Statistics, the Journal of Economic Growth, the Journal of Development Economics, and the Journal of Economic Literature.*

emphasise that economic historians must select topics of interest to economists, introduce a research question strictly connected with economic theory, and provide extensive robustness checks. Abramitzky (2015: 1244), studying economic history papers appearing in the top five economics journals since the 1970s, notes that:

> An economic history paper appears more likely to be published in a top five economics journal, relative to an economic history journal, when it studies the United States, when it has an identification strategy to get at a causal question, and when it uses economic theory to guide the analysis.

But causality is not necessarily top of mind when studying Africa's economic past. Much of the continent's historical statistics remains inadequately documented (Fourie 2016). Whereas wage series for Western Europe cover centuries, male unskilled wages in African cities were only recently reconstructed and go back to only the early twentieth century (Frankema and Van Waijenburg 2012). The same is true for population estimates, trade statistics, and much more. Given the limited availability of such historical data, focusing on the fundamental issue of 'historical reconstruction' may be a prerequisite for African economic historians before they can tackle more complex, causative research questions.

Another related trend in economic history is the shift from using aggregate data to individual-level data. The availability of full-count census data allows for more detailed and precise analyses, including the ability to study small subgroups, link data over time to examine mobility, and access administrative records for comprehensive insights into causal mechanisms (Gutmann et al. 2018). Such 'big data' is an exciting prospect for the field and has allowed economic historians, as Margo (2018) and Fernández-de-Pinedo, La Parra-Perez and Muñoz (2023) show, to deepen its integration with the broader field of economics. But the rise of 'big data' comes with a red flag for African economic history: if no such data exists or can be reconstructed, will African economic historians be left behind?

A second concern is the ability to engage scholars from Africa to participate in the renaissance in African economic history.[8] But why does representation matter in scholarship? As Fourie (2019) explains, African scholars introduce epistemological diversity, which is crucial because Africa lacks extensive written records. This means that to adequately interpret and understand the history, one needs to be familiar with local languages, cultures, beliefs, and customs. Oral histories, for instance, offer alternative sources that can fill the gaps left by written records. Experiences shaped by colonialism, slavery, and apartheid allow Africans to critically evaluate past power structures and the knowledge they have engendered. The notion of 'decoloniality' speaks to this, emphasising the importance of recognising who produces knowledge about Africa and from where.

Involving Africans in the discourse of African economic history is not only essential for an accurate representation but also carries significant policy implications. African scholars, given their proximity to and understanding of local contexts,

[8] In South Africa, the challenge has a racial dimension, with very few black South African economic historians producing economic history research. See Fourie (2018).

are best positioned to narrate their history, making it contextually relevant and more impactful. These locally grounded narratives can provide policymakers with a rich repertoire of historical analogies that are more pertinent and applicable to the African context. While global economic history offers valuable lessons, relying solely on them can sometimes lead to policies that may not align well with the unique challenges and opportunities present in Africa. By involving African voices, we ensure that the lessons drawn from history are not just generic but are tailored to the specificities of the continent. Such an inclusive approach ensures that when faced with challenges, like potential bank crises, policymakers can reference historical events that resonate more closely with the African experience, leading to more informed and effective policy responses.

Yet, as Table 1 shows, African scholars are notably underrepresented in economic history journals. It shows the share of papers published for each geographic region by authors based in those regions. For example, of the 1675 papers published in the top four economic history journals, 78.5% were written by scholars based in the Americas. Similarly, 82.2% of papers about European regions were published by scholars in Europe. Africa is the outlier. Only 10.4% of papers were published by scholars based on the continent. Most papers on Africa are, in fact, written by authors based in Europe.[9]

This underrepresentation is not because of a lack of demand or recognition for their work. In fact, Fourie (2019) shows that papers on Africa are not more likely to be rejected or to be cited less frequently than those from other regions. Path dependency is one explanation. The paucity may stem from methodological differences and the distinct development paths of economic history in Western and African institutions. Bar research on the Atlantic slave trade, the cliometric revolution of the 1960s—and the need it created for large historical datasets—contributed to a decline in interest in Africa's past by Western scholars. The divide between the humanities and social sciences in academic institutions on the continent further widened the gap. Put simply, by the early 2000s, there were few economic historians in Africa equipped with the econometric toolkit that would allow them to

Table 1 Geography of paper topics in the top four economic history journals by author location, percentage

Region	Obs	American	European	Asian	African
Africa	370	21.4	64.4	3.8	10.4
Americas	1675	78.5	17.8	3.7	0.0
Asia and Oceania	720	22.4	30.0	47.6	0.0
Europe	4920	13.5	82.2	4.2	0.1
Global	415	36.5	58.4	5.1	0.0
Other	80	24.7	75.3	0.0	0.0

[9] It is important to remember that this shows the location of authors and not their nationality. A Zimbabwean author based at a US university would count as American. Although counting nationality is intractable, the expectation is that the shares would not be substantially different.

publish in the top economic history journals. Another explanation, noted above, is that African economic history struggles with limited data documentation, and the costly creation of 'big data' now fashionable in the top economic history journals may further disadvantage African economic historians due to resource constraints.

Bridging the Gaps

Yet there is some evidence that concerns about fragmentation and underrepresentation can be addressed. In 2010, the *South African Journal of Economic History* rebranded as *Economic History of Developing Regions*. Not only did their focus expand but they also managed to attract papers by authors that usually publish exclusively in economics journals. In the first rebranded issue (Volume 25, Issue 1), Acemoglu and Johnson published a paper 'Why is Africa Poor?'; by 2023, the paper had attracted more than 400 Google Scholar citations. In a 2012 special issue for the World Economic History Congress, Nathan Nunn published 'Culture and the historical process', a paper that has been cited more than 300 times. By attracting significant citations, these papers not only elevated the journal's stature in the field of economic history but also bridged the divide between scholars who typically publish solely in economics journals and the wider economic history community.

But reducing fragmentation did not come at the cost of exclusion. In fact, as Table 2 reports, EHDR has been able to build up an impressive impact factor whilst publishing more papers on developing regions, notably Africa. Whilst the share of Africa papers in the other five economic history journals has not been more than 2%, 30% of papers in EHDR focus on Africa. Nor has African authors been excluded. Whereas 10.4% of papers on Africa were written by Africa-based authors when only considering the top four journals, this percentage increases to 33% when including *EHDR and Cliometrica*.

This has consequences for the research questions asked. Figures 3 and 4 report the word frequency in paper titles for the top four economic history journals and for *EHDR*, respectively. Although words like 'growth', 'development', and 'market' are common across both, they are the exceptions. 'Industrial', 'war', and 'trade' feature prominently on the first list but are completely missing from the

Table 2 Journal output in economic history journals by author location, percentage

Journal	Obs	American	European	Asian	African
EHR	2700	13.9	76.8	8.3	1.0
Explorations	1755	42.3	48.5	8.9	0.3
JEH	2205	47.4	43.5	9.0	0.1
EREH	1440	14.5	80.4	4.5	0.5
Cliometrica	955	33.5	59.2	5.8	1.6
EHDR	820	22.7	39.1	8.5	29.8

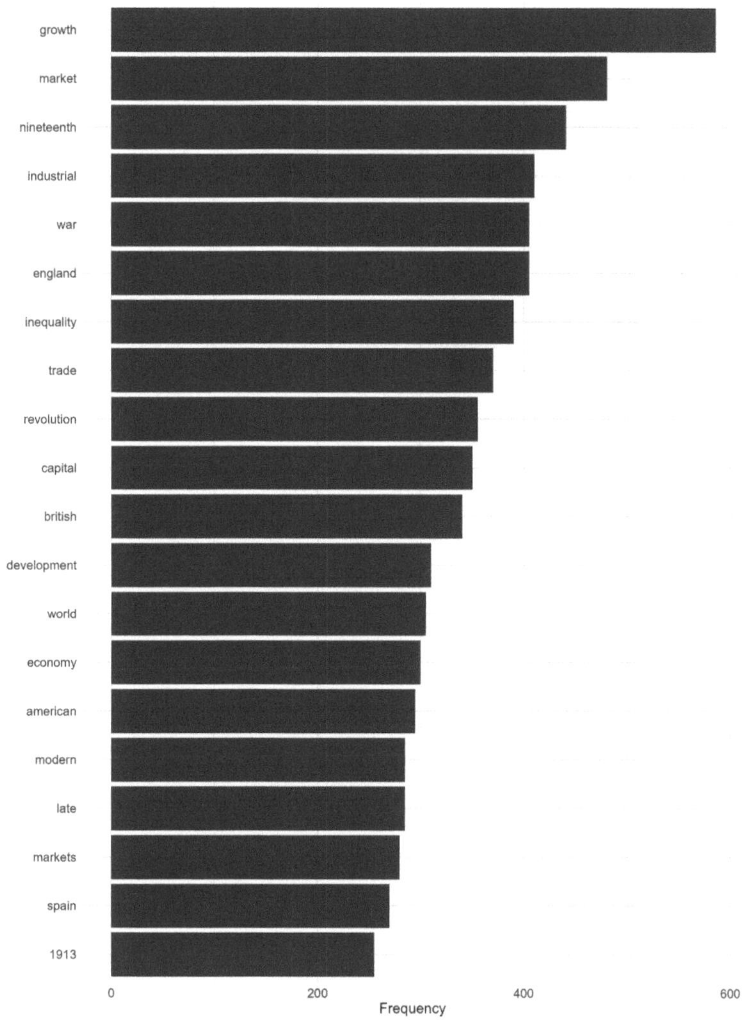

Fig. 3 Word frequency in paper titles, top four economic history journals, 2010–2022. Notes: Excluded words: century, economic, social, evidence

second. By contrast, 'colonial', 'inequality', and 'apartheid' are more prominent on the second.

Fourie (2019) proposed several additional steps to address the underrepresentation concern. Firstly, there is a need to promote the study of African economic history among African scholars, as only a handful of economic history departments remain in Africa, many under constant threat of closure (Kufakurinani 2022). The solution, Fourie proposes, is not to rebuild stand-alone departments but to integrate the subject into mainstream economic curricula. By showcasing the relevance of economic history in understanding Africa's development challenges and presenting

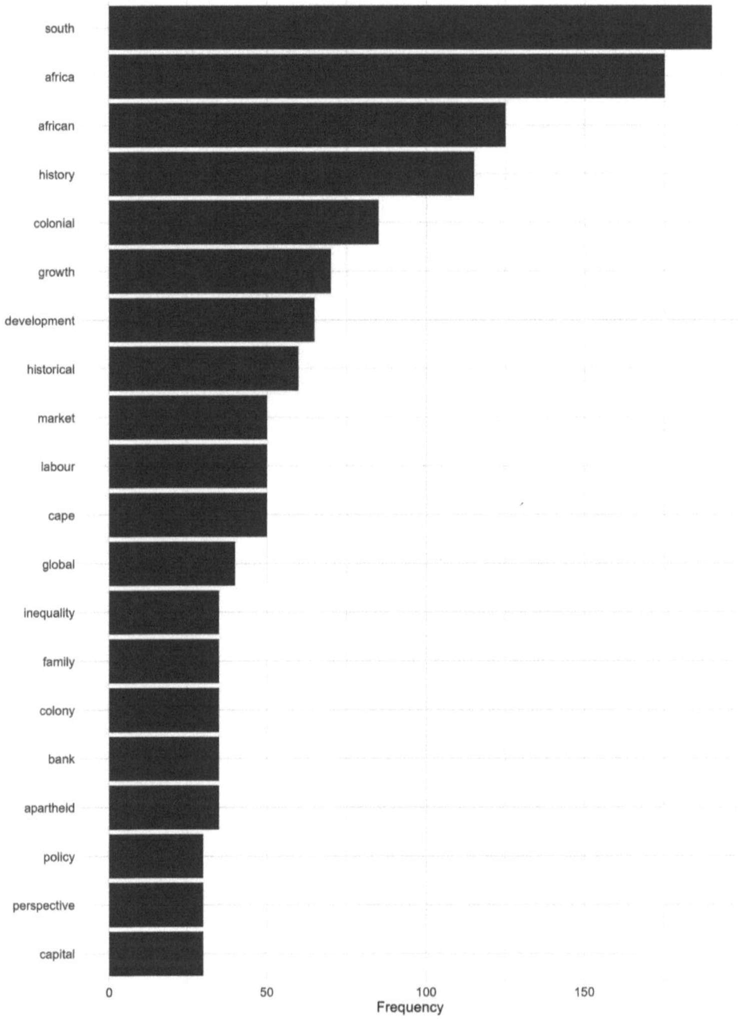

Fig. 4 Word frequency in paper titles, *Economic History of Developing Regions*, 2010–2022

it attractively, such as through cliometrics, the combination of historical context and quantitative analysis, it becomes more appealing to African students. A case in point are two new textbooks. The first—*The History of African Development*—was developed by scholars associated with the African Economic History Network and is available for free on its website. The second—*Our Long Walk to Economic Freedom*—is an accessible global economic history textbook for undergraduate economics students, written from an African perspective (Fourie 2022).

The second strategy involves breaking down network barriers. This may include inviting African economic historians to join editorial boards of top journals. There are, at the time of writing, no scholar based in Africa serving on any of the top four economic history editorial boards. Networks also emerge through closer partnerships between African universities and leading economic history departments in Europe and the USA. In terms of teaching, several African Economic History Network scholars teach a course in economic history at the African School of Economics in Benin. An online course hosted by the London Business School attracted several thousand participants in 2022. In terms of research, a few successful partnerships are now underway. Lund University's Department of Economic History, in collaboration with Stellenbosch University in South Africa, successfully applied for substantial funding to transcribe household level records of the Cape Colony, known as the Cape of Good Hope Panel project.[10] The 2021–2026 project employs several researchers and postdocs that have already published in top four journals (Ekama et al. 2021; Martins et al. 2023; Fourie and Garmon 2023).

Finally, a robust approach involves financially supporting promising African students both within the continent and abroad. The good news is that several African PhD students have recently graduated from economic history departments in Europe or have been employed there as postdoctoral students.[11] These students are very likely to stay in the profession and, given their training, publish in economic history journals, often with international scholars (Aboagye and Bolt 2021; Gwaindepi 2022; Cilliers et al. 2023; Chiseni 2023). South African universities are also increasingly producing PhD students with economic history topics.[12] The latter reflects the establishment of permanent centres of economic history within economics departments, like Stellenbosch University's Laboratory for the Economics of Africa's Past or the research focus area in economic history at the University of Pretoria. Such units are pivotal in producing research that reach economic history journals (Links et al. 2020; Walters et al. 2023; Funjika 2023). The importance of *Economic History of Developing Regions* to expose these scholars' work should not be underestimated. Consider Fig. 5, which compares the number of papers by region published in economic history journals including and excluding EHDR. Though more can be done, it is clear that more Africa-papers have found an outlet as a result of EHDR's focus on regions outside Europe and the United States.

The Way Forward

As previous gaps are addressed, new ones emerge. At a meeting of African economic historians in London in May 2023, two new challenges were identified: chronological and geographic gaps.

[10] Visit www.capepanel.org for more information.

[11] At Lund University, for example, PhD students include Prince Young Aboagye (Ghana) and Chanda Chiseni (Zambia). Postdocs include Jeanne Cilliers (South Africa) and Abel Gwaindepi (Zimbabwe).

[12] Calumet Links (Stellenbosch University), and Leoné Walters and Patricia Funjika (both University of Pretoria).

The structure of academic research often displays path dependence, leading scholars to work within established topics and methods, with supervisors guiding students to familiar areas (Gardner 2023). A significant gap observed is the chronological emphasis on the colonial period, given the wealth of data available from colonial bureaucracies and public interest in colonial legacies. However, this brief colonial period might not warrant the disproportionate scholarly attention it receives. It often sidelines significant epochs like Africa's vast history before colonialism or the process of decolonisation post-independence. While historians are leveraging interdisciplinary methods and new technologies to address these gaps, more long-term datasets covering the entire twentieth century, and indeed into the nineteenth and eighteenth centuries, are needed.

Geographical gaps also prevail in the field. Language barriers and accessibility issues mean former British and French colonies receive more attention than smaller empires or independent states. Using government archives often overshadows other valuable sources like business archives or oral histories. While digitisation can ameliorate some accessibility issues, its selectivity poses challenges.

Here, too, participation by African scholars can address some of these concerns. Overcoming institutional barriers and increasing funding opportunities are essential. Addressing these gaps is critical, especially since the study of African economic history is likely to play a pivotal role in shaping public policy on the continent.

Appendix

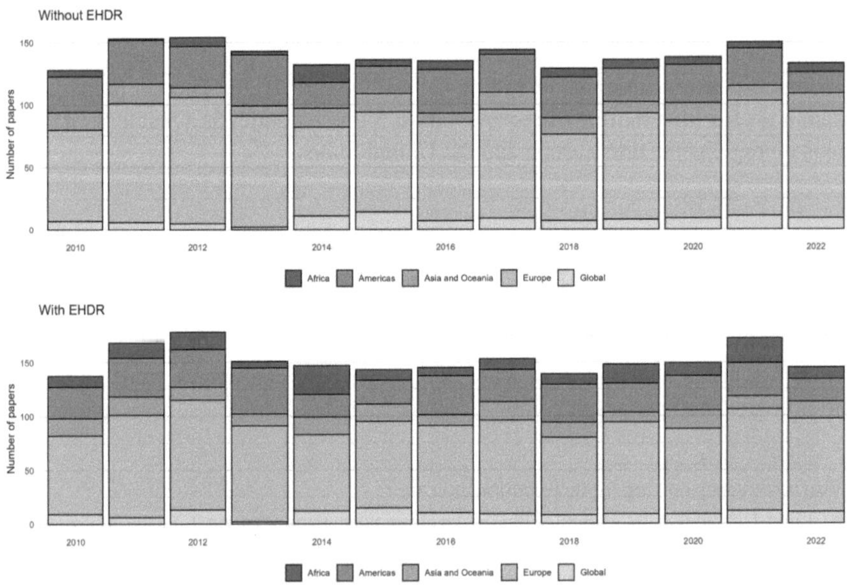

Fig. 5 Comparison of publication trends with and without papers published in *Economic History of Developing Regions*

References

Aboagye, P. Y., and J. Bolt. 2021. Long-term trends in income inequality: Winners and losers of economic change in Ghana, 1891–1960. *Explorations in Economic History* 82:101405.

Abramitzky, R. 2015. Economics and the modern economic historian. *The Journal of Economic History* 75 (4): 1240–1251.

Acemoglu, D., S. Johnson, and J. A. Robinson. 2001. The colonial origins of comparative development: An empirical investigation. *American economic review* 91 (5): 1369–1401.

Alesina, A., S. Michalopoulos, and E. Papaioannou. 2016. Ethnic inequality. *Journal of Political Economy* 124 (2): 428–488.

Alesina, A., S. Hohmann, S. Michalopoulos, and E. Papaioannou. 2021. Intergenerational mobility in Africa. *Econometrica* 89 (1): 1–35.

Alesina, A., S. Hohmann, S. Michalopoulos, and E. Papaioannou. 2023. Religion and educational mobility in Africa. *Nature* 1–10.

Alsan, M. 2015. The effect of the tsetse fly on African development. *American Economic Review* 105 (1): 382–410.

Austin, G. 2008. The 'reversal of fortune' thesis and the compression of history: Perspectives from African and comparative economic history. *Journal of International Development: The Journal of the Development Studies Association* 20 (8): 996–1027.

Bolt, J., and L. Gardner. 2020. How Africans shaped British colonial institutions: Evidence from local taxation. *The Journal of Economic History* 80 (4): 1189–1223.

Bolt, J., and E. Hillbom. 2016. Long-term trends in economic inequality: Lessons from colonial Botswana, 1921–74. *The Economic History Review* 69 (4): 1255–1284.

Burger, R., and S. Du Plessis. 2011. Examining the robustness of competing explanations of slow growth in African countries. *Studies in Economics and Econometrics* 35 (3): 21–48.

Chiseni, M. C. 2023. The sins of the church: The long-term impacts of Christian missionary praxis on HIV and sexual behaviour in Zambia. *Economic History of Developing Regions* 1–33.

Cilliers, J., E. Green, and R. Ross. 2023. Did it pay to be a pioneer? Wealth accumulation in a newly settled frontier society. *The Economic History Review* 76 (1): 257–282.

Cioni, M., G. Federico, and M. Vasta. 2021. The two revolutions in economic history. In *The handbook of historical economics*, 17–40. Academic Press.

Cioni, M., G. Federico, and M. Vasta. 2023. Is economic history changing its nature? Evidence from top journals. *Cliometrica* 17 (1): 23–48.

De Haas, M. 2017. Measuring rural welfare in colonial Africa: Did Uganda's smallholders thrive? *The economic history review* 70 (2): 605–631.

Ekama, K., J. Fourie, H. Heese, and L. C. Martin. 2021. When cape slavery ended: Introducing a new slave emancipation dataset. *Explorations in Economic History* 81:101390.

Englebert, P. 2000. Solving the mystery of the AFRICA dummy. *World development* 28 (10): 1821–1835.

Fenske, J. 2010. The causal history of Africa: A response to Hopkins. *Economic History of Developing Regions* 25 (2): 177–212.

Fenske, J. 2011. The causal history of Africa: Replies to Jerven and Hopkins: Debate. *Economic History of Developing Regions* 26 (2): 125–131.

Fernández-de-Pinedo, N., A. La Parra-Perez, and F. F. Muñoz. 2023. Recent trends in publications of economic historians in Europe and North America (1980–2019): an empirical analysis. *Cliometrica* 17 (1): 1–22.

Fourie, J. 2013. The remarkable wealth of the Dutch Cape Colony: Measurements from eighteenth-century probate inventories. *The Economic History Review* 66 (2): 419–448.

Fourie, J. 2016. The data revolution in African economic history. *Journal of Interdisciplinary History* 47 (2): 193–212.

Fourie, J. 2018. Cliometrics in South Africa. *Studies in Economics and Econometrics* 42 (2): 1–13.

Fourie, J. 2019. Who writes African economic history? *Economic History of Developing Regions* 34 (2): 111–131.

Fourie, J. 2022. *Our long walk to economic freedom: Lessons from 100,000 years of human history*. Cambridge University Press.

Fourie, J., and F. Garmon Jr. 2023. The settlers' fortunes: Comparing tax censuses in the Cape Colony and early American republic. *The Economic History Review* 76 (2): 525–550.

Fourie, J., and E. Green. 2015. The missing people: Accounting for the productivity of indigenous populations in Cape Colonial History. *The Journal of African History* 56 (2): 195–215.

Frankema, E., and M. Jerven. 2014. Writing history backwards or sideways: Towards a consensus on African population, 1850–2010. *The Economic History Review* 67 (4): 907–931.

Frankema, E., and M. Van Waijenburg. 2012. Structural impediments to African growth? New evidence from real wages in British Africa, 1880–1965. *The Journal of Economic History* 72 (4): 895–926.

Frankema, E., and van Waijenburg, M. 2023a. What about the race between education and technology in the Global South? Comparing skill premiums in colonial Africa and Asia. *The Economic History Review*.

Frankema, E., and M. van Waijenburg. 2023b. Bridging the Gap with the 'New' Economic History of Africa. *The Journal of African History*1–24.

Funjika, P. 2023. Historical African ethnic class stratification systems and intergenerational transmission of education. *Economic History of Developing Regions* 38 (1): 89–116.

Gardner, L. 2023. Where are the gaps in African economic history? *Our Long Walk* blog post. Available online: https://johanfourie.substack.com/p/where-are-the-gaps-in-african-economic. Accessed 26 Sept 2023.

Gutmann, M. P., E. K. Merchant, and E. Roberts. 2018. "Big data" in economic history. *The Journal of Economic History* 78 (1): 268–299.

Gwaindepi, A. 2022. Fiscal capacity in "responsible government" colonies: The Cape Colony in comparative perspective, c. 1865–1910. *European Review of Economic History* 26 (3): 340–369.

Heldring, L. 2021. The origins of violence in Rwanda. *The Review of economic studies* 88 (2): 730–763.

Hopkins, A. G. 2009. The new economic history of Africa. *The Journal of African History* 50 (2): 155–177.

Hopkins, A. G. 2011. Causes and confusions in African history: Debate. *Economic History of Developing Regions* 26 (2): 107–110.

Hopkins, A. G. 2019. Fifty years of African economic history. *Economic History of Developing Regions* 34 (1): 1–15.

Jedwab, R., F. Meier zu Selhausen, and A. Moradi. 2022. The economics of missionary expansion: Evidence from Africa and implications for development. *Journal of Economic Growth* 27 (2): 149–192.

Jerven, M. 2010. African growth recurring: An economic history perspective on African growth episodes, 1690–2010. *Economic History of Developing Regions* 25 (2): 127–154.

Jerven, M. 2011. A clash of disciplines? Economists and historians approaching the African past: Debate. *Economic History of Developing Regions* 26 (2): 111–124.

Kufakurinani, U. 2022. *A Promising Start and a Frustrating End: The Rise and Fall of the Economic History Department at University of Zimbabwe*. Paper presented at University of Pretoria History seminar series. 28 February.

Links, C., J. Fourie, and E. Green. 2020. The substitutability of slaves: Evidence from the eastern frontier of the Cape colony. *Economic History of Developing Regions* 35 (2): 98–122.

Lowes, S., and E. Montero. 2021a. Concessions, violence, and indirect rule: Evidence from the Congo Free State. *The Quarterly Journal of Economics* 136 (4): 2047–2091.

Lowes, S., and E. Montero. 2021b. The legacy of colonial medicine in Central Africa. *American Economic Review* 111 (4): 1284–1314.

Margo, R. A. 2018. The integration of economic history into economics. *Cliometrica* 12 (3): 377–406.

Martins, I., J. Cilliers, and J. Fourie. 2023. Legacies of loss: The health outcomes of slaveholder compensation in the British Cape Colony. *Explorations in Economic History* 89:101506.
Michalopoulos, S., and E. Papaioannou. 2013. Pre-colonial ethnic institutions and contemporary African development. *Econometrica* 81 (1): 113–152.
Michalopoulos, S., and E. Papaioannou. 2016. The long-run effects of the scramble for Africa. *American Economic Review* 106 (7): 1802–1848.
Michalopoulos, S., and E. Papaioannou. 2020. Historical legacies and African development. *Journal of Economic Literature* 58 (1): 53–128.
Moradi, A. 2010. Nutritional status and economic development in sub-Saharan Africa, 1950–1980. *Economics & Human Biology* 8 (1): 16–29.
North, D. 1990. *Institutions, Institutional Change and Economic Performance*. Cambridge: Cambridge University Press.
Nunn, N. 2008. The long-term effects of Africa's slave trades. *The Quarterly Journal of Economics* 123 (1): 139–176.
Nunn, N. 2020. The historical roots of economic development. *Science* 367 (6485): eaaz9986.
Nunn, N., and D. Puga. 2012. Ruggedness: The blessing of bad geography in Africa. *Review of Economics and Statistics* 94 (1): 20–36.
Nunn, N., and L. Wantchekon. 2011. The slave trade and the origins of mistrust in Africa. *American economic review* 101 (7): 3221–3252.
Schirmer, S., L. Chaudhary, M. Cosgel, J. L. Demonsant, J. Fourie, E. Frankema, G. Garzarelli, J. Luiz, M. Mariotti, G. Verhoef, and S. Yan. 2010. The state and scope of the economic history of developing regions. *Economic History of Developing Regions* 25 (1): 3–20.
Van Waijenburg, M. 2018. Financing the African colonial state: The revenue imperative and forced labor. *The Journal of Economic History* 78 (1): 40–80.
Walters, L., C. Chisadza, and M. Clance. 2023. The effect of pre-colonial ethnic institutions and European influences on contemporary education in Sub-Saharan Africa. *The Journal of Development Studies*1–22.

From Dependencia Back to the Original Sin: Economic History in South America in the Twenty-First Century

Adolfo Meisel

Abstract Since the 1950s, research on Latin American economic history has been dominated by the Marxist and Dependencia paradigms. However, since the beginning of the twenty-first century, there has been a trend toward an increasing influence of the cliometric and new institutionalist approach. As a result, there have been significant advances in research areas such as anthropometrics, social savings of railroads, and the long-term effects of colonial institutions, such as encomiendas and slavery.

In this article, I will discuss the state of economic history in South America at the beginning of the twenty-first century as well as some of the dominant trends that can be observed at the present time. First, I will briefly review the early stages of the economic historiography in the region and the main sources of influences. Then I will refer to the boom in economic history research in South America during the 1960s and the 1970s. This was a period when economic historians and other social scientists had a large influence in economic policies throughout the region. Thus, some analysts consider this to be a Golden Age of economic history studies in South America (Bértola and Weber 2015). Next, a discussion of some of the main reasons for the loss of influence of the paradigms that dominated South American economic history from the 1960s to the early 1980s is presented. Finally, we study how the New Economic History (NEH), born in the USA in the late 1950s, gradually began to gain ground. However, in this last period, there was also rapid spread of the New Institutional History (NIH) inspired among others by Douglas C. North, and given an enormous boost through the empirical research within this framework of Daron Acemoglu, Samuel Johnson, and James Robinson and their followers. Other strands of research are also discussed in the final section: mainly the research on monetary history inspired by Milton Friedman and Anna Schwartz's monetary history of the USA (Friedman and Schwartz 1963) and studies on free banking as well as on the birth of central banks in the region.

A. Meisel (✉)
Universidad del Norte, Barranquilla, Colombia
e-mail: ameiselroca@gmail.com

C. Diebolt, M. Haupert (eds.), *The State of Economic History*, Frontiers in Economic History, https://doi.org/10.1007/978-3-032-01624-9_9

The birth of South American economic history can be dated to the 1940s when several classics in this literature were published. I refer to the pioneering work of Caio Prado Junior (1942), Luis Eduardo Nieto Arteta (1942), Rodolfo Puigross (1940), and Sergio Bagú (1949). Each of these authors was a pioneer in the analysis of the economic history of their respective countries.[1] All of them followed a Marxist approach. However, none of them adhered to a dogmatic form of Marxism, which is perhaps why these books became so influential. An additional reason for their success was that at the time they wrote, Marxist ideology was becoming very influential among Latin American intellectuals.

In 1949, the United Nations Economic Commission for Latin America (ECLA) issued its very influential report, *The Economic Development of Latin America and its Principal Problems.* In this document, and under the guidance of ECLA's director, the Argentine economist Raul Prebisch, a contrast was established between an industrialized Center and an agrarian Periphery, where Latin America was located (Love 2005). There was an unequal exchange in foreign trade between the Center and the Periphery, since through time the terms of trade of exporters of agricultural and other primary goods deteriorated. Thus, ECLA recommended protectionist measures to promote the industrialization of the periphery as a way to escape this situation, industrialization by substitution of imports (ISI).

The Ideas of ECLA were widely accepted, especially in Brazil and Chile. They also had a large impact in Mexico and Argentina, not only among academics but also in policymaking. ECLA was able to spread its ideas through training programs for civil servants, country reports, producing enormous amounts of statistical information on the region, and through personal and institutional networks (Fajardo 2022).

The ideas of ECLA had an immediate effect on the economic historiography of the countries where it had the largest influence. This was particularly the case for Brazil (Furtado 1959), Chile (Pinto 1959), and Argentina (Ferrer 1963). All of these works followed the ideas of ECLA.

However, in the late 1960s, the views of ECLA started to lose ground even among some researchers on its staff. Building on the ideas of ECLA, a group of Latin American social scientists went beyond ECLA's view that industrialization plus international economic cooperation could lead to a convergence of the periphery with the center (Fajardo 2022). This new approach was known as *dependencia.*

The basic ideas where *dependencia* differed from ECLA's views were that "…ECLA's economic theories and critiques were not based on an analysis of social process, did not call attention to imperialist relationships among countries, and did not take into account the asymmetric relations between classes" (Cardosa and Faletto 1979).

In a sense, *dependencia* added Marxist class analysis to the center–periphery approach of ECLA. Furthermore, some of the main authors at the time envisioned: "a socialist form for the social organization of the future" for the region (Cardosa and Faletto 1979, p. 216).

[1] Brazil, Colombia, Chile, and Perú, respectively.

In the 1970s and the 1980s, *dependencia* became a dominant intellectual approach among Latin American social scientists. “No other single viewpoint pervaded the field of Latin American history, nor historicized Latin American studies, as did dependency theory” (Haber 1997, p. 10; Hernandez 2015). However, it must be said that among many Latin American historians, the French school of the Annales continued exerting a salient influence, especially among those who studied the rural sector and the colonial period (Bonett 2015). For example, the Colombian historian German Colmenares, who specialized in the colonial period and had studied in France under the direction of Pierre Vilar—a leading member of the Annales School, and a Marxist, was not himself a Marxist.

The dominance of *dependencia* started to disappear in the late 1980s due to multiple causes. One of them was the increasing difficulties of the process of ISI, and the questioning of some of its excesses. The rise of the successful Asian exporters, such as South Korea, was another. In addition, the scrutiny of the empirical evidence and economic logic of its main arguments on the part of a new generation of well-trained economists revealed many of its shortcomings (Sanchez 2003). The repression by military dictatorships and the closure of think tanks with progressive ideas in several South American countries led to a dispersion and lack of continuity in the work of some of its practitioners. Finally, the loss of legitimacy of Marxism after the fall of the Berlin Wall in 1989 was an additional factor.

An additional cause for the erosion of the hegemony of the dependency approach was the turn of historians toward cultural topics and the study of identities. Previous generations of Latin American social scientists had been under the influence of Marxism and the first generation of Annales, so the study of the economy was among their preferred areas of research. The new macro narratives favoring cultural studies eroded much of the interest in economic history.

New Economic History

What came to be known as the New Economic History (NEH) was born in the United States at the end of the 1950s. In the next decade, it became the dominant approach in the field in that country. In Latin America, however, that reception was delayed because of the enormous influence of Marxism, *dependencia,* and the Annales. In Latin America, the transition to the “new” economic history occurred in the 1980s. The new economic history gradually substituted, although it never completely eliminated, the schools of thought with which it competed: Marxism, Annales, and Latin American structuralism. “The critiques of structuralist, and particularly dependency models, centered their attacks on the lack of logically consistent theories and the failure to derive and test relevant hypothesis” (Coatsworth and Taylor 1998, p. 3).

Among the pioneers of the New Economic History, both Robert Fogel and Douglas North stand out. The contributions of Fogel in this field were mainly in three areas: estimates of the contributions of railroads to economic growth (he elevated the concept of social savings), the economics of slavery, and anthropometrics (Mitch 2019). In all of these areas, the NEH has had an important impact on Latin American economic historiography in the last few decades.

Robert Fogel's quantitative analysis of the profitability of railroads in the USA in the nineteenth century led him to conclude that railroads did not substantially alter the economic growth of the US economy. For that analysis, he used the concept of social saving, which was not new, but which he exploited to a greater degree, in particular calculating a specific measure of the actual economic impact of the railroad on American economic growth (Fogel 1970).

Following this methodology, Maria Teresa Ramirez (2001) published perhaps the first paper addressing railroad profitability in a Latin American country. Ramirez argued that according to the results of the social savings she estimated for Colombia, like the U.S. railroads, the industry had not been essential for the economic growth of Columbia between 1905 and 1950.

William R. Sumerhill (2005) calculated large social savings for the nineteenth- and early twentieth-century Brazilian railroads. The benefits were small for passengers but large for freight. In contrast to these results, Alfonso Herranz-Loncan (2011) concluded that the resource saving effects of railroads in Uruguay in the period 1870–1914 were negligible.

The social savings of railroads in Peru were calculated by Luis Felipe Zegarra (2013) at between 0.3 and 1.3% of GDP in 1890 but went up to 3.6–9.4% of GDP in 1918. Thus, they were like the results for the USA and Great Britain but below Brazil and Argentina. For Argentina, Herranz-Loncan (2014) estimated benefits for railroads in the range of 20–25% of income per capita before 1914. This was a country with one of the highest returns for railroads in the world and certainly higher than for those in the center of the world economy.

With the publication of *Time on the Cross: The Economics of American Negro Slavery* in 1974, Robert Fogel and Stanley Engerman changed many of the ideas prevalent among social scientists about the institution of slavery. They showed that before its abolition, slavery in the USA was economically rational and profitable. Furthermore, the slave plantations were as profitable as the family farms of the US north. Thus, slavery was not on a path toward extinction, and a political decision, and ultimately a civil war, was necessary to end it. The publication was highly controversial, but further research validated its main theses, and it continues to be highly influential in the economic historiography of slavery in the United States.

In South America, the impact of *Time on the Cross* has been limited. Perhaps the main reason being that with the exception of Brazil, which imported more slaves than the United States, in most countries the size of the slave populations was not comparable to what was observed in the southern United States. Among the research topics inspired by the work of Fogel and Engerman, the determinants of the price of slaves have been important. The pioneers of this line of research were Alfred Conrad and John Meyer (1958).

Carlos Newland and Maria Jesus San Segundo (1994, 1996) estimated the determinants of slave prices throughout Spanish America using a sample of 2347 slaves for the period 1767–1794. The majority of the observations refer to Peru (39.5%)

and La Plata (44.1%). The main explanatory variables are age, gender, health, training, type of economic unit, African born, and mixed race. Their results produced an R^2 of 0.57, and all their variables tested significant. The price of males exceeded that of females and the maximum price was achieved at an age of 28.4 years.

Based on 3800 observations of sales of slaves in Santiago, Chile in the period 1773–1822, Celia Cussen, Manuel Llorca-Jaña, and Federico Droller (2016) established that a simple OLS model including age and gender explains 47% of the variations in prices. Unlike most other studies, prices for females were higher than for male slaves. The explanation is that in an urban setting, like the one they studied, women can attain a higher price than in rural settings perhaps because most work is less physically demanding and could involve more human capital.

Using the inventories of haciendas and mines for the Caribbean region of the Viceroyalty of New Granada, Meisel and Granger (2019) estimated that age, height, and dummy variables to account for gender, health, training, and employment in the mining sector determined the price of slaves. Rebeca Riella (2021) used a dataset of post-mortem inventories of slaves of deceased owners for the period 1700–1825, in Montevideo. She follows the majority of the literature in that she uses OLS to estimate an equation in which the price is explained by age, gender, health, and training. Consistent with the South American slavery literature, each of her explanatory variables are significant and the results are robust. The weakness of her study is in the relatively small sample size of 206 observations.

Following the work of Fogel and Engerman (1974), Wiliam F. Sharp (1976) studied the mining region of Colombia. Sharp calculated the annual rate of return for 12 mines for the period 1690–1803. The average rate of return to the use of slaves was 17.2%, quite an attractive rate for the period, and higher than the 10% average that Conrad and Meyer found in the antebellum United States. The profitability of the 12 mines Sharp analyzed was as high as 49.2%.

Anthropometrics

Perhaps the largest impact of the New Economic History, and in particular Fogel, in South America in the last few decades is the use of anthropometric data, especially height, as an indicator of biological well-being. Fogel (1996) revealed that his interest in anthropometrics was an intellectual externality of his research on the efficiency of slavery. He was a pioneer in the field of anthropometrics, and his research, as well as that of his students, including Richard Steckel, Kenneth Sokoloff, George Villaflor, and John Komlos, led the field to prominence among economic historians.

In 2019, Joe M. Martinez-Carrion and Ricardo Salvatore evaluated the state of research in anthropometrics in the Iberian and Latin American countries with references to several countries in South America: Colombia, Peru, Chile, Argentina, and Brazil. They concluded that anthropometric history was a well-established discipline in Iberia and Latin America. Argentina, Colombia, and Chile lead the way in anthropometric research in South and Central America, although a few studies have also been published for Peru, Brazil, and Uruguay.

One of the earliest works authored in South America under the influence of the New Economic History on anthropometrics was published in 1998 by Ricardo Salvatore. He found that height declined in the late eighteenth century and reached its lowest point in 1800–1804. After that date and until the late 1920s, height increased, with a short dip in the late 1820s.

In a paper where he presents the height of military recruits and prisoners, which corresponded to the lower classes of Argentina, Salvatore (2007) concludes that in the era of liberal progress, 1850–1899, there were very small advances in the height of the lower classes. He discovered a similar occurrence for the period 1900–1929. In contrast, in the 1930s, there were large advances in biological welfare as measured by height. The evolution of average heights in the regions of Argentina was not homogeneous. For example, according to Salvatore (2016), in the northwest, the average height increased in the first half of the twentieth century. Also, average heights went through a process of convergence among the different subregions of the northwest. This heterogeneity in what happened with height in Argentina in the early twentieth century was also observed between social classes. Salvatore (2019) found that average height decreased at an annual average rate of 0.052 cm for the working poor between 1890 and 1929. Although from 1930 to 1939, height increased 1.01 cm, over the 1890–1939 period the total gain was only 0.49 cm.

The rates for the Argentine Pampas showed stagnation from the 1850s to the 1880s. This is somewhat surprising in a food rich economy. The data for this study (Salvatore 2020) was obtained from 84,500 recruits, prison records, and electoral records. The rates declined after the 1880s from 15.3% to 5.6% in the late 1940s, and then stagnated. In contrast, average height of recruits increased from 167 cm around 1910 to 170.5 cm in 1940. Finally, Salvatore (2010) shows that there were minor declines during World War I and the Great Depression.

An early work in the field of anthropometrics in Brazil was conducted by Leonardo Monasterio and Luiz Paulo Noguerol (2006). Using a dataset numbering 40,000 observations they found a significant increase in the average height of men, which increased from 1.65 m in 1940 to 1.71 m in the 1980s. This is an increase of more than 1 cm per decade. They also observed a difference of 6 cm between the highest and the lowest income quintiles. The Northeast registered a height which was 1.87 cm below the average and 4.84 below that of the South.

For the period 1889–1914, Monasterio (2014) used 13,000 registries of male height for those living in the state of Rio Grande do Sul. Local residents were tall for the period by the Brazilian standards of the time, 167 cm, and immigrants had a similar height. Finally, Monasterio shows that stature was stagnant in the region during this period, and even declined in the final years of the nineteenth century.

Using a sample of prisoners in the jails of Rio de Janeiro in the nineteenth century, Zephyr Frank (2006) traced the behavior of the height of that population. The height of Brazilian born slaves declined from the 1830s through the beginning of the 1860s. Slaves born in the city of Rio do Janeiro were shorter than their free counterparts throughout the period. However, slaves from the Northeast were taller than those born in Rio, and as tall as their free counterparts.

Perhaps the most complete study on the evolution of height in Brazil is the work of Daniel Franken (2019), who exploited 16,000 military records, and combined that with data from 6000 Passports, to trace the behavior of height from 1850 to 1950. He found lower average height for the North and Northeast. Height increased 2.5 cm between the 1880s and the 1910s. However, in the North and Northeast, height remained stagnant until the decade of 1910. In the 1920s, the average height remained constant and fell slightly in the 1930s. Finally, in the 1940s and the 1950s, height grew again, but not as fast as in the period 1880–1920.

Colombia is one of the countries with better records for the study of heights. This is especially true for the twentieth century, during which time authorities recorded the height of all citizens upon reaching the age of 21. Beginning in 1975, they recorded height at age 18. In all of Latin America only two other countries, Cuba and El Salvador, both less populous than Colombia, have a citizen card where the height is recorded. The database obtained from that source includes more than nine million observations for those born between 1905 and 1985 (Meisel and Vega 2007a, b). This database has the advantage that it includes women and the place of birth.

In 2005, Adolfo Meisel and Margarita Vega published the first paper written in Colombia under the influence of the work of Robert Fogel and his associates on anthropometrics. They constructed a database from the archives of the foreign ministry containing information on those Colombians who were issued passports, with their names, gender, age, activity, destination, and reason for traveling. The group was comprised mainly of members of the elite. The average height of men born in 1870–74 was 167.4 cm and women 158.1. Men born between 1900 and 1904 measured 168.3 cm, and women 158.2. That is a negligible increase, which is a reflection of almost no growth in per capita GDP in this period and essentially no advances in terms of quality of the water supply and sanitation. However, it should be noted that by international standards of the time this was a fairly tall group, which was also taller than the rest of the Colombian population, for which men averaged 160 cm in height and women 150 cm.

Using heights collected from three different sources, Meisel and Vega (2007a, b) conducted an exhaustive examination of anthropometric data for Columbian citizens for the period 1870 to 1985 In addition to the aforementioned passport data, they use the information on height obtained from citizenship cards, to document an increase of 8.96 cm for men and 8.95 for women for those born between 1905 and 1985. Thus, an increase of more than 1 cm. per decade. Additionally, they found that in the same period, there was a steady reduction in interpersonal and interregional inequalities in height, as measured by the coefficient of variation.

Finally, they utilized a database of white-collar workers containing the height of all employees of the Colombian Central Bank between 1923 and the early twenty-first century, a total of 16,909 persons, of which 64% were men. The trend is similar to that obtained with the citizenship cards, but the Central Bank employees on average were 4 cm. taller, which is similar to the height of urban dwellers in the same period.

Karina Acosta and Adolfo Meisel (2013) used information from a Colombian national health and nutrition survey to study the height of Afro-Colombians and the Indigenous population, according to self-reporting of ethnicity, for those born between 1965 and 1990.

Meisel et al. (2019) used a large-scale dataset of 225,000 individuals gathered from the judicial certificates to study the height of those born between 1921 and 1990. The certificates include data on height, gender, date and place of birth, level of education, and occupation. They found that during the period 1920–1990, there was a process of convergence in heights between individuals and between the regions of Colombia.

Using the same database obtained from the judicial records, Meisel and Ramirez (2023) trace the evolution of gender dimorphism for those Colombians born between 1920 and 1990. Using quantile regressions they conclude that in hard economic times men are more penalized. Thus, the height gap between men and women becomes smaller in bad economic situations and increases during booms.

Chile is a source of great advancement in South American anthropometric studies. Most of the contributions have been made by Manuel Llorca and his associates, who have constructed new databases resulting in an exceptionally good understanding of the evolution of biological welfare in that country over the last three centuries.

Llorca et al. (2018) published the first study on adult height for the Chilean population. They used eighteenth-century military records, which restricted their study to the male population. They found that the height of military recruits remained stagnant between the 1740s and the 1770s, and then declined from the 1780s to the 1800s. However, on average Chilean men were 167 centimeters tall, similar to the contemporary Swedes and taller than the Mexicans.

Borrego et al. (2019) explored the relationship between early-life diseases, proxied by infant mortality in the first year of life, and adult height. They obtained the data on height from the National Health Surveys of 2003 and 2009. The sample includes 3644 observations for 13 regions of Chile. All the regions experienced a decline in infant mortality and an increase in height. The cohort of 1960–1964 had an average height of 162 cm and it was 164.4 for the 1985–1989 cohort. They concluded that the majority of the increase in height can be attributed to the improvements in the health of infants.

Llorca et al. (2019) constructed a database for height of Chilean men in the nineteenth century. They used 3283 observations from the 1810s to the 1890s. Their results show that the average height of Chilean men started to decline in the 1850s and then stagnated in the 1890s. Average height fell significantly from 169 cm in the 1840s to 166.7 cm in the 1890s. This occurred in a period of export boom and growth of GDP per capita.

Using information from the main jail of Santiago de Chile, Manuel Llorca et al. (2020) created a database with records on height for 20,325 prisoners. The results show that those with a university degree, legitimate birth, European surname, and who were literate were taller than average.

For the whole of the twentieth century, Llorca et al. (2021) analyzed military records from the Archivo Historico del Ejercito to trace the evolution of the average height of Chilean men. Height increased in every decade in the twentieth century except the 1940s, when it fell 0.5 cm. In the first decade of the century, height was on average 166.2 cm, but by the 1990s it was 172.4 cm, an increase of 6.2 cm. The authors also found that there was a negative correlation between height and dark skin pigmentation, and that those born in the center of the country were taller.

The behavior of gender dimorphism in Chile in the period going from the 1860s to the 1990s has been researched by Llorca et al. (2022). They found that from the 1920s, gender dimorphism in height increased until the 1990s. While both genders experienced a height increase, men grew more rapidly. Their hypothesis is that male height is more responsive to changes in overall socioeconomic conditions.

Only a few anthropometric studies exist for Peru, Bolivia, and Uruguay. There are currently no publications on this topic for Venezuela, Ecuador, and Paraguay. For Peru, Baten et al. (2009) used prison data to explore the behavior of male height during the nineteenth century. They found no significant differences in height by occupation. However, there are large variations by ethnicity. Whites born in the 1880s were 8 cm taller than Indians, who were also shorter than Mestizos and Asians. Overall, heights in this sample stagnated from the 1820s to the 1880s, when the average height decreased from 162.4 cm to 161.4 cm, with a small increase from the 1850s to the 1860s. There was no stature convergence between ethnic groups. Only the height of whites increased in this period. In the 1880s, both blacks and whites were taller than Indians by more than 7 cm.

Branisa et al. (2020) conducted the first anthropometric study for Bolivia, using the National Identification Card records. Their sample covers males in La Paz from mostly the upper and middle classes. During the period 1880–1929, heights were stagnant around 163 cm. This happened even though GDP per capita grew at a rate of 2% annually between 1903 and 1929. They attribute this result to the fact that there were no improvements in agricultural production or health services during those years. They also found that non-Indigenous males were 3 cm taller than Indians and those who were literate achieved 3.32 cm more in height.

In a recent study, Daniel Ferrari exploited Uruguayan military records to study the height of males during the twentieth century. He finds no evidence of improvement in biological well-being for those born after 1955 through 2001. Uruguayans born in the period 1956–1960 were on average 171.18 cm tall, those born in 1997–2001 were 171.06 cm. The coefficient of variation of height was quite stable during this period, indicating that there were no reductions in interpersonal differences in height.

Financial History

The schools that dominated the economic historiography in Latin America, at least until the early 1970s—Marxism, Annales, and structuralism—were not attracted to the history of monetary policy and banks, perhaps because they lacked a well-developed theoretical framework in this field and because they considered money as an epiphenomena. The structuralists considered the underlying determinants of inflation to be concentrated in agrarian land concentration, not monetary policy. They argued that this led to the rigidity of food supplies and the inadequate and unstable purchasing power of exports, which in turn hindered the importation of foodstuffs (Sunkel 1958). The hyperinflation experiences in several Latin American economies in the 1970s discredited this structuralist approach. As a result, economists more inclined toward a neoclassical view of macroeconomics started to dominate the discussion of monetary policies in most of South America. Since those studies usually make explicit use of economic theory and econometric techniques when applied to historical experiences, it can be argued that they are representative of the growing influence of the New Economic History in South America.

It was in this context that a growing interest in the monetary and banking history of the region emerged in the 1980s. Beginning in 1989 with Chile, Jacome (2016) highlighted the trend toward granting autonomy to the central banks: Colombia (1991), Costa Rica (1995), Honduras (1996), Mexico (1993), Peru (1993), Uruguay (1995), and Venezuela (1992). Several of these central banks have published their histories, which are basically the monetary history of their respective countries (Martinelli et al. 2023; Uribe 2023; Carrasco 2009).

After the former Spanish American colonies obtained their independence from Spain in the 1820s, there was a period of political instability caused by civil wars, as well as fiscal and monetary chaos. This led to decades of economic stagnation. As a result, few banks were created in South America in the period 1820–1850. This changed in the period 1850–1873 when more than 90 domestic banks were created in the region (Marichal 2021).

The early 1990s saw an uptick in the interest of research on free banking, which existed in the late nineteenth century in Colombia, Peru, Uruguay, and Chile (Meisel 1990, 1992; Zegarra 1993; Echeverri 1994). Free banking refers to a regime where multiple private banks issue their own money, the barriers to entry are low, and there is no government bank of issue or central bank. Meisel (1990) examined the Colombian experience with free banking, which lasted from 1871 to 1885. He showed that in the Colombian experience, most banks were successful and that there was never a generalized panic. Free banking ended after the government established a bank of issue that overextended its circulation in an effort to finance public spending. As a result, the government suspended the convertibility of its paper money to gold, effectively making it a fiat currency.

In Peru, the period of free banking extended from 1862 to 1878, a period of financial stability (Zegarra 1993). However, the government began to intervene in

1873 and by 1875 it suspended convertibility of banknotes to gold, bringing the free banking experiment to an end.

Chile was another South American country which experimented with free banking in the nineteenth century. Similar to the experiences in Colombia and Peru, the period was free of bank panics and ended only when the government began to issue banknotes through the Treasury and then suspended gold convertibility in 1878 (Marichal 2021).

The Uruguayan free banking period lasted from the 1870s to 1913. Unlike the other examples discussed previously, the Uruguayan government intervened and even declared inconvertibility in some subperiods (Diaz 2018). Free banking was debated, but never implemented in Brazil and Argentina.

The 1920s saw a process of central bank creation in South America. In the Andean countries, which were increasingly falling under the economic influence of the United States, Princeton economist Edwin W. Kemmerer established central banks in Colombia (1923), Chile (1925), Ecuador (1927), and Bolivia (1929). In 1931, he reformed the Peruvian central bank, which had been created in 1922—the first one in South America (Meisel et al. 1994; Flores 2021). A few years later, central banks were created in Argentina (1935) and Venezuela (1939).

To understand the economic history of South America in the twentieth century, it is necessary to understand its monetary history. One country where this is particularly true is Argentina. Once one of the richest countries in the world, it entered into a period of economic decline at the beginning of the twentieth century, which does not seem to have ended a century later. della Paolera and Taylor (2003) argue that Argentina had a combination of economic prosperity and a deficit of institutions, which led to financial and monetary instability. Thus, the outcome was a quasi-permanent decline. They arrived at this conclusion after studying the monetary and financial history of that country between 1880 and 1935.

The popularity of studying monetary history in the region has grown in recent decades (Sanchez 2003; Hernandez 2004; Banco Central de Bolivia 2015; Contreras 2016; Llona 1997). In 2019, the Becker and Friedman Institute carried out a project to review the monetary and fiscal history of the last half century for the 10 Latin countries in South America (Venezuela, Ecuador, Colombia, Peru, Chile, Argentina, Uruguay, Brazil, Paraguay, and Bolivia).

The Influence of Douglass North

New institutional history is one of the most influential approaches to South American economic history in the first decades of the twenty-first century. The initial impulse derived from the work of Douglass C. North (1981), whose contributions are nicely summarized by John Wallis (2016). Lloyd and Lee (2018) argue that North's primary contribution has been "to elevate the analysis of institutions to a more macro level—linking institutions to economic growth and development." For North, institutions, understood as rules of the game that determine human interaction, are the reason why some economies prosper in the long-run.

The contributions of North for the study of the determinants of economic prosperity in the long-run were mainly analytical. However, following in his footsteps, Daron Acemoglu, Simon Johnson, and James A. Robinson have published a series of papers on the role of institutions for the understanding of economic growth of nations, which include explicit economic models and empirical analysis based on econometric estimates (Acemoglu et al. 2001; Acemoglu and Robinson 2008). That is, their approach to study the past is basically that of the New Economic History. In particular, in their 2001 article, they argue that in Africa, Central America, and South America, the Caribbean, and South Asia, the European powers established colonies with highly extractive institutions. For example, in the Americas, Spain established encomiendas, mitas, and the slavery of Africans. In contrast, in North America, Australia, and New Zealand, English colonists set up more inclusive institutions. These colonization strategies depended on the number of colonizers and on the mortality rates they faced. Thus, in the Caribbean, the English set up extractive institutions, such as slavery, because of the high mortality rates that predominated, and in North America they enforced property rights "for a broad cross section of the society" (Acemoglu and Robinson 2008).

Acemoglu and his coauthors influenced many economists and economic historians whose research illustrates the long-term impact of institutions on the prosperity of nations. Two criticisms often formulated in relation to this literature are that the way institutions are modeled and measured is often rudimentary, and the role of geography and culture is completely ignored (Lloyd and Lee 2018).

In the case of South America, there have been many recent economic history studies using the institutionalist approach. I will mention only a few to illustrate the type of analysis on which they base their results. One of the most influential papers was published by Engerman and Sokoloff (1997). They consider that the independence of institutions from factor endowments has been exaggerated and that the role of factor endowments has thus been underestimated. Reviewing the evidence for the Americas, Canada, and the USA, they conclude that if local conditions were appropriate for crops that exhibited economies of scale (e.g., sugar, cotton, coffee), then slavery was introduced. In other Spanish American countries where there were large numbers of Native Americans, other exploitative institutions, such as encomiendas and mitas, were established. These institutions led to a large concentration of wealth, human capital, and power, which benefitted a small elite and lowered the possibilities for long-term prosperity.

Evaluating the long-term impact of the mita in Peru, Melissa Dell (2021) concluded that the districts where it had existed felt its negative influence. The mita was a labor system that forced Indian communities to send one seventh of the adult population to work in the silver mines of Potosí or the mercury mines of Huancavelica every year. This system of labor existed in the Viceroyalty of Peru between 1573 and 1812. Dell found that in the long run, the mita lowered household consumption by 25%. In districts where there was no mita, the Spanish authorities allowed the formation of a greater number of haciendas. These members of the landed elite were able to secure more public goods for their districts, such as roads and human capital, which facilitated long-term growth.

Nathan Nunn (2008) tested the Engerman–Sokoloff hypothesis for the Americas as well as across the US states and districts. He found that slave use was negatively correlated with subsequent economic development. However, there was no evidence that the previous relationship was driven by large-scale plantation slavery or that it manifested through slavery's effect on economic inequality.

Joana Naritomi et al. (2012) studied the differential long-term impact of the sugar boom and the gold boom in Brazil. Sugar was associated with an oligarchic society and there was great inequality in the distribution of land. In the case of gold, there was a presence of the heavily inefficient Portuguese state, which led to inefficiencies in governance and access to justice. The authors find that in those municipalities that grew sugar cane in the colonial period, land distribution is more unequal today. And those which mined gold have worse governance and less access to justice today.

Final Comments

In the first decades of the twenty-first century, it is evident that Latin American economic history is increasingly dominated by the New Economic History (NEH) and the New Institutional History (NIH). In the case of the NEH, the approach is fundamentally microeconomic (for example, railroads, slavery, anthropometrics) or sectoral (such as monetary and fiscal history). While the NIH asks the big questions in economic development, it does not have the teleological attraction of Marxism, for which historical analysis was seen as a guide for political action, or the clear policy recommendations of dependencia. Thus, one can expect that over the next few decades, economic history in Latin America will advance under the influence of the NEH-NIH and produce research of a high technical quality but for a specialized and reduced audience. This tendency is amplified because currently the history profession has taken a cultural turn and almost completely abandoned its interest in economic history. Perhaps this result is just a reflection that the field of economic history has achieved a stage of professional maturity.

The results of the New Institutional History lead to the conclusion that the reason that South American countries are much less prosperous than Canada and the USA is the lasting impact of colonial institutions. This diagnosis coincides with the view of many of the Latin American liberal intellectuals of the nineteenth century, who blame the colonial legacy for retarding the economic growth of the region. For example, the Argentinian Esteban Echeverria said that: "...we are independent but we are not free; the arms of Spain no longer oppress us, but her traditions weigh us down...the social emancipation of Latin America can only be achieved repudiating the heritage bequeathed by Spain" (Velíz 1980). In the decades after independence, many of the institutions which were inherited by the new republic, including mita, resguardos, the tax system, mortmain, slavery, the inquisition, and the lack of separation between church and state, were eliminated. But there was a strong persistence in the concentration of wealth, land, power, and human capital among the elite. This legacy was often cited by the Latin American intellectuals of the late nineteenth century as an original sin that has proven difficult to eliminate. This dismal message seems to be corroborated by the New Institutional History. However, as a philosopher of nineteenth century once said, it is human beings that make history, even if they face enormous limitations.

References

Acemoglu, Daron, and James Robinson. 2008. *The Role of Institutions in Growth and Development.* Working Paper No. 10, Commission on Growth and Development, Washington.

Acemoglu, Daron, Simon Johnson, and James A. Robinson. 2001. The Colonial Origins of Comparative Development : A Empirical Investigation. *American Economic Review* 91 (5).

Acosta, Karina, and Adolfo Meisel. 2013. Anthropometric Measurement by Ethnicity in Colombia, 1965-1990. *Economics and Human Biology* 11.

Arteta, Luis Eduardo Nieto. 1942. *Economía y cultura en la historia de Colombia.*

Bagú, Sergio. 1949. *Economía de la sociedad colonial.*

Banco Central de Bolivia. 2015. *Historia monetaria de Bolivia.* La Paz: Banco Central de Bolivia.

Baten, Joerg, Ines Pelger, and Linda Twrdek. 2009. The anthropometric history of Argentina, Brazil, and Peru during the 19th and early 20th century. *Economics and Human Biology* 7.

Bértola, Luis, and Javier Rodríguez Weber. 2015. *Latin American Economic History Looking Backwards for the Future.* Documento On Line, No. 37, abril. Facultad de Ciencias Sociales, Universidad de la República.

Bonett, Diana, ed. 2015. *Una obra para la historia: Homenaje a German Colmenares.* Bogotá: Editorial Universidad del Rosario.

Borrego, Florencia, Carlos Guillermo Bozzoli, and Federico Droller. 2019. Early life environment and adult height: The case of Chile. *Economics and Human Biology.*

Branisa, Boris, Jose Peres, and Nigel Caspa. 2020. The biological standard of living in La Paz (Bolivia), 1880s-1920s: Persistent stagnation and inequality. *Economics and Human Biology* 37.

Cardosa, Fernando Henrique, and Enzo Faletto. 1979. *Dependency and Development in Latin America.* Berkeley, CA: University of California Press.

Carrasco, Camilo. 2009. *Banco Central de Chile 1925-1964, Una historia institucional.* Santiago: Banco Central de Chile.

Coatsworth, John H., and Alan M. Taylor. 1998. Introduction. In *Latin America and the World Economy Since 1800, The David Rockefeller Center Series on Latin America*, ed. John H. Coatsworth and Alan M. Taylor. Harvard University.

Conrad, Alfred H., and John R. Meyer. 1958. The Economics of Slavery in the Ante Bellum South. *Journal of Political Economy* LXVI (2).

Contreras, Carlos. 2016. *Historia de la moneda en el Perú.* Lima: Banco Central de Reserva.

Cussen, Celia, Manuel Llorca-Jaña, and Federico Droller. 2016. The Dynamics and Determinants of Slave Prices in an Urban Setting: Santiago de Chile, 1773-1822. *Revista de Historia Económica.*

Dell, Melissa. 2021. The Persistence Effects of Peru's Mining Mita. *Econometrica* 78 (1, Winter).

della Paolera, Gerarrd, and Alan M. Taylor. 2003. *Tensando el ancla, La caja de conversión Argentina y la búsqueda de estabilidad macroeconómica, 1880-1935.* Fondo de Cultura Económica, Argentina.

Diaz, Gaton. 2018. *The Uruguayan Monetary and Banking System, 1857-1913.* Universidad de la República, Uruguay (mimeo).

Echeverri, Lina. 1994. *Banca Libre: La experiencia colombiana en el siglo XIX*. en Fabio Sanchez, compilador, Ensayos de historia monetaria y bancaria de Colombia, Tercer Mundo Editores, Bogotá.
Engerman, Stanley L., and Kenneth L. Sokoloff. 1997. Factor Endowments, Institutions, and Differential Paths of Growth Among New World Economies. In *How Latin America Fell Behind, Essays in Economic History of Brazil and Mexico, 1800-1914*, ed. Stephen Haber. Stanford, CA: Stanford University Press.
Fajardo, Margarita. 2022. *The World That Latin America Created, The United Nations Economic Commission for Latin America in the Development Era*. USA: Harvard University Press.
Felipe Zegarra, Luis. 2013. Transportation Costs and the Social Savings of Railroads in Latin America. The Case of Peru. *Revista de Historia Económica* 31 (1).
Ferrer, Aldo. 1963. *La economía argentina desde sus orígenes*.
Flores, Juan. 2021. Money Doctors and Latin American Central Banks at the Onset of the Great Depression. *Journal of Latin American Studies* 53.
Fogel, Robert, and Stanley Engerman. 1974. *Time on the Cross: The Economics of American Negro Slavery*. New York: Little, Brown and Company.
Fogel, Robert W. 1996. *A Life of Learning*. American Council of Learned Societies, Occasional Paper, No. 34.
Fogel, Robert W. 1970. *Railroads and American Economic Growth, Essays in Econometric History*. Baltimore: John Hopkins Press.
Frank, Zephyr. 2006. Stature in Nineteenth Century Rio de Janeiro: Preliminary Evidence from Prison Records. *Revista de Historia Económica* XXIV (3).
Franken, Daniel. 2019. Anthropometric History of Brazil, 1850-1950: Insights From Military and Passport Records. *Revista de Historia Económica* 37 (2).
Friedman, Milton, and Anna J. Schwartz. 1963. *A Monetary History of the United States, Princeton*. NJ: Princeton University Press.
Furtado, Celso. 1959. *A Formacao economica do Brasil*.
Haber, Stephen. 1997. Introduction. In *How Latin America Fell Behind, Essays on the Economic Histories of Brazil and Mexico*, ed. Stephen Haber, 1800–1914. Stanford, CA: Stanford University Press.
Hernandez, Antonio. 2004. *La moneda y el debate monetario en Colombia*. Bogotá: Retina.
Hernandez, M. Silva. 2015. Entrevista con Carlos Marichal.A propósito de la historia economica de America Latina. *Revista de Historia,* 7, enero-junio.
Herranz-Loncan, Alfonso. 2011. The role of railways in export-led growth: The case of Uruguay. *Economic History of Developing Regions* 26 (2).
Herranz-Loncan, Alfonso. 2014. Transport Technology and Economic Expansion: The Growth Contribution of Railways in Latin America Before 1914. *Revista de Historia Económica* 32 (1).
Jacome, Luis I. 2016. A Historical Perspective on Central Banking in Latin America. *IMF eLibrary*, October.
Junio, Caio Prador. 1942. *La formacao do Brasil contemporáneo-Colonia*.
Llona, Augustin. 1997. Chilean Monetary History, 1860-1925: An Overview. *Revista de historia económica* XV (1).
Llorca, Manuel, Juan Navarrete, Federico Droller, and Roberto Araya. 2018. Height in eighteenth century Chilean men: Evidence from military records, 1730-1800s. *Economics and Human Biology* 29.
Llorca, Manuel, Juan Navarrete, Federico Droller, and Roberto Araya. 2019. The Physical Stature of Men in 19th Century Chile: Another Case of Stagnation During an Export Boom. *Revista de Historia Económica* 37:1.
Llorca, Manuel, Javier Rivas, Damian Clarke, and Diego Barria. 2020. Height of Male Prisioners in Santiago de Chile During the Nitrate Era: The Penalty of Being Unskilled, Illiterate, Illegitimate, and Mapuche. *International Journal of Environmental Research and Public Health* 17:6261.

Llorca, Manuel, Juan Navarrete, Roberto Araya, Federico Droller, Martina Allende, and Javier Rivas. 2021. Height in twentieth-century Chilean men: Growth with divergence. *Cliometrica* 15.
Llorca, Manuel, Roberto Araya, and Juan Navarrete. 2022. Adult Female Height and Gender Gap in Chile, 1860s to 1990's. *Journal of Interdisciplinary History* 53 (2): Autumn.
Lloyd, Peter, and Cassey Lee. 2018. A Review of the Recent Literature on the Institutional Economic Analysis of the Long-Run Performance of Nations. *Journal of Economic Surveys* 32:1.
Love, Joseph L.. 2005. The Rise and Decline of Economic Structuralism in Latin America: New Dimensions. *Latin American Research Review* 40:3
Marichal, Carlos. 2021. *El nacimiento de la banca en América Latina.* El Colegio de Mexico: Finanzas y política en el siglo XIX.
Martinelli, Cesar, et al. 2023. *Historia del Banco Central y de la política monetaria.* Banco Central de la Reserva del Perú, Tomo 1, Lima.
Martinez-Carrion, Jose M., and Ricardo Salvatore. 2019. Inequality and Well-Being in Iberian and Latin American Regions since 1820: New Approaches From Anthropometric History. *Revista de Historia Económica* 37:2.
Meisel, Adolfo. 1992. *"Free Banking", in Kevin Dowd, The Experience of Free Banking.* USA: Routledge.
Meisel, Adolfo, "Los bancos comerciales en la era de la banca libre, 1871-1885", in Adolfo Meisel, et al., *El Banco de la República, Antecedentes, Evolución y Estructura,* Banco de la República, Bogotá, 1990.
Meisel, Adolfo, Alejandro Lopez, and Francisco Ruiz. 1994. Compiladores, Kemmerer y el Banco de la República, *Diarios y documentos,* Banco de la República, Bogotá.
Meisel, Adolfo, and Angela Granger. 2019. Determinantes del precio de los esclavos en el Caribe neogranadino en el siglo XVIII. *Tiempo y economía* 6 (1): enero-junio.
Meisel, Adolfo, and Margarita Vega. 2005. La estatura de la elite colombiana antes de la industrialización, 1870-1919. *Revista del Banco de la República* 932.
Meisel, Adolfo, and Margarita Vega. 2007a. The Biological Standard of Living (and its Convergence) in Colombia, 1870-2003, A Tropical Success Story. *Economics and Human Biology* 5:1.
Meisel, Adolfo, and Margarita Vega. 2007b. *La calidad de vida biológica en Colombia, Antropometría histórica, 1870-2003.* Cartagena: CEER, Banco de la República, CEER.
Meisel, Adolfo, and María Teresa Ramirez. 2023. Gender Height Dimorphism: An Approximation of the Living Standards in Colombia, 1920-1990. *Investigaciones de Historia Economica* 19.
Meisel, Adolfo, María Teresa Ramirez, and Daniela Santos. 2019. Socioeconomic Determinants and Spatial Convergence of Well-Being, 1920-1990. *Revista de Historia Económica* 37 (2).
Mitch, David. 2019. The Contributions of Robert Fogel to Cliometrics. In *Handbook of Cliometrics*, ed. Claude Diebolt and Michael Haupert. Cham: Springer.
Monasterio, Leoanardo. 2014. Stature and Immigration in Southern Brazil, 1889-1914. *America Latina en la Historia Económica,* Año 21, Numero 1.
Monasterio, Leonardo, and Luiz Paulo Nogueral. 2006. Growth and Inequalities of Height in Brazil (1939-1981). *MPRA Paper* 769.
Naritomi, Joana, Rodrigo R. Soares, and Juliano J. Assuncao. 2012. Institutional Development and Colonial Heritage Within Brazil. *Journal of Economic History* 72 (2).
Newland, Carlos, and María Jesus San Segundo. 1996. Determinants of the Price Life Cycle of a Slave: Peru and La Plata in the eighteenth Century. *Journal of Economic History* 56 (3).
Newland, Carlos, and María Jesus San Segundo. 1994. Un análisis de los determinantes del precio de los esclavos hispanoamericanos en el siglo XVIII. *Revista de Historia Económica* (3).
North, Douglas C. 1981. *Structure and Change in Economic History.* USA: W.W. Norton and Company.
Nunn, Nathan. 2008. Slavery, Inequality, and Economic Development in the Americas: An Examination of the Engerman-Sokoloff Hypothesis. In *Institutions and Economic Performance*, ed. Elhanan Helpman. Cambridge, MA: Harvard University Press.
Pinto, Anibal, Chile un caso de desarrollo frustado, 1959

Puigross, Rodolfo, De la colonia a la Revolución (1940)
Ramirez, Maria Teresa. 2001. Los ferrocarriles y su impacto sobre la economía colombiana. *Revista de Historia Económica* XIX (1).
Riella, Rebeca. 2021. *Precio de esclavos en inventarios post mortem 1700-1825*. Uruguay, octubre: Instituto de Economía, Universidad de la Republica.
Salvatore, Ricardo. 1998. A Most Difficult Case of Estimation: Argentinian Height, 1770-1840. In *The Biological Standard of Living in Comparative Perspective*, ed. John Komlos and Joerg Baten. Stuttgart: Franz Steiner Verlag.
Salvatore, Ricardo. 2010. Better-off in the Thirties: Welfare Indices for Argentina, 1900-1940. In *Living Standards in Latin American History, Height, Welfare, and Development, 1750-2000*, ed. Ricardo Salvatore, John Coatsworth, and Amilcar Challú. DRCLAS, Harvard University, USA.
Salvatore, Ricardo. 2007. Height, Nutrition, and Well-Being in Argentina, ca. 1850-1950. *Revista de Historia Económica* 25 (1).
Salvatore, Ricardo. 2020. Stunting Rates in a Food-Rich Country: The Argentine Pampas from the 1850s to the 1950s. *International Journal of Environmental Research in Public Health* 17 (21).
Salvatore, Ricardo. 2019. The Biological Well-Being of the Working-Poor: The Height of Prisoners in Buenos Aires Province, Argentina, 1885-1939. *Economics and Human Biology* (34).
Salvatore, Ricardo. 2016. Stature, Nutrition, and Regional Convergence in the Argentine Northwest in the First Half of the Twentieth Century. *Social Science History* 28 (2).
Sanchez, Omar. 2003. The Rise and Fall of the Dependency Movement: Does It Inform Under Development Today? *E.I.A.L.* 14 (2).
Sharp, William F. 1976. *Slavery on the Spanish Frontier, The Colombian Chocó, 1680-1810*. USA: University of Oklahoma Press.
Sumerhill, William R.. 2005. Big Social Savings in a Small Laggard Economy: Railroad Led Growth in Brazil. *Journal of Economic History* 65 (1).
Sunkel, Osvaldo. 1958. La inflación chilena: Un enfoque heterodoxo. *Trimestre económico* XXV, No. 4.
Uribe, Jose Dario, ed. 2023. *Historia del Banco de la República*. Banco de la República, Bogotá: Cien Años.
Velíz, Claudio. 1980. *The Centralist Tradition of Latin America*. Princeton, New Jersey: Princeton University Press.
Wallis, John J.. 2016. The New Economic History and Beyond: The Scholarship of Douglas C. North. *Journal of Economic History* 76 (3).
Zegarra, Luis Felipe. 1993. Free Banking and Financial Stability in Peru. *Quarterly Journal of Austrian Economics* 16 (2). See also, Eduardo Moron, *La experiencia de la banca libre en el Perú, 1860-1879,* Universidad del Pacífico, Lima.

Recent Trends in Economic History in Mexico

Gustavo A. Del Angel

Abstract This chapter examines the recent evolution of economic history research in Mexico through a bibliometric analysis of 656 academic papers published between 1994 and 2021 in four Mexican journals, as well as presentations at the The Inter-Institutional Economic History Seminar (SIHE) in that country. The study identifies trends in thematic focus, co-authorship patterns, gender participation, and historical periods analyzed. It reveals a significant growth in publication volume since 2010. Research on the twentieth century has increased notably, while business history, fiscal history, and financial institutions have emerged as salient topics. In Mexico, the field remains predominantly housed in history departments, though interdisciplinary collaboration, especially with economists, is growing. A gender gap is observed, with decreasing female authorship over time. The study also highlights the increasing internationalization of Mexican economic history scholarship, with over half of the analyzed articles focusing on countries other than Mexico. The findings suggest that research output has become more collaborative and diversified in both topics and historical periods. This chapter contributes to understanding the institutional, thematic, and methodological development of economic history in Mexico and its role within broader Latin American and international academic contexts.

The author thank the invaluable help as research assistants of Daniel Fernández and Alejandro Romero; Daniel worked in the organization of the database and Alejandro in the analysis of the data. The author also thank conversations with Antonio Ibarra, Aurora Gómez-Galvarriato, Michael Haupert, Sandra Kuntz, Carlos Marichal, and Manuel Bautista; and the participants at the Session The State of Economic History: A Global Perspective in the XIX World Economic History Congress in Paris, 2022.

G. A. Del Angel (✉)
Department of Economics at CIDE, Centro de Investigación y Docencia Económicas (CIDE), Mexico, Mexico
e-mail: gustavo.delangel@cide.edu

C. Diebolt, M. Haupert (eds.), *The State of Economic History*, Frontiers in Economic History, https://doi.org/10.1007/978-3-032-01624-9_10

Introduction

This chapter studies the production, characteristics, and trends of recent research in economic history in Mexico, focusing on academic papers published in Mexican journals (one of which specializes in the subject) between 1998 and 2021. Research in this field has certainly expanded in Latin America in the last 25 years, but this is not a new thing. Mexico has had an economic history tradition since the first quarter of the twentieth century. Today, it is also a regional hub in the field with active participation of academics from different institutions and countries and with a range of approaches, all of whom combine to form an ecosystem.

That being said, the patterns in the research have changed and therefore the following questions arise: How has published research in Mexico evolved in the last 25 years? What are the most-studied themes and periods? In this chapter, I show that there has been growth in the research published in Mexico; the number of countries studied in the publications has increased; research into the twentieth century has increased; and some subjects have become higher profile, such as business history and fiscal history. One thing that has remained fairly constant is that local research production comes mostly from academics in the discipline of history and less so from economics.

Studying the research production patterns in economic history is important because it holds a unique position within the social sciences. It is akin to an indispensable sibling to both history and economics, but one that not everyone wants to have anything to do with. However, it is a cornerstone for the advancement of both disciplines.

In this chapter, the term "economic history" is used interchangeably to refer to research in business, economic, and financial history—they can all be considered subfields of economic history. It is also used interchangeably to refer to research produced within the spheres of both economics and history. The latter is important because, despite the dialogue between the two disciplines and the research that results from an amalgamation of the two, the methods and discussions in economics and history are different.

It is important to note that, in Anglo-American academia between the 1990s and the 2000s, there was a reluctance among historians to tackle economic issues and even more so to use methods from economics. This has represented a high cost for history as a discipline. Consequently, the most influential works of economic history were mainly produced within economics, even though economic history has not been a dominant field within economics research.

This has been different in other parts of the world, not least in Europe and Latin America, where economic history has largely been the work of historians. In Mexico, economic history predominantly lies in academic departments of history; nonetheless, there have always been economists in the field and even today there is a healthy dialogue between researchers from both disciplines.

At the international level, there is an important discussion about economic history to understand it as the amalgamation of two disciplines: economics and history.

This discussion seeks to identify which discipline has been most relevant in research into the historical nature of economic problems, how methods have evolved, and which discipline has had a bigger impact on the production of economic historians. For example, Cioni et al. (2023) analyze a database of around 2500 papers published between 2001 and 2018 in the 5 main economic history journals and eight leading economics journals. The study's results do not confirm the narrative of economic history becoming more integrated with economics. Despite recent interest from economists, economic history—and the theme of legacy studies in particular—remain marginal in economics journals. Moreover, according to that paper, very few authors have published in both economics and economic history journals.

Fernández-de-Pinedo et al. (2023) study the integration of economic history into economics, using a dataset of 11,143 papers written by 919 researchers in economic history and published in leading journals in the field between 1980 and 2019. In addition, they analyzed the authors' biographical information to study geographical trends and individual factors that influence publication in different types of journals. The authors utilized a probit regression and found that, since 1980, the probability of economic historians publishing in economics or finance journals has increased. This integration is more pronounced in North America than in Europe due to differences in the academic training of economic historians. The authors found that economic history is much more integrated within economics in North America.

Economic history research conducted in economics departments is characterized by a constant incorporation of new methods for analyzing historical data. Certainly, this is essential for better understanding the economic problems. The amalgamation of quantitative history, statistical and econometric methods, economic theory and historical sources is known as cliometrics. Diebolt and Haupert (2022) show that cliometrics was a revolution in economic history because it introduced a new way of studying the past by utilizing economic theory and quantitative methods. Cliometrics has enabled economic historians to reevaluate previous findings and gain a deeper understanding of the past, which has significantly improved the discipline as a whole. The interdisciplinary approach of cliometrics has enabled economic historians to work with experts in other areas, such as computing and statistics, to improve their ability to compile and analyze data and thereby offer a more complete perspective on economic phenomena over time.

In another paper, Diebolt and Haupert (2019) examine the influence and impact of cliometrics on economics, arguing that the former has provided valuable tools, new approaches, and datasets to the study of economic history, and this has enabled a better understanding of economic growth and development. Cliometrics has also facilitated the reevaluation of previous findings and, as a result, has led to a deeper and more accurate understanding of the past. It has also been the basis for the emergence of new approaches in the study of economics. A noteworthy example is institutional economics, which expanded in the 1980s and extended the conversation with other disciplines such as political science, business, law, psychology, and sociology.

Regarding these debates, Mexico and the rest of Latin America have not been out of sync with international tendencies. However, they have their own features, which

I will try to discuss in this chapter. For this purpose, the next section explains the context of Mexico's economic history in the last three decades. Section "Analysis of Publications in Mexican Journals" provides an analysis of a database of papers published in Mexico between 1994 and 2021, and section "Concluding Remarks" gives concluding remarks.

The Context of Economic History in Mexico

In Mexico and Latin America, studies into the evolution of the field of economic, business, and financial history in the region have also focused on the disciplinary interaction between economics and history. The growth of this field of research has led to several questions. For example, how does research in Latin America link up with research from other regions? How can it contribute to a better understanding of the region's economic problems? How can it help to identify how the region's phenomena have a global nature and relate to the big trends in the world, such as capitalism or the emergence of the welfare state?

Unlike in Anglo-American academia, economic history in Latin America remains a constant presence in historians' work. In Mexico, this is due to a historiographical tradition of dealing with economic issues that dates back to the nineteenth century, but that became explicit in the 1920s and emerged formally as a field of research for historians from the 1960s. To some extent, this is undoubtedly explained by the fact that economic problems in the region attract constant attention from academics. Historical analysis of economic phenomena, ever-present for economists since the origins of their profession in Mexico in the first quarter of the twentieth century, has primarily been a way of evaluating the country's economic trajectory in the long run.

Avella (2020) makes a thorough assessment of how economic history became a field in its own right, weaving together the two disciplines of economics and history. The author proposes three broad periods: the first of forerunners (1927–1955), another when it became work of academic nature (1956–1975), and a third that saw the professionalization and consolidation of the field (1976–1989). In the first two stages, publications by economists and historians coincided, although not necessarily by theme or spaces of discussion. However, there was a small amount of noteworthy dialogue between the two disciplines (proven by citations between them). Avella (2020) pinpoints some major milestones, such as the publication of works by the historian Enrique Florescano at the end of the 1960s and the beginning of the 1970s that made way for, and generated interest in, the emergence of projects on the history of economic development (from within the discipline of history) and quantitative history, similar to that done in other countries (Florescano 1970, 1980).

Avella's exploration ends as a new stage began in the 1990s, which we address in this study. But there are two major milestones that mark that stage. The first was the establishment of a journal in 1990, first called the *Boletín de Fuentes para la Historia Económica de México* (Bulletin of Sources for Mexican Economic History), which published essays on archival sources for economic history. In 1994, the *Boletín* became the journal *América Latina en la Historia Económica* (Latin America in Economic History). The journal upheld in its early years its original purpose of investigating archival sources and later became a more wide-ranging journal with research papers, as well as undergoing the process of becoming indexed in international databases.

The other milestone was the foundation of the *Asociación Mexicana de Historia Económica* (Mexican Association of Economic History; AMHE) in October 1998. The AMHE's creation was the result of an exchange of ideas and communication between colleagues in Mexico and other countries. This milestone shows that there was interest in institutionalizing the information exchanges about research and teaching that were taking place among a professionalized community of researchers.

It is important to add that in 1992, previous to the AMHE, a group of historians from institutions in the northern States of México formed the *Asociación de Historia Económica del Norte de México* (Association of Economic History of the North of Mexico). The scope of their activities has been regional and focused on the regional business history of the Mexican northern states.

With the AMHE came conferences that always had international participation as well as attendees from Mexico. Conferences are part of the AMHE's mandate, enshrined in its by-laws. As such, the first Economic History Conference organized by the association was held in October 2001 at the UNAM *Instituto de Investigaciones Históricas* in Mexico City. Interestingly, attendance at the conferences has seen constant growth. This clearly shows that they are a rigorous and professional space for the exchange of ideas and, as such, are attractive to colleagues. It also suggests that colleagues from other fields see them that way, such as academics who study historical periods without necessarily focusing on economic themes and who converge at them through their own journey of research and discovery.

One important characteristic has been the internationalization of academic activities in economic history, in part due to the flow of researchers from other countries into Mexico to conduct research or to present their results. Likewise, there is constant participation by Mexican academics in international conferences. This internationalization has mainly occurred through exchanges with other Latin American countries, as well as the United States and Spain.

Some academics have analyzed the research output of scholars dedicated to economic history in Mexico and Latin America. One watershed moment in this type of analysis was the publication in 2003 of a special number of the journal *Historia Mexicana* (Mexican History)—"Mexican Economic History in the Nineties"—which discussed recent contributions in the field (Ibarra 2003). Some features of the papers in that special edition are, among others, an increase in the production of research, the consolidation of a hub of research about Mexico, and a greater link with the global literature and discussions.

The discussion has not been limited to Mexico but covers research production across Latin America. Haber (1997) opened up a debate about Latin American economic history and the need to generate research with refutable hypotheses that belongs to the social sciences. Haber argued that approaches such as dependency theory, which were widespread in the 90s and 80s in the Latin-American academica, restricted the possibilities of logic refutation and limited explanations of complex long-run phenomena. More recently, other authors such as Simonassi et al. (2021) and Bértola (2016) have emphasized the importance of dialogue between the two disciplines—economics and history—as a minimum (and if possible, to converse with others such as sociology, political science, and anthropology too) to enable more robust research. For those authors, the problem does not lie in the approach but rather in the challenges to craft research that combines historical work with social science frameworks. The authors also draw on the fact that scholarship in the field has been consolidated in various Latin American countries.

On a different note, Szmrecsanyi and Topik (2004), as well as Dávila (2008, 2013), study the increasing production of business history research in Latin America, which has been notable in the last two decades. They discuss how business history produced in those countries has been linked to a global discussion. They argue that the findings of Latin American business history enable a better understanding of global phenomena, and, at the same time, there is greater insertion of the regional issues in the global literature.

Analysis of Publications in Mexican Journals

This section presents an analysis of papers published in the four Mexican journals that are most relevant for economic history in Mexico and are high profile in Latin America. To enable this, I have created a bibliometric database of papers from these journals' catalogs.

Working with this database of papers presents some restrictions when it comes to understanding the publication patterns in the field. First, publications in books are not considered, whether from local academic publishers or commercial ones. Books make up a large proportion of the publications in economic and business history in Mexico, but information about them is sparse and the standards of publication are not comparable between publishers. Second, publications in the main international journals and academic press are not considered either. These make up only a fraction of publications, but there has been a significant increase in the number of academics across Latin America that publish in these journals.

For this research, I analyzed 656 academic papers published in the four most prolific specialized journals on the subject between 1998 and 2021. In total, there were 790 authors involved in these papers. The four academic journals in question, according to the number of works on economic, business, and financial history that featured in them during the period studied, are *América Latina en la Historia Económica* (Latin America in Economic History; ALHE), *Historia Mexicana* (Mexican History; HM), *Estudios de Historia Novohispana* (Studies on New Spain History; Novohispana), and *El Trimestre Económico* (The Economic Quarterly; Trimestre). Two of the journals are from the discipline of history, one is from economics, and one specializes in economic, business, and financial history. Only the research publications from these journals are considered, not reviews.

Table 1 Journals analized in this paper

Journal name and discipline	Publisher, year of establishment, and publication language	Scimago ranking	Sample
***América Latina en la Historia Económica* (Latin America in Economic History)** Economic, business, and financial history	Instituto Mora, 1994, publishes mostly in Spanish but also in English, Portuguese, and French	Q1 in history, Q3 in economics	462 articles (all published articles), 1994–2021
***Historia Mexicana* (Mexican History)** History (general)	El Colegio de México, 1951, Spanish	Q2 in history (showing improvement)	109 articles, 1998–2021
***El Trimestre Económico* (The Economic Quarterly)** Economics (general, mostly empirical)	Fondo de Cultura Económica, 1934, Spanish	Q4 in economics (showing decline)	41 articles, 1998–2021
***Estudios de Historia Novohispana* (Studies on New-Spanish History)** History (general)	UNAM—IIH, 1966, Spanish	Not available	44 articles, 1998–2021

Table 1 shows the journals, the discipline to which they belong, information about the publisher, the year of establishment, the language of the journal, and the Scimago Journal Rankings (SJR),[1] as well as the sample size taken. ALHE represents the majority of the publications in the database. ALHE has between 40% and 75% of all the papers for the period from 1994 to 2008, and that increases to between 63% and 84% of the total for the period from 2009 to 2021.

The database includes all the papers published in the journals in question between January 1998 and the last 2021 edition, except for ALHE which includes articles from 1994. All the papers published in ALHE are taken into account in this study, given it is the journal that specializes in this field. For the other three journals, the criteria for determining whether or not to include papers involved the identification of a common theme and certain methodological proximity within broad parameters. In this sense, there may have been a (small) margin of error in the selection of papers. The most difficult was *El Trimestre* because some economics papers that were included contain a historical or long-term perspective and are contiguous to economic history, and yet they do not necessarily fit into a discussion of the economic, business, and financial history literature.

In the database, the papers are categorized by historical period and theme of research. Each of the papers was assigned two themes or research areas that it could belong to, as well as a historical period. The database also categorizes papers by the

[1] The rankings are published at: https://www.scimagojr.com/journalrank.php

country they study (using contemporary borders). The number of authors per paper is also indicated, including how many are female. The data is presented by year.

Tables 2 and 3 show the classification of the historical periods and themes or research areas. The historical periods are segmented in a way that is relatively traditional and accepted in historiography, as established in *Historia Económica General de México* (General Economic History of Mexico), coordinated by Kuntz (2010). I also added a category for works that develop a long-term, multi-secular analysis, and an additional category is for papers that do not belong to any specific period but are rather contemporary discussions of economic history (for example, papers about

Table 2 Historical periods

1	New Spain and Iberian empires
2	Wars of independence and nation building, nineteenth century (first half)
3	Global capitalism in the nineteenth century (extended second half, up to 1914)
4	Twentieth century (1914–)
5	Long-term analysis (multi-secular)
6	Contemporary discussion about Economic History and its sources

Table 3 Themes or areas of research

1	Historiography and economic thought
2	Mining
3	Agriculture and the rural economy
4	Energy industries
5	Industrial activity
6	Domestic trade and consumption, merchants
7	Globalization, international trade, commodities, and migration
8	Labor and salaries
9	Slavery
10	Indigenous population
11	Transport and communications
12	Credit, savings, banks, and financial institutions
13	Money, monetary policy, prices
14	Taxes and fiscal history
15	Public debt, domestic, and foreign
16	Growth and economic fluctuations
17	Public institutions, law, public policy, and property rights
18	Innovation and technology
19	Enterprises, entrepreneurs, and business networks
20	Inequality, income distribution, and social mobility

sources, historiographical papers, and those about methods). More precise historical divisions could be mapped out, but most of the papers fit into these broad categories.

The classification of themes or research areas is adapted from those used by others, such as by Florescano (1980), which uses bibliographic criteria, and that of the *Journal of Economic Literature*, so as to avoid discrepancies as far as possible. While there is an element of arbitrariness on the part of the author of this paper, the classification captures the research themes that are worked within Mexico. An alternative would have been to directly use the classification from the *Journal of Economic Literature*; however, this would reduce precision and many elements of local research would not be captured. The order in which they appear in Table 3 is random and does not represent any sort of hierarchy.

I also analyzed information from 108 presentations at the *Seminario Interinstitucional de Historia Económica* (Inter-Institutional Economic History Seminar; SIHE) between 2008 and 2018. This is an academic seminar that has taken place regularly since 2008, organized jointly by academic institutions in Mexico City: primarily El Colegio de México, the Instituto Mora, the Instituto de Investigaciones Históricas (Institute of Historical Research) at the National University, the UNAM, the Facultad de Economía (School of Economics) also at UNAM, CIDE, and Anáhuac University. It is the most important academic seminar in its field in Mexico and always hosts presenters from other countries. The seminar database is separate from the bibliographical database because it does not deal with publications. The presentations generally correspond to works in progress but can also be research updates as well as presentations of published books. The information from SIHE also reveals research trends. I analyzed the SIHE presentations using the same categories of historical periods and themes as the papers, but the information is more limited.

Main Findings

This section presents the analysis of the bibliometric database and the SIHE, mainly through figures and tables. First, the number of papers published in economic and business history increased during the period from 1998 to 2004, and particularly from 2010 onward. This is driven by significant growth in the number of papers published in the journal ALHE from 2009. The numbers for *Historia Mexicana* and *Novohispana* remain relatively steady, while there was a significant drop in papers in the field in *Trimestre* from 2007. This is due to the better positioning of ALHE as a journal, while *Trimestre* possibly became less attractive to researchers in economic history.

An important observation from the data is the increase in the number of papers, and an increase in the number of authors involved in the papers, which might be the result of more researchers working in the field. This shows an increase in coauthored papers. However, it is not clear what drives that increase: the single fact that there are more researchers in the field, or more economic historians aiming to publish a journal article (instead of a book or a book chapter), or the fact that the journal became better positioned in its ranking and hence it became more attractive for economic historians (and other scholars) to publish in it.

Coauthorship became more common over time, and the average number of authors per paper also increased significantly after 2009. This indicates that there are more collaborations between researchers, leaving behind the tradition of single-author projects (namely, the commonplace of the lonely historian). Chart 1 shows the number of papers and authors per year, while Chart 2 presents the average number of authors per paper for each year.

An important aspect to highlight is the participation of women as authors. Unlike other fields, economic and business history have always had a strong presence of female researchers. However, there is a big difference between history—where there are more women—and economics—where there are fewer. Chart 3 shows the proportion of authors per year that are female. According to the figure, the percentage of female authors has dropped consistently since 2007: having reached 50% in previous years, it reduced to as low as 18% in 2018. This downturn goes hand in hand with the increase in the number of papers, suggesting that most of the new authors are men.

The classification of papers by the historical period they study shows—as expected—a significant frequency for the periods of New Spain and the Iberian empires, as well as Global Capitalism in the nineteenth century, which were the periods traditionally studied in recent decades. In fact, New Spain and the Iberian empires were the most-studied periods up to 2004. The dominance of these periods can be explained by the availability of archival sources, debates started by economic historians in the region, in the United States and Europe, as well as an interest to

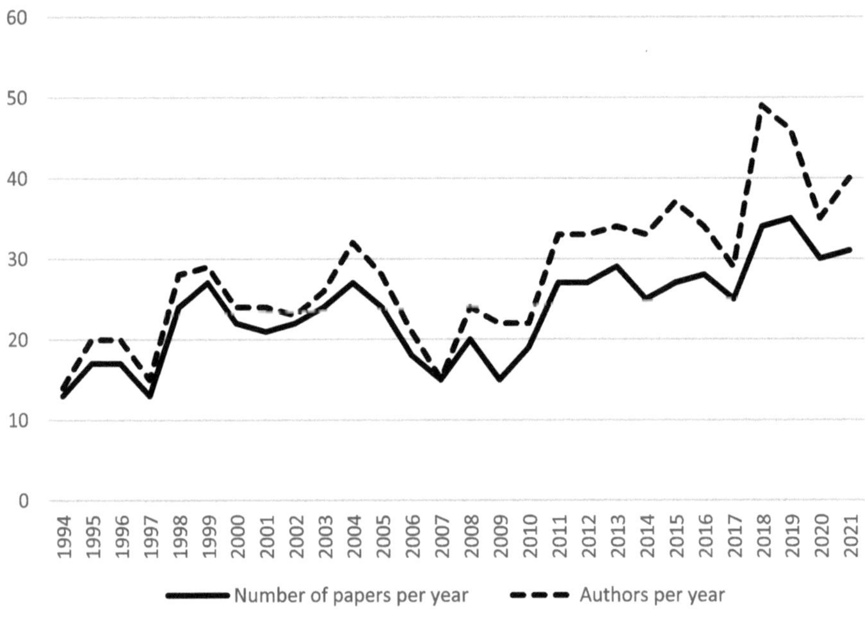

Chart 1 Number of papers and authors per year

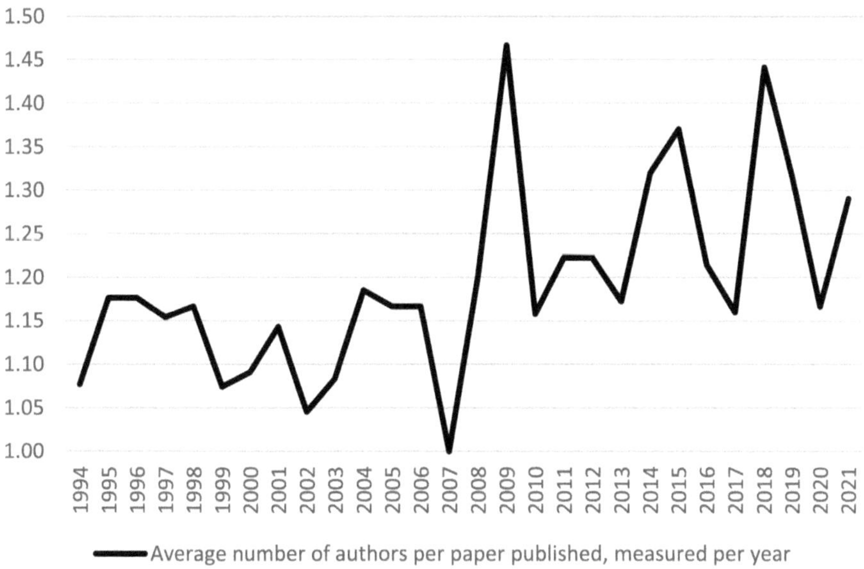

Chart 2 Average number of authors per year

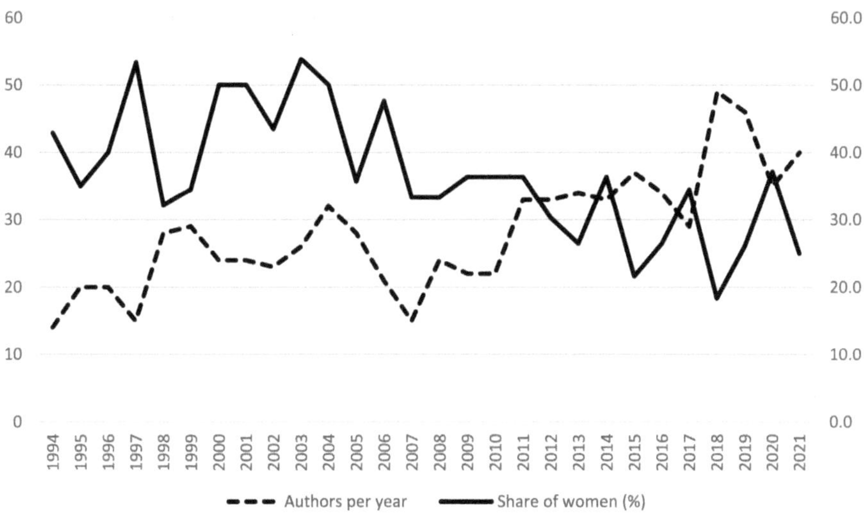

Chart 3 Authors and share of women per year

better understand periods that were understudied in the past and interpreted with commonplaces of very traditional national history.

Nonetheless, there is a notable increase in papers studying twentieth century, such that they make up the majority of the sample analyzed. These papers began to increase steadily from 2010. In the case of research about Mexico, most papers

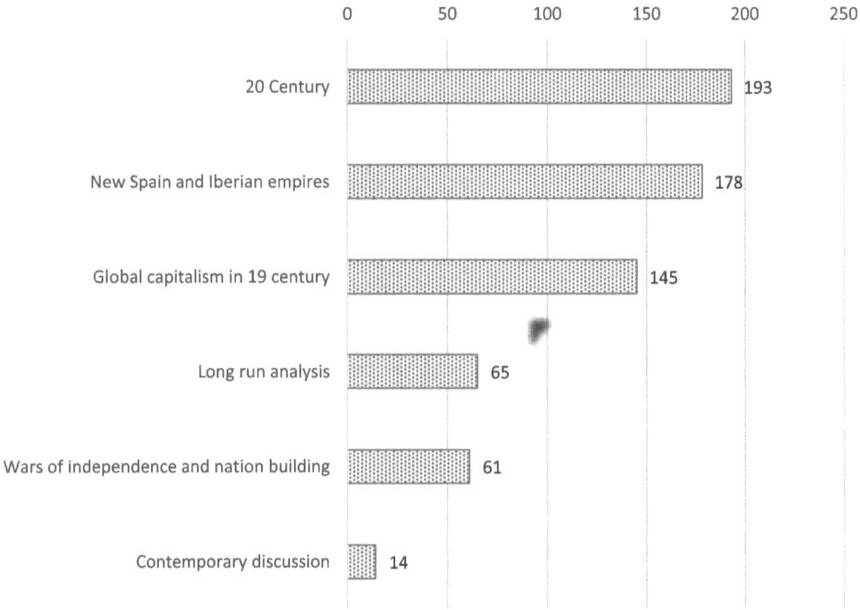

Chart 4 Articles classified by historical period of analysis

focus on the first half of the twentieth century, particularly the Mexican Revolution and the post-Revolution period. This trend reflects, mostly, new interests of historians, however influenced by debates among economists about the causes of economic performance in the twentieth century. Other historical periods remain stable over time. When classifying the historical periods by the percentage of women authors, it shows that more women research more remote periods in the past. But it is unclear what can explain this. Chart 4 shows how the papers are classified into different historical periods, while Chart 5 shows the growth in the three most-studied periods between 1994 and 2021. Table 4 shows the percentage of woman authors per period of analysis.

The themes of research reveal emergent areas of interest. Again, this is related to availability of archival sources and local as well as international debates that stimulate the interest of scholars. Charts 6, 7, and Table 5 show the themes ordered from most to least commonly recurring. Chart 6 shows the number of articles classified and ranked by the main theme of the articles, and Chart 7 shows that number classified and ranked by two main themes (in the database two themes were assigned to each paper, main and second).

There are predominant themes within the research, but it should be noted that those themes cover a wide range of subthemes. For example, research that analyzes agriculture and rural economy (agriculture, cattle farming, and other aspects of the rural extractive activities) are most prevalent, as well as domestic trade, domestic merchants, and taxes and fiscal history. International trade is an important theme, which along with the study of globalization processes is one of the most recurrent

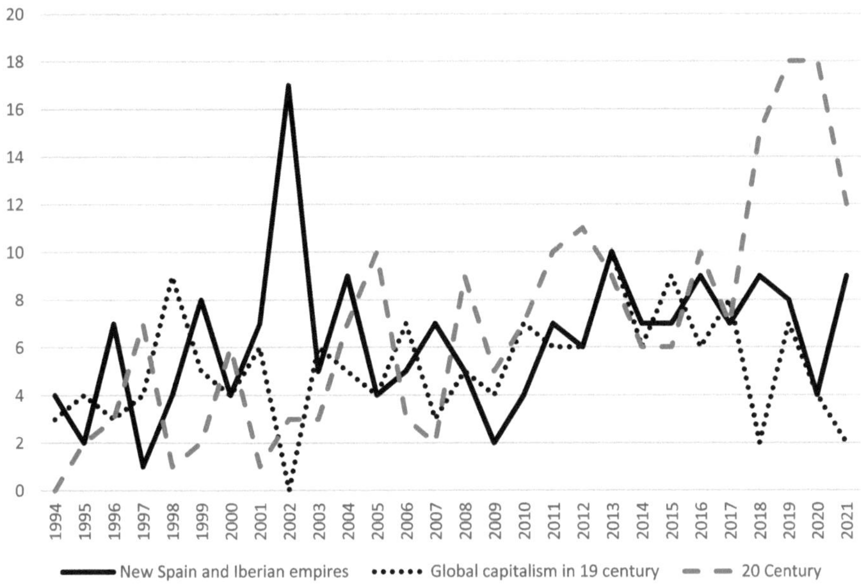

Chart 5 Trend of most studied historical periods

Table 4 Percentage of woman authors per period of analysis

New Spain and Iberian empires	44.0
Wars of independence and nation building, nineteenth century (first half)	42.0
Global capitalism in the nineteenth century (extended second half, up to 1914)	36.2
Twentieth century (1914–)	28.0
Long-term analysis (multi-secular)	25.3
Contemporary discussion about Economic History and its sources	21.0

themes. Likewise, financial history and the history of financial institutions represent a significant proportion of the publications.

When analyzing using the papers classified by two themes, as shown in Chart 7, the patterns persist, but there are some variations. In this ranking, public institutions, law, public policy, and property rights, first, historiography and economic thought, second, and agriculture and the rural economy, third, become the leading three themes in the research. Enterprises, entrepreneurs, and business networks rank as fourth, showing that business history emerges as a relevant area. Also, globalization, international trade, commodities, and migration are areas that are recurrent in our sample of the published research.

Moreover, the patterns of publications over time in each theme reveal interesting information. For example, themes relating to enterprises, entrepreneurs, and

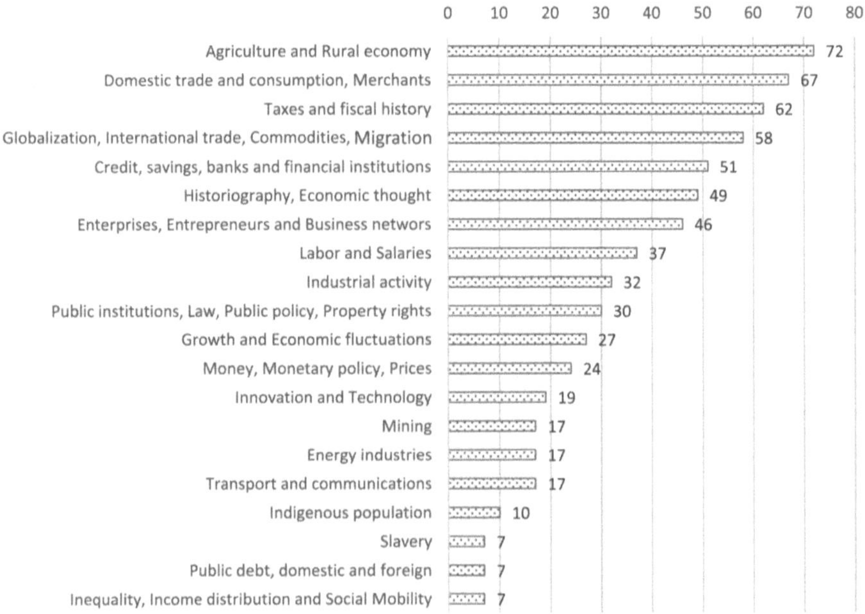

Chart 6 Themes of research in the published articles. Classified and ranked by the main theme of the articles. Number of articles per theme

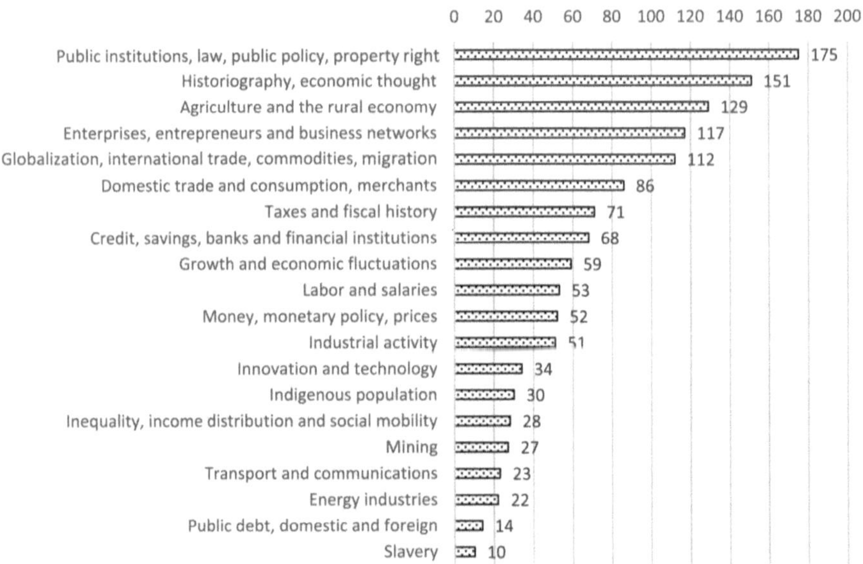

Chart 7 Themes of research in the published articles. Classified and ranked by the two themes of the articles. Number of articles per theme

Table 5 Themes of research in the published articles

	Total 1994–2021	1994–2000	2001–2005	2006–2010	2011–2015	2016–2021
Agriculture and rural economy	72	16	14	13	11	18
Domestic trade and consumption, merchants	67	7	21	15	14	10
Taxes and fiscal history	62	15	11	3	12	21
Globalization, international trade, commodities, and migration	58	8	8	6	19	17
Credit, savings, banks, and financial institutions	51	14	9	5	11	12
Historiography and economic thought	49	15	14	3	5	12
Enterprises, entrepreneurs, and business networks	46	9	6	10	9	12
Labor and salaries	37	3	5	4	10	15
Industrial activity	32	9	4	2	6	11
Public institutions, law, public policy, and property rights	30	6	4	1	11	8
Growth and economic fluctuations	27	3	3	7	4	10
Money, monetary policy, and prices	24	4	4	6	5	5
Innovation and technology	19	0	3	1	3	12
Mining	17	6	3	3	4	1
Energy industries	17	6	3	2	2	4
Transport and communications	17	5	2	2	4	4
Indigenous population	10	6	0	1	0	3
Slavery	7	0	1	1	2	3
Public debt, domestic, and foreign	7	1	1	2	0	3
Inequality, income distribution, and social mobility	7	0	2	0	3	2

Classified and ranked by the main theme of the articles. Number of articles, total and by segment of years business networks have increased consistently in recent years. The same can be said for the labor history and salaries, as well as innovation and technology. New themes have emerged too, or at least new perspectives on existing themes, such as more sophisticated methods for studying economic growth and fluctuations—a theme that saw growth in the quantity of research. Likewise, the history of slavery and more recently studies of inequality, income distribution, and social mobility in historical perspective have also grown under new methodological guidelines.

One of the most interesting aspects is the internationalization of these journals. Chart 8 shows the papers classified by the country they analyze (according to contemporary borders). As expected, given they are Mexican journals, the single most-studied country in the papers is Mexico. However, the majority of the papers do not refer to Mexico, as 54% are studies of other countries. This happens because the journals have reach and reputation across Latin America—particularly ALHE and Trimestre, and to a lesser extent HM. This reflects the international nature of these journals. There is generally a convergence between the country studied and the location of the institutions where the authors work, although this is not the case for all the papers.

After Mexico, Argentina and Brazil are the most discussed in these journals' papers, followed by Chile, Colombia, Peru, Uruguay, Spain, and Cuba. Some papers cover multiple countries, for example, when they study trade relations or economic

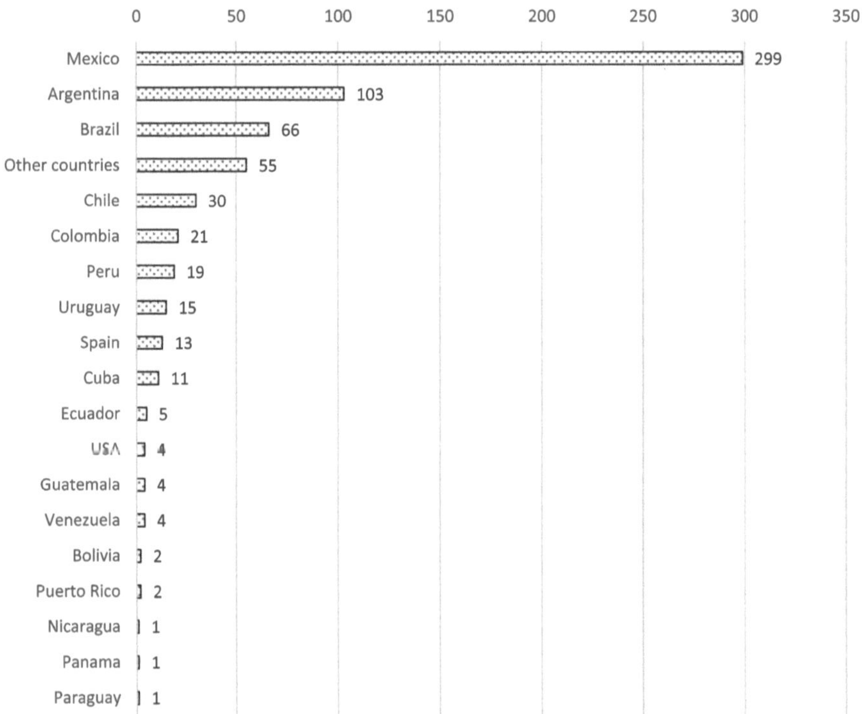

Chart 8 Articles classified and ranked by country of analysis

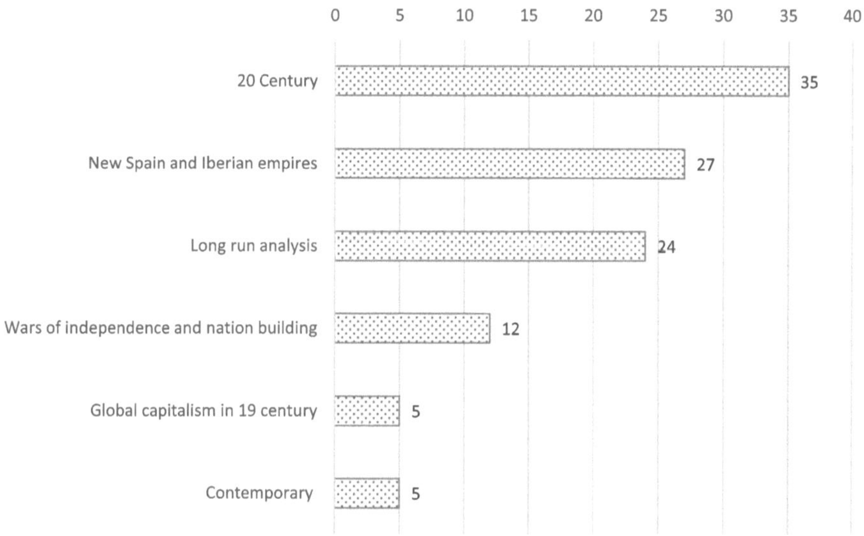

Chart 9 Seminario Institucional de Historia Económica

regions. However, in most cases, they refer to a base or axis country from which they generate the narrative.

Meanwhile, the information from the SIHE seminar reveals with some anticipation the research trends that are subsequently published. Charts 9 and 10 show the classification of SIHE presentations by historical period and theme of research, respectively. Chart 9 shows that twentieth-century research again has the highest number of observations, mostly referring to the first half of the twentieth century, followed by the period of New Spain and Iberian empires. However, there are a significant number of observations from the seminar for long-run analysis and studies on the first half of the nineteenth century referring to the wars of independence and nation building. The latter is because the seminar involves presentations by researchers from various countries, and there is a trend in international economic history of studies on historical legacies in the very long term.

Regarding the themes of research, public institutions, law, public policy, and property rights are the most recurring themes. This is surely a result of the advance of institutional (or institutional analysis) approaches to economic history, which have been adopted by many historians to have a more precise framing of their analysis. Globalization, international trade, commodities, and migration, followed by historiography and economic thought are other themes that the presentations in the seminar mostly address. The former is expected due to the fact that international participants in the seminar present research that elaborate about international issues and economic/trade relations among different regions of the world. Certainly, agriculture and the rural economy, fiscal history and business history are less present in the seminar than in the publications.

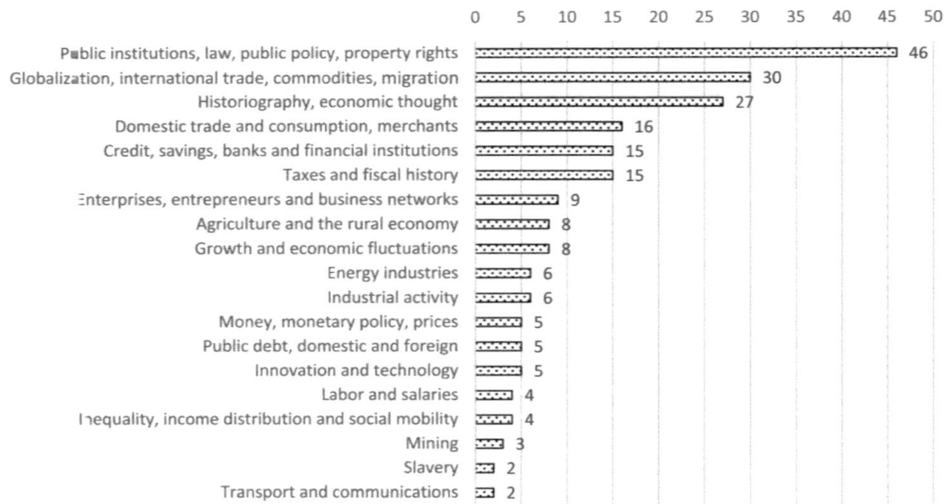

Chart 10 Themes of research in the presentations at the SIHE. Classified and ranked by the two themes of the articles. Number of articles per theme

Concluding Remarks

This chapter has presented a simple analysis of a database of publications and a seminar. The results indicate patterns in the economic history produced and published in Mexico. However, the database allows for a deeper analysis that could be carried out in the future, e.g. studying network connections, methods, and the cited literature. Likewise, a question that remains open is whether these trends tell us something about the future of this research area.

At the international level, some scholars suggest important opportunities for the future of economic history in the face of technological change represented by digitalization [for example, Abramitzky et al. (2021), as well as Claude Diebolt, and Michael Haupert (2019)]. Without a doubt, the digital economy is contributing to better databases being constructed, as well as better data mining and analysis. This will certainly motivate more economists to tackle economic history topics and, above all, to collaborate on research between disciplines.

Likewise, digitalization contributes to the construction of other types of databases using data that require a different type of analysis, e.g. digital archives upon which more text analysis can be done, systematic banks of digital imagery, geospatial information, etc. This is already part of the research in various countries, including economic history in Mexico, although it is being adapted more slowly or at least by a more limited number of researchers.

Much of the future of economic history in Mexico will depend on the relationships that local researchers can form between disciplines, but mainly with academics from other countries. Incentives to adopt leading methodologies and publish in global journals will also be relevant to the advance of the field.

References

Abramitzky, R., L. Boustan, K. Eriksson, J. Feigenbaum, and S. Pérez. 2021. Automated Linking of Historical Data. *Journal of Economic Literature* 59 (3): 865–918.

Avella Alaminos, I. 2020. *Génesis y configuración disciplinar de la historia económica en México (1927-1989)*. México: Universidad Nacional Autónoma de México. Facultad de Filosofía y Letras.

Bértola, L. 2016. *Los desafíos de la Historia Económica de América Latina. Boletín de la AMHE. Año 11, Núm. 3. Sept-Dic, 2016*. México: Asociación Mexicana de Historia Económica.

Cioni, M., G. Federico, and M. Vasta. 2023. Is Economic History Changing Its Nature? Evidence from Top Journals. *Cliometrica* 17:23–48. https://doi.org/10.1007/s11698-022-00242-z.

Dávila, C. 2008. Introduction. Business in Latin America. *Business History Review* 82 (3): 439–444.

Dávila, Carlos. 2013. The Current State of Business History in Latin America. *Australian Economic History Review* 53 (2): 109–120.

Diebolt, C., and M. Haupert. 2019. *How Cliometrics has Infiltrated Economics – and Helped to Improve the Discipline*. Working Papers of the Association Française de Cliométrie (AFC), 5.

Diebolt, C., and M. Haupert. 2022. *Cliometrics and the Future of Economic History*. Document de Travail n° 2022 – 23.

Fernández-de-Pinedo, N., A. La Parra-Perez, and F.-F. Muñoz. 2023. Recent Trends in Publications of Economic Historians in Europe and North America (1980–2019): An Empirical Analysis. *Cliometrica* 17 (1): 1–22.

Florescano, E., coordinador. 1970. *Perspectivas de la historia económica cuantitativa en América Latina*. México: El Colegio de México.

Florescano, E., coordinador. 1980. *Bibliografía general del desarrollo económico de México, 1500-1976*. México: Instituto Nacional de Antropología e Historia.

Haber, S. 1997. Introduction: Economic Growth and Latin American Economic Historiography. In *How Latin America Fell Behind: Essays on the Economic Histories of Brazil and Mexico, 1800-1914*, ed. Stephen Haber, 1–33. Stanford University Press.

Ibarra, A. 2003. A modo de presentación: Historia económica mexicana de los noventa, una apreciación general. *Historia Mexicana* 52 (3): 613–647.

Kuntz, S., coordinadora. 2010. *Historia Económica General de México*. México: El Colegio de México.

Simonassi, S., C. Marichal, A. Regalsky, and L. Bértola. 2021. La historia económica en América Latina hoy. *H-industri@: Revista de historia de la industria, los servicios y las empresas en América Latina* 29:121–137.

Szmrecsanyi, T., and S. Topik. 2004. Business History in Latin America. *Enterprise & Society* 5 (2): 179–186.

MIX
Papier aus verantwortungsvollen Quellen
Paper from responsible sources
FSC® C105338

If you have any concerns about our products,
you can contact us on
ProductSafety@springernature.com

In case Publisher is established outside the EU,
the EU authorized representative is:
Springer Nature Customer Service Center GmbH
Europaplatz 3, 69115 Heidelberg, Germany

Printed by Libri Plureos GmbH
in Hamburg, Germany